365
SPORTS CARS
YOU MUST DRIVE

JOHN LAMM, with LARRY EDSALL and STEVE SUTCLIFFE

motorbooks

Brimming with creative inspiration, how-to projects, and useful information to enrich your everyday life, Quarto Knows is a favorite destination for those pursuing their interests and passions. Visit our site and dig deeper with our books into your area of interest: Quarto Creates, Quarto Cooks, Quarto Homes, Quarto Lives, Quarto Drives, Quarto Explores, Quarto Gifts, or Quarto Kids.

Inspiring | Educating | Creating | Entertaining

© 2011 Quarto Publishing Group USA Inc.
Text © 2016 John Lamm
All photographs are from the author's collection unless noted otherwise.

First published in 2011 by Motorbooks, an imprint of The Quarto Group, 100 Cummings Center, Suite 265-D, Beverly, MA 01915, USA.
T (978) 282-9590 F (978) 283-2742 www.QuartoKnows.com

Motorbooks titles are also available at discount for retail, wholesale, promotional, and bulk purchase. For details, contact the Special Sales Manager by email at specialsales@quarto.com or by mail at The Quarto Group, Attn: Special Sales Manager, 100 Cummings Center, Suite 265-D, Beverly, MA 01915, USA.

20 19 18 17 16 15 14 13

Library of Congress Cataloging-in-Publication Data

Lamm, John.
  365 sports cars you must drive / John Lamm with Larry Edsall and Steve Sutcliffe.
     p. cm.
  ISBN 978-0-7603-4045-5 (softcover w/ flaps)
  1. Sports cars. I. Edsall, Larry. II. Sutcliffe, Steve. III. Title. IV. Title: Three hundred sixty five sports cars you must drive.
  TL236.L36 2011
  388.3'421—dc23
                                                                    2011023803

Editors: Jeffrey Zuehlke
Design Manager: Kou Lor
Layout by: Chris Fayers
Cover designed by: Rob Johnson, Toprotype, Inc.

On the cover: Behind the wheel of Ferrari's F430 Spider.
On the frontispiece: The Jaguar XJ13
On the title pages: The view from the roof of a Ruf Rt 12.

Printed in China

Sports cars are more than mere transportation. They are the stuff of dreams, designed to be driven, admired, and lusted after. Your tastes in these performance machines says much about you—they define your self image and what you expect from life.

This book is more than just your typical "car of the day" compilation; it truly is an eclectic mix of sports cars that covers the broadest possible spectrum—from two seats to four doors. This is a blend of the familiar and expected—who wouldn't want to see Ferraris, Lamborghinis, and Porsches—and the unexpected, like Tojeiro, Dual-Ghia and even a Bosley. There is just the right balance of the old and the new, the exotic and affordable, obscure and famous, foreign and domestic, production and concept. If it's got wheels and any pretense of performance, it's in here.

The photos, compiled and mostly shot by John Lamm, also tell a story—there are action shots, images from auto shows, statics and even guest appearances by notables ranging from Phil Hill to Carroll Shelby. In addition to the great pictures, John and veteran writers Larry Edsall and Steve Sutcliffe provide a taste of history, basic specs, and little known facts about these dream machines.

All in all, this is a remarkable collection of remarkable automobiles. From sublime lightweight roadsters to all-out fire breathing supercars, these are the kinds of cars that get car guys and gals' blood pumping. It's the kind of book that you can open up to any page and get lost in these wheeled wonders. Like the open road that beckons us all, these cars are calling you . . . enjoy!

—Matt DeLorenzo, Editor-in-Chief, *Road & Track* magazine

This is like the ultimate automotive bar bet:

Okay, pal, you've got a garage with 365 spaces and unlimited funds. What will you slot in each space? What will you wheel into spot 365? What's number one?

Chronological? Park the 1886 Benz—not just the first sports car, but also the first car—in space 1?

How about the 1962 Ferrari 250 GTO, arguably the most luscious vehicle ever created? That would put you head-to-head with many McLaren F1 guys . . . no argument.

But let's be practical. Mazda's Miata belongs in a place of honor. Ditto with any of several Alfa Romeos and MGs.

A horsepower guy? Park a Cobra, a Viper, or a 'Vette.

And so you get a little sense of what it's like to create a book like this. We all have our automotive loves and when you narrow it down to sports cars, ouch, it gets even more difficult.

To some it's their first love; in my case a Bugeye Sprite or Triumph TR4. Others opt for what they can afford right now, like a Miata, a nicely maintained Toyota "MR 2," or a low-mileage Corvette. For those who prefer to dream, this is the chance to mull over a Ruf CTR3, a Ferrari 458 or something really out there, like an Aston Martin One-77. And there are those who will slip into the past, to an Alfa Romeo 8C 2900 or one of many Bugattis.

With luck, wherever your dreams take you, there are examples in this book. You'll find all the favorites, but we also kept an open mind, so don't be surprised by a few curveballs, from pony cars to a three-wheeler.

That is, however, the fun of assembling a book about sports cars. There are classic definitions of the type and then those that give a little space.

Maybe that's the real bet. What is a sports car?

—John Lamm, Summer 2011

Abarth

Simca   1962–1965

- Austrian Karl Abarth founded his eponymous company in 1949.

- About 300 Abarth Simcas were built.

- The project ended when Chrysler bought Simca.

- Abarth Simcas weighed around 1,500 pounds.

Engine: 2.0-liter dohc inline four	**Top speed:** 168 mph
Horsepower: 199	**Price when new:** $9,000
0–60 mph: 5.2 seconds	**Value now:** $100,000

We read these days about carmakers cooperating with each other, but it's nothing new. Back in the 1960s, Fiat owned a portion of France's Simca. Trying to up Simca's sex appeal, Fiat had Abarth start with Simca platforms, shorten them, wrap a beautiful aluminum body around them, and install an Abarth drivetrain. First came 1.3-liter fours, but later were 1.6- and 2.0-liter versions. Not particularly streetable, they were Porsche beaters on tracks and in hillclimbs. —*JL*

AC

Ace 5.0   1994–1998

The first Ace was built by AC in the 1950s, a beautiful two-seat sports car that became the basis for the legendary Shelby Cobra. In the early 1990s, the modern AC company, which built Cobra replicas off the original tooling, developed a new Ace. It was also a two-seat sports car that lacked the sublime beauty of the original Ace, but it was cute enough. Production ended in 1998. —*JL*

- The Autokraft/AC factory was located within the historic Brooklands racetrack, southwest of London, England.

- Aces used an automatic transmission.

- 50 AC Aces were built.

- Famed engineer Len Bailey was involved in the car's design.

Engine: 4.9-liter ohv V-8	**Top speed:** 139 mph
Horsepower: 260	**Price when new:** $110,000
0–60 mph: 6.8 seconds	**Value today:** N/A

- The forerunner to the NSX was the HP-X (Honda Pininfarina Xperimental) concept car.

- Racers Ayrton Senna and Bobby Rahal helped develop early versions of the NSX.

- Gordon Murray, designer of the McLaren F1, has said the Honda NSX was his benchmark for a light, fast, and well-balanced supercar.

- The red car pictured is an Acura NSX; the white car is an NSX-R GT.

Engine: 3.0-liter V-6	Top speed: 165 mph
Horsepower: 270	Price when new: $92,000
0–60 mph: est. 5.8 seconds	Value now: $29,000

Like Porsche, Honda believes you can achieve world-class performance with fewer than 8, 10, or 12 cylinders. In 1989, it unveiled the NSX (short for New Sports car Xperimental). Designed by Pininfarina, the low wedge-shaped but well-rounded two-seater celebrated Honda's Formula One racing success with a lightweight package that featured an aluminum body and a midmounted, high-revving, 270-horsepower V-6 engine. The car was sold in the United States by Honda's upscale Acura division.

For racing in Japan, a lightweight R version of the car was developed with race-tweaked suspension. A few years later, Honda released the NSX-R GT, which featured a wider body and a snorkel-style air intake that stuck up over the driver's compartment. —*LE*

Alfa Romeo

6C 1750 Gran Sport   1930–1932

Credit for the 6C 1750 goes to Vittorio Jano, the technical magician who designed many of the great pre-war and early-post-war Italian performance cars. He began with the 6C 1750 Super Sport and shortened the wheelbase. More importantly, perhaps, was the introduction of a Roots-type supercharger. What makes the car so beautiful is the Zagato bodywork that graced most of the 6C 1750 Gran Sports. Built to be race cars, they were quite successful, the most famous win being by Tazio Nuvolari in the 1930 Mille Miglia when he raced in near darkness with this lights turned off to fool a competitor. The stuff of legends. This particular car is different; while it was built in Milan, Italy, its familiar Alfa radiator badge says "Paris" instead of "Milano," as it was built for the French importer. —JL

- Alfa Romeo debuted the 6C 1750 at the motor show in Rome in 1929.
- The 1.7-liter supercharged engine provided an impressive 117 lb-ft of torque.
- It's said more than 250 Gran Sports were built, although exact numbers are elusive.
- Vittorio Jano went on to do major design work for Lancia and Ferrari.

Engine: 1.7-liter supercharged dohc inline four
Horsepower: 85
0–60 mph: 14 seconds

Top speed: 90 mph
Price when new: $4,200
Value now: $1,100,000

Alfa Romeo ▮▮

- One of the Mille Miglia cars is now owned by renowned fashion designer Ralph Lauren.

- Alfa Romeo built the 8C 2900s in two wheelbase lengths, 110.2 and 118.1 inches.

- Vittorio Jano designed the 2.9-liter engine.

- These Alfas featured aluminum bodies on steel frames.

Engine: 2.9-liter supercharged dohc inline eight	**Top speed:** 120 mph
Horsepower: 180	**Price when new:** N/A
0–60 mph: N/A	**Value now:** $10,000,000

These are the sorts of cars you see taking Best of Show on the awards ramp at the Pebble Beach Concours, and several have. Toward the end of the 1930s, Alfa Romeo's 8C models had developed into the 2900, which stood for the 2.9-liter displacement of their engines. These are magnificent engines, long and beautiful, with a pair of Roots-type superchargers and Weber carburetors. The four-speed transmission is mounted in back as a transaxle, and the car has an independent rear suspension. Only about 30 8C2900s were built, but each has a story. Most have Touring bodies, wonderful sculptures often with rear-wheel spats. Among the most famous are the open cars built for the 1938 Mille Miglia *(below)* and the sleek low-roof 1938 Le Mans Speciale *(inset).* —JL

Alfa Romeo

8C Spider   2009–2010

When Alfa Romeo unveiled the 8C Competizione concept at the Frankfurt Motor Show in 2003, the world took one step back and just smiled. For here, at last, was a genuinely beautiful-looking Alfa that was—thank the Lord—rear-wheel-drive and powered by a 450-horsepower Ferrari V-8 that was as potent as it was melodic. The production car appeared a few years later, but it wasn't until Alfa unveiled the Spider concept in 2005 at the Pebble Beach Concours D'Elegance, and subsequently enlisted the services of Maserati to help build the open version in 2009, that the true genius of the 8C's design became apparent. And with a top speed of 180 miles per hour the thing doesn't exactly disappoint on the road, either. —SS

- Just 35 of the 500 8C Spiders built made their way to the United States.

- The windshield frame is made of carbon fiber, which helped keep the front/rear weight balance at a perfect 50/50.

- The Spider concept was built by Carrozeria Marazzai, but the production models were all made at Maserati.

- Top speed is just 5 mph less than the coupe, not bad considering how much extra drag the Spider has.

Engine: 4.7-liter Ferrari V-8
Horsepower: 444
0–60 mph: 4.2 seconds
Top speed: 180 mph
Price when new: $241,000
Value now: $300,000

1952–1953   Disco Volante

- Flying Saucer? UFOs were a hot topic in the early 1950s.

- There were also 3.0- and 3.5-liter Disco Volantes.

- You can see the Disco Volantes in Alfa's museum in Arese, Italy.

- It is said that the Disco Volante's coefficient of drag is an impressive 0.26.

Engine: 2.0-liter dohc inline four	**Top speed:** 140 mph
Horsepower: 158	**Price when new:** N/A
0–60 mph: N/A	**Value now:** Est. $1,000,000

How can you not love a car nicknamed the "Flying Saucer"? Alfa Romeo's legendary Alfetta 158/159 Grand Prix car had become obsolete by 1952, but the Milanese automaker had already moved on to sports car racing with a machine based on the mechanicals in its 1900 models. Carrozzeria Touring, the coachbuilder long associated with Alfa, created the slippery body that allowed the car to reach 140 miles per hour despite its small engine. The author had the pleasure of running the Italian retro Mille Miglia in this car with Phil Hill. Five Disco Volantes were built, including coupe versions, which aren't as pretty but just as interesting as the open Disco. The cars never captured any great race victories, but they certainly captured the hearts of many enthusiasts. —JL

Giulia TZ-2   1965

For reasons that become obvious the moment you set eyes upon it, the beautiful little Alfa Giulia TZ2 (Tubolare Zagato) became known as the "mini Ferrari GTO" soon after it was introduced to the world in 1965. It was an ultra-lightweight racing car, pure and simple, and was designed by Ercole Spada (of Zagato) and engineered by Carlo Chiti (from Alfa's Autodelta racing division) to compete on the world GT stage. And compete it did, albeit briefly, winning five times internationally in 1966, having failed to leave its mark at Le Mans in 1965. Only 12 examples were made by Autodelta, each featuring a highly tuned 170 horsepower version of the company's inimitable 1570cc twin cam engine. This was sufficient to accelerate the TZ2 to 160 miles per hour, and straight into the history books. —SS

- The TZ2 was just 41 inches tall.

- Its so-called Kamm tail made it look remarkably like a Ferrari 250 GTO from the rear.

- The car's glass-reinforced plastic bodyshell was more than 200 pounds lighter than the metal-bodied TZ1.

- Alfa bought Autodelta outright to ensure the build of the TZ-2 took place entirely in-house.

Engine: 1.6-liter twin-cam inline four
Horsepower: 170
0–60 mph: 5.0 seconds (approx)

Top speed: 160 mph
Price when new: N/A
Value now: $300,000

Alfa Romeo 🇮🇹

- The four-door GTV sedan was known simply as The Berlinetta.

- In total, Alfa Romeo produced some 43,965 GTVs from 1967 to 1972.

- The optional alloy wheels for the GTV were almost identical in style to those fitted to the Montreal.

- The GTV pictured here is competing in the legendary Trans-Am production car racing series in 1971.

For 2.0 liter version	
Engine: 2.0-liter inline four	Top speed: 121 mph
Horsepower: 130	Price when new: $5,600
0–60 mph: 8.9 seconds	Value now: $11,500

Each of Alfa's impossibly pretty 105/115 series coupes was designed by Giorgetto Giugiaro while he worked for Bertone. In 1967, the GT Veloce was created, first with a 1,750cc twin cam engine and 122 horsepower, then in 1971 as a more potent version with a 1,962cc lump. All 2.0-liter GTVs claimed a rousing 150 horsepower when fitted with carburetors. Unfortunately, the ones sold in the United States had fuel injection, which trimmed output back to a mere 130 horsepower. Hmm. —*SS*

Alfa Romeo 🇮🇹

The 1600 Junior Zagato was a rebodied, limited-production-run homologation version of the regular Junior GT. It was produced by Alfa primarily to go racing, but also as a styling exercise. It was much lighter than the original and much more dramatic to look at too, thanks to the fetching design from Ercole Spada at Zagato. Most of the 402 cars made were used in competition, using a modified 1,570cc twin cam engine. —*SS*

- Ercole Spada was chief stylist at Zagato and did cars for Aston Martin, Ferrari, and Maserati. He also did the E34 BMW 5-Series (1989–1996).

- Zagato is based in Milan and was founded by Ugo Zagato, who put aircraft construction techniques into cars.

- The floorpan of the 1600 Junior Zagato was almost 4 inches longer than that of the similar-looking 1300 JZ.

- The 1600 JZ had a bigger fuel tank than the 1300, plus a bulge in its rear bumper that housed the spare tire.

Engine: 1.6-liter twin cam inline four	Top speed: 118 mph
Horsepower: 125	Price when new: about $12,000
0–60 mph: N/A	Value now: $20,000

■ Alfa Romeo

Spider Duetto 1965–1969

The classic Alfa Spider, based on the Giulia 105 series cars and known affectionately simply as the Duetto, suffered from a troubled introduction to the world. Fiat was struggling financially at the time, which meant there was an unusually large gap between the car being unveiled in 1961 and it rolling down Pinifarina's production line at the end of 1965. But that didn't matter, because when the 1,570cc Duetto arrived it was such a charming little car, both to look at and to drive, the politics behind its creation took a back seat. One of the first road cars to have crumple zones engineered into its front end, the Spider Duetto lasted until 1967, when it became known as the Spider Veloce instead. —*SS*

- The Alfa Spider is perhaps most well known in the United States as the car driven by Dustin Hoffman's character in the 1967 film *The Graduate*.

- The Duetto was the last car that Battista "Pinin" Farina personally designed for the company.

- The nickname "Osso di Seppia" is sometimes given to the car (which means cuttlefish bone) because of its long tail design.

- Spiders sold in the United States had fuel injection, and as a result developed less power than the carburetor-fed versions.

Engine: 1.6-liter inline four	**Price when new:** $2,000
Horsepower: 109	(2,195 Lire)
0–60 mph: 11.3 seconds	**Value now:** $12,000
Top speed: 115 mph	

- The T33's 2.0-liter V-8 engine was designed by Alfa's chief race engineer, Carlo Chiti.
- *Top Gear* voted the T33 as the 15th sexiest car ever.
- The Stradale was based on the Autodelta Alfa T33 racing car.
- The three design study models of the T33 Stradale were called 33.2, Iguana, and Carabo. (See the Carabo profile under "Bertone.")

Engine: 2.0-liter V-8	Top speed: 160 mph
Horsepower: 230	Price when new: $17,000
0–60 mph: 5.5 seconds	Value now: More than $1 million

It's a rare one, this, but arguably one of the world's most beautiful cars ever. To the best of our knowledge, just 18 T33 Stradales were made, with a further three examples appearing as design studies, all of which were created to demonstrate how much of Alfa's racing technology was available to the general public (even though at $17,000 it was also the most expensive car to go on sale in 1968). Designed by Franco Scaglione and engineered by Alfa's racing division, the T33 used an oversquare, dry-sumped 2.0-liter V-8 that used no fewer than 16 spark plugs, could rev to 8,800 rpm, and, if pushed, would deliver an earsplitting 230 horsepower. That was good enough for a 0–60 mph time of 5.5 seconds, which was appropriately insane for 1968. —SS

After World War II, Englishman Sydney Allard quickly figured out that the United States was the place to sell cars. And the best way to power machines that would satisfy horsepower-hungry Americans was to install U.S.-made V-8 engines. While Allard did offer full-bodied models such as the P1 and the Palm Beach, the versions that captured everyone's imagination were the cycle-fendered J2 and J2-X. The cars also captured their fair share of race victories in the early years of competition, including at Pebble Beach and Watkins Glen. It's possible to think of Allard as a hot rodder, first fitting his race cars with Ford flathead V-8s, but he would move on to using more powerful Cadillac and Chrysler Hemi powerplants. Drivers like Carroll Shelby raced Allards, but arguably the most famous driver to compete in these cars was Bill Pollack, who won major events at Pebble Beach. —*JL*

- Corvette godfather Zora Arkus Duntov created flathead V-8 speed parts that were used on Allards.
- The J2 was equipped with a de Dion rear suspension.
- A split-beam axle was used up front.
- The transmission was a three-speed manual.

Engine: Cadillac 5.4-liter ohv V-8	**Top speed:** 114 mph
Horsepower: 160	**Price when new:** N/A
0–60 mph: 9.0 seconds	**Value now:** $200,000

- The A110 was also called the Berlinette.

- Alpines were built in Dieppe, France.

- Alpines got their name from Rédélé's competition success in the Alps.

- Many early A110s had engines tuned by Amédée "The Sorcerer" Gordini.

Specs for 1973:	
Engine: 1.6-liter twin-cam inline four	0–60 mph: 6.3
	Top speed: 130 mph
	Price when new: N/A
Horsepower: 140	Value now: $65,000

Jean Rédélé was a Renault dealer in Dieppe, France, who rallied in Renault automobiles. He then built a series of cars based on the automaker's mechanicals. The first model, the A106, wasn't too pretty, but its successor, the A108, was, made even better in 1963 as the A110. Following Lotus' lead, the car had a center backbone chassis and fiberglass body. Built for more than a dozen years, the A110s went through a variety of engines, from rather stock 1,108cc fours to Renault twin cam engines with 1.6-liter displacement. The Alpine A110 is best remembered for its many victories in the World Rally Championship, and as the winner of the inaugural WRC title in 1973. The most lasting image of the car is on the Monte Carlo Rally, sliding sideways through snowy Alpine passes. —JL

▌▌ Alpine-Renault

A310   1971–1984

By 1971, the Alpine A110 was entering its 10th year of production, and the company was poised to replace it with the new A310. A pretty little car, the A310 again had a backbone rear-engine chassis and fiberglass body, with the majority of its components coming from Renault. The early models shared much with the A110, but in 1976 the car was somewhat restyled to accept the new PRV V-6 engine. (The initials stand for Peugeot, Renault, and Volvo, after the automakers that jointly funded development of the aluminum engine.) The A310 would not enjoy the A110's glory in the World Rally Championship; Renault instead put its rally efforts behind the 5 Turbo, but A310s did enjoy success in circuit racing under Group 4 sports car racing regulations. —JL

- John DeLorean would use the same V-6 for the DMC-12.
- A310s offer a much more civilized driving experience compared to the A110s.
- Alpine built A310s until 1984.
- Renault took a majority interest in Alpine in 1973.

Engine: 2.7-liter dohc V-6   **Top speed:** 142 mph
Horsepower: 150   **Price when new:** $30,000
0–60 mph: 6.9 seconds   **Value now:** $30,000

- AMG would go on to build even more outrageous versions in the form of the SL70 and SL73.

- AMG was founded in 1967 by a pair of ex-Mercedes engineers.

- AMG became part of Mercedes in 1999, when Mercedes aquired 51 percent of the company.

- The SL60 was restricted to 155 mph but could do 185 without its limiter.

Engine: 6.0-liter V-8	Top speed: 155 mph
Horsepower: 384	Price when new: $80,000
0–60 mph: 5.8 seconds	Value now: $20,000–$40,000

In the early days, long before they were swallowed by and subsequently blossomed within the vast empire of Teutonic excellence that is Mercedes-Benz, folks did things a bit differently at AMG. And cars like the outrageously rapid AMG SL60 were the result. No one was quite sure just how much power was produced by the AMG-tuned engine in this Mercedes-Benz SL-class roadster; some say it was around the 380 horsepower mark, others claim well over 400. Either way, it was a monster of a machine, with huge amounts of energy available via its modified 6.0-liter V-8 engine (that's what AMG stood for originally; engine production and development ltd). Mated to the already superb SL chassis with a few well-judged tweaks to tires and suspension, the SL60 was truly a sign of things to come from AMG. —*SS*

🇬🇧 Ariel

Atom 2000–

What a thrill ride. Imagine riding inside a motorcycle. That's roughly what it's like to drive an Ariel Atom, a truly unique vehicle that features an exoskeleton frame. Light weight is the key to the vehicle's abilities: It weighs just 1,350 pounds—half that of a Mazda Miata, but with roughly twice the horsepower. Ariel offers three versions, producing 200, 245, or 300 horsepower through a six-speed gearbox. —JL

- Among Arial Atom owners is comedian Jay Leno.
- Atom suspensions have a race car–like rocker arm/pushrod design.
- *Autocar* magazine got an Atom to 100 mph and back to a standstill in 10.88 seconds.
- American Atoms are made in the United States by TMI Auto Tech in Alton, Virginia.

Engine: 2.0-liter dohc supercharged inline four
Horsepower: 300
0–60 mph: 2.8 seconds
Top speed: 140 mph
Price when new: $49,980
Value now: Same

🇺🇸 Arnolt

Arnolt-Bristol 1953–1959

Stanley Howard Arnolt's enterprises included automotive lubricants, boat engines, steel frames for furniture, galley equipment for trains, and landing gear for military airplanes. He also imported British cars to the Midwest and commissioned hybrid versions that he sold under his own brand. Among his most memorable models was the Arnolt-Bristol, which featured Bertone bodywork in the form of an exotic design by Franco Scaglione, and a 2.0-liter six-cylinder powerplant from British automaker Bristol. —LE

- Arnolt earned the nickname "Wacky" after he proved the capability of his inboard marine engine by motoring a 13-foot boat across a choppy Lake Michigan.
- "Wacky" Arnolt was the American distributor for Solex carburetors.
- Arnolt and Bertone produced 254 Arnolt Bristol roadsters and three coupes. . .
- . . .Half were fully outfitted, and the others came without tops and were intended primarily for road racing.

Engine: 2.0-liter inline six
Horsepower: 130
0–60 mph: N/A
Top speed: N/A
Price when new: $3,994 (Bolide version without a top)
Value now: $175,000 for Bolide, $275,000 for DeLuxe version

1958–1963 DB4 and DB4GT Zagato

- So rare and so valuable is the GT Zagato, there is a budding replica business that turns DB4s into DB4 GT Zagatos.

- The Zagato never won at Le Mans.

- The most famous DB4 GT Zagatos bear the registration plates 1 VEV and 2 VEV; both cars competed at Le Mans in 1961.

- The original DB4 was styled by Carrozzeria Touring, based in Milan, but was built at Newport Pagnell in the U.K.

(For Zagato):	
Engine: 3.7-liter inline six	**Top speed:** 153 mph
Horsepower: 314	**Price when new:** $18,025
0–60 mph: 6.1 seconds	**Value now:** More than $2 million

If the standard Aston Martin DB4 (*inset*) that appeared in 1958 wasn't quite powerful enough to drive or beautiful enough to look at, then the stunning DB4GT Zagato (*below*) that Ercole Spada produced two years later at the London Motorshow was surely the remedy to end all remedies. Not that the stoically handsome DB4, with its 3.7-liter, 240-horsepower straight-six engine, was in any way a disappointing car to drive. It's just that the Zagato took the idea of the DB4 and turned it into some kind of legend, with a breathtakingly gorgeous bodyshell clothing an uprated engine and chassis that were good enough to compete at Le Mans. Just 19 such cars were produced, and nowadays they are each worth over $2 million. —*SS*

 # Aston Martin

DB7   1994–2004

It would not be unduly dramatic to say that without the DB7 Aston Martin may well not have survived. For when this car arrived in 1994, the famous Newport Pagnell era at Aston had just about ground to a halt, which meant the DB7 was genuinely a make-or-break car for the company. Fortunately, the styling of the DB7 (courtesy of Brits Ian Callum and Keith Helfet, both of whom went on to work for Jaguar) was enough on its own to ensure the car was a success. The fact that it drove rather well too—on account of its muscular 3.2-liter straight-six engine, which was later joined by a rousing 6.0-liter V-12—was almost a bonus in the end. Some bonus, some car. —SS

- When *Autocar* magazine first road tested the DB7, the test car caught fire. But the fault (with the exhaust's heat shielding) was rectified before the car went on sale.

- The DB7 was Aston Martin's highest-selling model for many years, with over 7,000 examples being produced before it was replaced by the DB9.

- Beneath its skin the DB7 is, in fact, merely a development of the far older Jaguar XJS.

- Aston built 150 Alfred Dunhill Edition DB7s in 1998, each one featuring a built-in humidor.

Engine: 3.2-liter inline six	**Top speed:** 157 mph
Horsepower: 335	**Price when new:** $169,000
0–60 mph: 5.8 seconds	**Value now:** $50,000

- The DBS V-12 has actually appeared in two Bond films, *Casino Royale* and, briefly, *Quantum of Solace*.

- The original DBS was unveiled in 1967 and was powered by a straight-six motor. It, too, made a Bond appearance in *On Her Majesty's Secret Service*.

- The optional sound system in a DBS is a bespoke Bang & Olufsen item that has 13 speakers and features Acoustic Lens Technology, which is nice.

- The DBS is available with a six-speed manual transmission or Aston's Touchtronic 2 automatic transmission, operated via a steering wheel paddle shifter.

Engine: 6.0-liter V-12	Top speed: 188 mph
Horsepower: 510	Price when new: $269,000
0–60 mph: 4.3 seconds	Value now: $260,000

It's the car in which James Bond very nearly met his end when he crashed in spectacular style in the 2006 film *Casino Royale*. It's also one of Aston Martin's most focused machines, featuring a tuned 510-horsepower version of AM's venerable 6.0-liter V-12 with an appropriately uprated chassis and suspension system to match. You can pick out the DBS from the outside by noting that it has a much deeper front splitter (with which to scoop up whatever baddies may stand in its path), and from its more, shall we say, thrusting side skirts and tail spoiler styling. The DBS may not be Aston Martin's most graceful creation ever, but, on the road, it's certainly one of its fastest cars. —SS

One-77 2010–

First revealed in 2009, the One-77 provided more proof that English automaker Aston Martin lives at the top of the list of exotic carmakers. At the heart of this rare machine is a light, quite rigid carbon fiber monocoque. Around this is dramatic aluminum bodywork with bulging fenders that remind one of German DTM race cars. Inside is a sporting-yet-elegant mix of leather and carbon fiber. Upper and lower A-arm suspension are employed front and rear, matched to what Aston calls Dynamic Suspension Spool Valve technology, which allows the driver to vary the shock absorbers' characteristics. For motive power, Aston upgraded its V-12 to 7.3 liters and improved handling by adding a dry sump oiling system to lower the engine in the car, dropping the center of gravity. —*JL*

- Aston Martin plans to build just 77 of these spectacular supercars.
- The One-77's aluminum body panels are all hand-crafted.
- A six-speed sequential manual gearbox backs the V-12.
- The One-77 features a Carbon Ceramic Matrix brake system.

Engine: 7.3-liter dohc V-12	**Top speed:** 200-plus mph
Horsepower: 700	**Price when new:** $1.5 million
0–60 mph: 3.5 seconds	**Value now:** Same

- British heritage aside, Rapides are assembled in Graz, Austria.

- You can lock or unlock your Rapide remotely if you own the matching $25,000 Jaeger-LeCoultre watch.

- The Rapide's "swan wing" doors open out and up at 12 degrees to avoid hitting curbs.

- Aston Martin raced a nearly stock version of the Rapide at the Nürburgring 24 Hours in May 2010, taking second in its class.

Engine: 5.9-liter V-12	**Top speed:** 184 mph
Horsepower: 470	**Price when new:** $199,999
0–60 mph: 5.0 seconds	**Value now:** Same

When you think of modern four-door exotic cars, two names quickly come to mind: the Porsche Panamera and the Aston Martin Rapide. While the former has questionable exterior styling but a roomy interior, the Aston sacrifices interior space for a scrumptious exterior. The Rapide's sculpting from end to end is truly stunning. Its front is identical to Aston's DB9 back to the first pillar, but the sedan's wheelbase is 11.6 inches longer, and that space is used to make a more comfortable passenger compartment. While those up front have plenty of room, the rear seats are best left to children—and they would be quite comfortable. Regardless, everyone inside would barely notice that they are riding in a four-seater, since the Rapide has all the speed and litheness of a true supercar. —JL

 # Aston Martin

V8 Vantage — 1972–1989

To begin with, the model that would evolve into the Aston Martin V8 wasn't actually powered by a V-8 at all because the V-8 engine wasn't ready. Hence, the car originally went on sale in 1967 as the DBS, featuring a straight six from the DB6 Vantage. When Tadek Marek's new 5.3-liter V-8 was finally ready, though, the straight six was phased out and the DBS-V8 was born, just one year after Neil Armstrong went for a walkabout way up there on the moon. By 1972, the V8 had become the epitome of the big, hairy Aston, its long hood projecting proudly toward the horizon, and 1977 saw the introduction of the V8 Vantage, which was hailed as Britain's first supercar and was the fastest production car in the world at the time. It had a heavy gearbox, brakes that required a reasonable degree of optimism about life in general, and an engine note to die for. It lasted, and lasted well, until October 1989. —SS

- Roger Moore drove an Aston V-8 in the 1971–1972 TV series *The Persuaders.*

- Timothy Dalton drove a V8 Vantage in the 1987 James Bond film *The Living Daylights.* . .

- . . .Well, sort of. He actually drove a V8 Volante (convertible) in one scene, and was later shown driving a car badged as a V8 Vantage, but which was not, in fact, a V8 Vantage.

- Aston Martin famously refused to release official power outputs for the V-8, though the estimate was 320 horsepower for the base model.

Engine: 5.3-liter V-8	**Top speed:** 146 mph
Horsepower: 320	**Price when new:** $27,500
0–60 mph: 7.2 seconds	**Value now:** $75,000

2010–   V8 Vantage and V12 Vantage

- The V12 Vantage comes with a six-speed manual gearbox and carbon-ceramic brakes as standard.

- Aston Martin announced plans to build just 1,000 units of the V12 Vantage; sadly, none of them will be sold in the United States.

- A racing version of the V8 Vantage, running exclusively on E85 fuel, was campaigned in the United States in 2008.

- The V8 model uses a paddle shift transmission developed by Italian gearbox maker Graziano, which also makes transmissions for Ferrari and Lamborghini.

(For V12 Vantage):

Engine: 6.0-liter dohc 48-valve V-12

Horsepower: 510

0–60 mph: 4.1 seconds

Top speed: 190 mph

Price when new: $183,000 (V-12)

Value now: Same

When the first new-era, so-called VH (vertical-horizontal) platform V8 Vantage (*below*) appeared, it was perhaps just a tad on the weedy side in terms of power and performance, especially considering the badge it wore so proudly on its rump. The 4.3-liter engine sounded good enough and delivered perfectly decent performance, but the car's drop-dead gorgeous looks and its luscious cabin design were most definitely the stars of the show. And then, of course, Aston Martin dropped first a 4.7-liter V-8 into the nose of the car, and then a 6.0-liter V-12 (*inset*)—and at a stroke the car's performance was transformed. In V12 guise especially, the combination of noise and pure, unadulterated acceleration is enough to make grown men weep. In many ways the V12 Vantage remains AM's most accomplished sports car. —SS

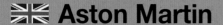

Aston Martin

V8 Vantage Zagato   1986–1990

Looking to reignite a once blissful relationship with the famous Italian design house, in the mid-1980s Aston asked coachbuilder Zagato to dream up an exotic body that could be fitted to a lightened, shortened V8 chassis. The result divided opinion. Gone were the luscious curves of Zagato's Aston revamps of the 1960s, and in their place were brutal straight lines and angled edges, with an extensive use of flush-fitting glass. The Zagato was dramatic to look at but not exactly beautiful in the traditional sense, and critics found it hard to get over the resemblance to contemporary Japanese sports coupes. On the other hand, only 89 were ever built, which means the Zagato is still monstrously rare and, of course, highly valuable today. —SS

- When it first announced the Zagato at the 1985 Geneva auto show, AM showed only drawings of the car. This was enough, however; within a few months the company had received enough orders to sell out the entire planned production run.

- The design was intended to be a modern interpretation of the original DB4 GT Zagato. Hmm. . . .

- The original list price was $156,600, but by the end of the 1980s cars were changing hands for over $500,000.

- British TV star Rowan Atkinson bought the first-ever right-hand-drive Zagato.

Engine: 5.3-liter V-8	Top speed: 186 mph
Horsepower: 432	Price when new: $156,600
0–60 mph: 5.0 seconds	Value now: $200,000

2012   **Virage**

- Torque spins out to 420 lb-ft.

- The two-person convertible version is called Volante.

- Behind the 20-inch wheels are carbon-ceramic brakes.

- Buyers can select one of two styles of recessed hood vents for added personalization.

Engine: 6.0-liter dohc V-12	Top speed: 186 mph
Horsepower: 490	Price when new: $210,000
0–60 mph: 4.5 seconds	Value now: Same

This can get a bit confusing. Aston offers a wide range of models—12 altogether when you include hardtop and roadster versions—each based on the VH platform. These include the DBS, DB9, Vantage, and the newest model, the lovely Virage. Each features styling that is as pretty as any in the business, but quite similar car to car. The Virage leads with a five-bar grille in the Aston frame and glides back via taut surface tension to the vertical tail. Under the hood is a powerful 6.0-liter V-12 backed by a six-speed Touchtronic 2 automatic gearbox with paddle shifting. Inside is an interior of leather and luxury with 2+2 seating—the best seat, of course, being the driver's seat. —JL

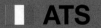

ATS

2500 GT   1963–1964

When the group of engineers that had led Ferrari and Phil Hill to the 1961 Formula 1 title defected from the famed Italian company, they joined an all-new automaker called Automobili Turismo e Sport (ATS). Engineer Carlo Chiti planned to create both a Formula 1 and sports car, both powered by versions of the same V-8. Classic A-arm suspensions were designed for the car's space frame, which was clothed in a beautiful body by famed designer Franco Scaglione. Sadly the ATS venture was doomed by a variety of happenings, including a recession in the Italian economy. Only a handful of the pretty mid-engine ATS 2500 GTs remain, although they are prized by collectors and occasionally appear at such famed shows as the Pebble Beach Concours d'Elegance. —JL

- Legendary Italian engineer Giotto Bizzarrini also had a hand in the design of the ATS 2500 GT.
- This was one of the first modern mid-engine production sports cars.
- Two ATS GTs were built with 3.0-liter 300-horsepower V-8s.
- It's estimated that just eight ATS GTs were built; only five still exist.

Engine: 2.5-liter dohc V-8	**Top speed:** 150 mph
Horsepower: 220–250	**Price when new:** N/A
0–60 mph: N/A	**Value now:** $525,000

- Electric motors drive the front wheels and the V-6 drives the rear set. Audi says torque vectoring allows each wheel to be turned or braked independently, "creating extremely precise, dynamic handling" and "the quattro drive of the future."

- Instead of traditional gauges, the e-tron Spyder provides information to the driver via a digital display screen.

- Whether it gets an electric or hybrid powertrain, word on the street is that Audi will have a 2012 production model based on the e-tron design.

- In addition to traditional auto show venues, Audi displayed the e-tron Spyder at the 2011 Consumer Electronics Show in Las Vegas.

Engine: 3.0-liter twin turbocharged V-6, plus two electric motors
Horsepower: 387
0–60 mph: Est. 4.3 seconds
Top speed: Est. 155 mph
Price when new: Concept car, not yet for sale
Value now: N/A

At the Frankfurt auto show in the fall of 2009, Audi unveiled its first e-tron concept car. The always-lowercase label is Audispeak for a high-performance sports car with an electric drivetrain.

A year later, at the Paris show, Audi peeled the top off the concept and gave it more angular styling, which resulted in the e-tron Spyder shown here. But now instead of a pure electric drivetrain, the concept sported a plug-in diesel-electric hybrid system—a twin turbocharged, 300-horsepower 3.0-liter V-6 with a pair of electric motors that added another 87 horsepower. This was a concept that looked like it could become reality.

Audi said the e-tron Spyder could sprint to 60 miles per hour in about 4.3 seconds yet could travel as far as 30 miles purely on electric power, all whilst returning the overall equivalent fuel economy of 107 miles per gallon. And don't fret about range anxiety: Audi claimed the car could cruise for more than 620 miles before its fuel tank needed to be refilled. If all goes well, consumers may have an opportunity to put these claims to the test in just a few years. —LE

Audi

Quattro 1981–1991

In March 1980, Audi unveiled a vehicle that would have a major impact on both road and racing cars for years to come. This was the Quattro, the first high-performance street car to feature four-wheel drive, the first in what would be a long line of performance cars that made use of all four wheels for maximum grip and control. Within a few years, every Audi model would feature its trademark(ed) "quattro" (Italian for "four") system.

A turbocharged street-legal rally car, the Quattro was a true driving enthusiast's vehicle, and, spurred on by changes to the World Rally Championship regulations that allowed four-wheel drive, Audi campaigned increasingly robust versions of its boxy beast in the early and mid-1980s, with dominating results. In 1981, Quattro driver Michele Mouton became the first woman to win a WRC event. The following year Audi won the first of two WRC manufacturers' titles, and in 1983 Hannu Mikkola earned the drivers' championship behind the wheel of the Audi Quattro A1. —LE

- Michele Moulton also drove an Audi Quattro to victory in the Pikes Peak Hill Climb in 1985. Walter Rohrl repeated her Race to the Clouds victory in 1987.

- Rally versions of the Audi Quattro were rated at as much as 470 horsepower.

- To distinguish it from the many "quattro" models that followed, the original Quattro is often referred to as the Ur-Quattro ("Original" Quattro).

- In 1985 and 1986, Audi offered a Sport Quattro version of the car, with 480 horsepower and nearly no turbo lag. These cars also had enhanced aerodynamics, could accelerate to 60 mph in less than four seconds, and have become prized by car collectors, who pay as much as $120,000 for one.

Engine: 2.1-liter inline five	Top speed: 130 mph
Horsepower: 160	Price when new: $35,000
0–60 mph: Est. 11 seconds	Value now: $15,000

- The Audi Quattro Concept takes styling cues from the original Audi Quattro—note the C pillar—but gives them a very 21st-century twist.

- The concept's LED (light-emitting diode) headlamp display changes the car's appearance from squinty-eyed to eyes wide open.

- Audi says the 408-horsepower engine would be rated at 27.6 miles per gallon in the United States.

- Reports in early 2011 hinted that the Quattro could see production by the middle of the decade.

Engine: 2.5-liter turbocharged inline five	**Top speed:** 155 mph
Horsepower: 408	**Price when new:** concept car, not for sale
0–60 mph: Est. 3.8 seconds	**Value now:** N/A

Audi celebrated the 30th anniversary of its original Quattro model by unveiling a new Quattro Concept at the 2010 Paris auto show.

The new concept is based on Audi's RS 5 model, though it has a shorter wheelbase and seats only two within an aluminum body with carbon fiber hood and hatch. The concept draws power from the inline-five-cylinder engine used in the Audi TT RS. This lump pumps out more than 400 horsepower, but the car's light weight gives it the same power-to-weight ratio as the Audi R8, the company's V-10–powered supercar. Thus the concept should sprint to 60 miles per hour in about 3.8 seconds.

In keeping with the car's historic name, the concept features a sport differential that enhances handling by sending more power to the outside rear wheel. Homage to the original Quattro's success in rallying includes a co-driver's-style route book that displays on the navigation screen. —LE

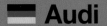

Audi

R8 and R8 V-10 — 2006–

The original Audi R8 was a Le Mans race car. To celebrate its success—the R8 won the 24-hour race five times in six years—Audi launched a mid-engine supercar by the same name. The R8 road car (*inset*) is based on the Lamborghini Gallardo (both Audi and Lamborghini are part of the Volkswagen Group) and is held together by an Audi aluminum space-frame chassis. Initially, power for the R8 road car came from a 4.2-liter V-8 that provided 414 horsepower. In 2008, Audi launched the R8 5.2 (*below*), which took its name from the 525-horsepower 5.2-liter V-10 fit into the car. To top off the R8 line, Audi announced plans to build 333 Audi R8 GTs. These cars will benefit from carbon fiber components, which will make the car some 180 pounds lighter, and from a modified 5.2-liter V-10 engine that will provide 560 horsepower and a top speed of 199 miles per hour. —*LE*

- The successor to the R8 Le Mans racer was the R10 TDI that added four more 24-hour race victories in a five-year span through 2010.

- The R8 road car was previewed by the Audi Le Mans Quattro concept car unveiled at the Geneva auto show in 2003. The production version of the R8 made its debut at Paris in the fall of 2006.

- The R8 and R8 5.2 (V-10) are available as closed coupes or as open spyders.

- The R8 was featured in the 2008 and 2010 movies *Iron Man* and *Iron Man 2* as part of Tony Stark's impressive garage full of supercars.

Tech specs (V-10):
Engine: 5.2-liter V-10
Horsepower: 525
0–60 mph: 3.7 seconds

Top speed: 185 mph
Price when new: $149,000
Value now: Same

- The TT was named for the famed Tourist Trophy races staged on the Isle of Man in the Irish Sea.

- The original design of the TT was done at Volkswagen's California design center and was the work of Freeman Thomas and J Mays.

- After some early high-speed crashes, TTs were equipped with electronic stability controls, revised suspension, and rear spoilers.

- The TT RS was the safety (pace) car for the 2009 24 Hours of Le Mans.

Tech specs (2011 model):

Engine: 2.0-liter turbocharged DOHC inline five

0–60 mph: 5.3 seconds

Top speed: 130 mph

Price when new: $38,300

Value now: Same

The Mazda Miata re-ignited interest in two-seat roadsters in the early 1990s, and many other manufacturers joined the party—some sooner, some later. In 1998, Audi introduced the TT, first as a closed 2+2 coupe in the fall, and then as a two-seat roadster convertible the following summer.

A second-generation TT was introduced for the 2007 model year after being previewed in the form of a "shooting brake" (two-door station wagon) concept car at the 2005 Tokyo auto show. The second generation has more angular styling, uses aluminum in the front bodywork to enhance weight distribution, and is longer and wider than the earlier version.

In Detroit in 2008, Audi showed off a high-performance S version of the car—the TTS—which featured a 272-horsepower engine, lowered suspension, and other enhancements. A year later in Geneva, the car's dynamic potential was enlarged with a TT RS version with a 340-horsepower five-cylinder engine. —LE

🇬🇧 Austin-Healey

100 and 3000 — 1953–1968

Looking to tap the lucrative postwar American auto market, British carmaker Austin turned to Donald Healey, a rally racer and former technical director at Triumph, who had recently turned to making touring cars and sports cars. Healey and his designer, Gerry Coker, devised a two-seat roadster around Austin Atlantic mechanical components. Healey called the car the Healey 100 (*below right*) when it was displayed at the London auto show, but it became the Austin-Healey 100 when it went into series production as a joint venture.

The nimble car would prove to be a huge hit, and over time the car evolved from the 100 to the 100-Six (with a new six-cylinder engine) to the 3000 (*bottom*), the "Big Healey," which took its name from its 3,000cc (actually 2,912cc) inline six-cylinder engine. The 3000 was available as a two-seat roadster or in a 2+2 seating configuration. Not only was the 3000 more powerful, it also featured front disc brakes. Austin-Healey 3000s were very successful as rally cars and have become very popular with classic car collectors. —*LE*

- Donald Healey drove a modified 100 to speeds as high as 142 mph on the Bonneville Salt Flats in October 1953.

- The Austin-Healey 100 was priced at just less than $3,000 in the United States, around a thousand dollars more than an MG and a thousand less than a Jaguar.

- A Mark II version of the Austin-Healey 3000 used a trio of carburetors to boost horsepower to 132.

- For 1963, the 3000 was switched to 2+2 configuration and got roll-up windows.

(For 3000):
Engine: 3.0-liter inline six
Horsepower: 124–150
0–60 mph: Less than 10 seconds
Top speed: 115 mph
Price when new: $3,300
Value now: $65,000

- The Sprite was launched at the 1958 Monaco Grand Prix.

- Production for the Mark I (shown here) was 48,987 units from 1958 to 1961.

- Sprites proved to be successful competition cars, and many are still raced today.

- Need to get to the engine? You lift the entire front bodywork.

Engine: 948cc inline four	**Top speed:** 83 mph
Horsepower: 43	**Price when new:** $2,000
0–60 mph: 20 seconds	**Value now:** $12,000–15,000

For many of us, the Sprite was the perfect first sports car. It was small, but also rugged, cheap, and a blast to drive. By the late 1950s, Donald Healey had already found success with his big sports car (see previous entry) and decided to build a less expensive model based on components from the British Motor Corporation. The engine, for example, was a tiny, slightly upgraded four from the Austin A Series. What really sold the little car, however, was its exterior design. Gerry Coker, who did the big Healey, drew this small rounded box and originally planned on including retracting headlights. When that proved too pricey, they plopped the pair atop the hood and the Sprite was forever known as a Bugeye. They weren't fast, but it's tough to drive a Sprite without smiling. —JL

Autokraft

Cobra Mk IV — 1982–1996

- Autokraft's factory was in the infield of the famous Brooklands race circuit.

- Autokraft began as a Cobra restoration shop.

- Some 480 Autokraft Cobras were built.

- Looks like a Cobra, drives like a Cobra...very quick.

Engine: 4.9-liter ohv V-8	Top speed: 134 mph
Horsepower: 250	Price when new: N/A
0–60 mph: 5.1 seconds	Value now: $105,000

After Carroll Shelby finished with the Cobra, the equipment used to build the cars eventually ended up in the hands of Brian Angliss. He continued Cobra production during the 1980s and early 1990s with a company called Autokraft, using the same machines that formed the original frames and bodies. Not surprisingly, this led to legal battles between Shelby and Angliss, but Autokraft continued while cooperating with Ford. —JL

Beck

550 Spyder — 1986–

- James Dean was killed in a Porsche 550 Spyder.

- Among the engine options available for the Beck 550 is a water-cooled 2.5-liter Subaru engine.

- Prices for the 190-horsepower Subaru version start at $37,500.

- Beck also makes a Porsche Speedster replica.

Engine: 1.9-liter flat four	Top speed: 130 mph
Horsepower: 125	Price when new: $33,306
0–60 mph: 5.8 seconds	Value now: Same

Yup, it sure looks like a Porsche 550 Spyder from the 1950s, but it's a brand-new vehicle with a smooth fiberglass body. And they aren't made in Germany, but rather Bremen, Indiana. Beck starts with a fiberglass body over a tubular space frame. Inside are leather-upholstered seats, and there's a folding top and side curtains. Okay, they are replicas, but also a great deal of fun at a fraction of the originals' prices. —JL

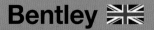

1927   **4 1/2-litre**

- To fund his auto-building effort, Bentley turned to wealthy British sportsman, Woolf Barnato. Barnato drove Bentleys to victory at Le Mans three times.

- The most famous Bentleys, the 4 1/2-liter Blower Bentleys, weren't successful race cars.

- Bentley built 655 non-supercharged 4 1/2s, 55 with the blower.

- Bentley's first car was previewed at the 1919 London auto show, although its engine wouldn't be ready for another two years.

Engine: 4 1/2-liter ohc 16-valve inline four	**Top speed:** 100 mph
	Price when new: N/A
Horsepower: 110	**Value now:** more than $1,000,000
0–60 mph: N/A	

Walter Owen (W. O.) Bentley was an engineer who had spent World War I helping the British military improve its aircraft engines. The "3-litre" Bentley was the first motorcar built by his post-war automaking enterprise, and was available from 1921 to 1929 in Blue, Red, and Green Label versions, each with a different length wheelbase. Bentley's wealthy young benefactors—the so-called Bentley Boys—won five of the first seven runnings of the 24 Hours of Le Mans race, twice (in 1924 and 1927) with cars powered by 3.0-liter four-cylinder engines. When Bentley owners needed more power, the company produced a 4 1/2-liter (seen here), then supercharged it despite W.O.'s protests. Next came the 6 1/2-liter versions, and then the big boy, the 8.0-liter. While the Bentley Boys went off racing, European royalty—princely and theatrically—furthered Bentley's reputation by driving them on the streets. —LE

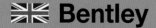
Continental GT Speed — 2009

When W. O. Bentley's benefactor, Woolf Barnato, withdrew his support from the company in 1931, the Bentley operation was taken over by British Central Equitable Trust, a front for Rolls-Royce. Soon after, W. O. left the firm that continued to bear his name, moving on to pursue engineering for Lagonda and later for Armstrong-Siddeley.

In 1998, Rolls and Bentley both were absorbed into Volkswagen, which later sold Rolls to BMW but retained and revived Bentley with new models, which for the 2009 model year included the Continental GT Speed, a higher-performance version of the Continental GT. With a 600 horsepower W-12 engine, this large, sporty car can accelerate to 60 miles per hour in less than 4 1/2 seconds, to 125 mph in less than 13, and on up to make it the first 200-plus Bentley. Not bad for a car that weighs nearly 5,300 pounds. —*LE*

- Bentley showed a Zagato-bodied version of the Continental GT, the GTZ, at the Geneva auto show in 2008.
- The Supersports extracts 621 horsepower from its engine, and Bentley claimed a 0–60 sprint of less than 4 seconds.
- In 2007, Bentley hired former World Rally Champion Juha Kankkunen to set a world record to top speed on ice.
- Kankkunen ran the Continental GT Speed at 199.83 mph on the frozen Baltic Sea off the coast of Finland.

Engine: 6.0-liter twin-turbo W-12	**Top speed:** 200-plus mph
Horsepower: 600	**Price when new:** $230,000
0–60 mph: 4.4 seconds	**Value now:** Same

1886 Patent Motorwagen

- Benz built three variations of the Patent Motorwagen from 1886 to 1892.

- Twenty-five copies were built and sold of variation No. 3, known as Model 3.

- Benz's wife, Bertha, helped to convince her husband of the Motorwagen's suitability by taking it on an extended journey from Mannheim to her hometown of Pforzheim and back again.

- In case you're wondering, yes, that is 1961 Formula 1 World Champion Phil Hill driving the Patent Motorwagen replica in the photo.

Engine: 954cc single	**Top speed:** 10 mph
Horsepower: 2/3 [fraction]	**Price when new:** N/A
0–60 mph: Ha! See top speed	**Value now:** Priceless

On January 29, 1886, Karl Benz of Germany patented a three-wheeled "Patent Motorwagen"—and the very first commercially available car was born. Actually, that's not quite true, because before that date Herr Benz had been experimenting with all sorts of motorized vehicles—the Victoria and the Vis-à-Vis being the two most famous. These things take time, though, and it wasn't until Benz produced the Velo in 1894 that the idea of the first volume-produced automobile became a reality; some 1,200 Velos were eventually produced. And the rest, as they say, is history.
—SS

Bertone

Alfa Romeo *Carabo* 1968

What is this wild green show car doing in this book? If you ask many of today's top car designers which automobiles influenced them, most, if not all, will mention the *Carabo*. The wedge-shaped design that came to be used in several automobiles—such as the Lotus Esprit and Lancia Stratos—arguably started with the *Carabo*. Penned by Marcello Gandini, who was working at Bertone at the time, one can see how it influenced his later design of the Lamborghini Countach, including the swing-up doors. Introduced at the Paris auto show in 1968, the *Carabo* was named after a beetle that shares the same iridescent color. Under that amazing body is an Alfa Romeo Tipo 33 mid-engine chassis, a type that was raced quite successfully. —*JL*

- The *Carabo* now resides in Alfa Romeo's museum.
- Mated to the V-8 is a six-speed transmission.
- Suspension is the classic upper and lower A-arm race car layout.
- The glass is reflective one-way.

Engine: 2.0-liter dohc V-8	**Top speed:** Est. 150 mph
Horsepower: 230	**Price when new:** N/A
0–60 mph: Est. 6.4 seconds	**Value now:** Priceless

1963   Cheetah

- A Cheetah appeared in the 1966 movie *Spinout*, starring Elvis Presley.

- Chevrolet got an early Cheetah and extensively tested it.

- A company called BTM builds continuation Cheetahs today.

- One Cheetah was "converted" into a roadster: Racer Ralph Salyer had the roof of his Cro-Sal Special race car chopped off to spare himself from the relentless heat of the car's tiny, cramped cockpit.

Engine: 6.2-liter ohv V-8	**Top speed:** 210 mph
Horsepower: 520	**Price when new:** $12,000
0–60 mph: N/A	**Value now:** $100,000

Spectacular automobiles, the Bill Thomas Cheetahs are quite rare—maybe 12 exist. Most were built as race cars, although apparently at least one has lived its life as a street machine. What gets you about the Cheetah is the layout, the long hood with the cockpit shifted well rearward. This was done to get the Chevrolet V-8 as far back as possible for good weight balance. In fact it was so far back the transmission was basically connected to the differential. Weighing just 1,700 pounds and with a booming Chevy V-8 in race trim, the Cheetahs were famous for their speed. Some were drag raced. But they also had reputations for quirky handling. Thomas hoped to build 100 cars to compete in the production race car classes, but a factory fire ended these ambitious plans. —*JL*

Bizzarrini

5300 Spyder S.I.   1966–1969

None other than the late Phil Hill would have told you of the engineering expertise of Giotto Bizzarrini. The Italian worked first at Alfa Romeo, then Ferrari through 1961 before moving on to ATS, then Lamborghini, and finally Iso Rivolta. There Bizzarrini engineered the Iso Grifo AC3/C, and after Renzo Rivolta's death, Bizzarrini took over production of the car, renaming it the 5300 GT Strada. Powered by a Chevrolet 327 V-8 with four Weber carburetors, the cars were well regarded for their power and handling, with an independent front suspension and DeDion rear layout. It's estimated that 115 5300 GT Stradas were built, and there were also competition versions. The little-known Italian design house Stile Italia (hence the S.I.) turned three of the 5300 chassis into targa-style roadsters with a removable center section roof, as shown here. —JL

- Giorgetto Giugiaro, working at Bertone, styled the 5300 GT.
- The first Spyder S.I. was uncovered at the 1966 Geneva auto show.
- Bizzarrini was based in Livorno, Italy.
- The Bizzarrini bodies were done in aluminum.

Engine: 5.3-liter ohv Chevrolet V-8	Top speed: 174 mph
Horsepower: 350	Price when new: N/A
0–60 mph: 5.5 seconds	Value now: $575,000

- BMW's internal code for this series of models was E9.

- 3.0 CSLs won the European Touring Car Championship in 1973 and then from 1975 through 1979.

- The car shown here is a CSL. The CSLs were lightened via the use of light alloy doors, hood, and trunk lid.

- The CSL's radical shape earned it the nickname the "Batmobile."

Engine: 3.0-liter sohc inline six	Top speed: 134 mph
Horsepower: 180	Price when new: $15,000
0–60 mph: 7.5 seconds	Value now: $30,000

In the late 1960s, BMW was just beginning to make headway into the lucrative American market, thanks to its nifty 02 Series of four-cylinder coupes. The company's model line became even more exciting and attractive with the introduction of the now-famous inline six-cylinder engine powering larger sedans and coupes. Then came 1971, when the six was opened up to a displacement of 3.0 liters, creating the CS and the 202-horsepower fuel-injected CSi. The following year, BMW launched the homologation special CSL (*leicht,* or "light") and went racing—to considerable success. Those who drove the cars would come to appreciate the smoothness of the drivetrain, but what really made the BMW was its exterior design. The classic BMW kidney grille up front, the sleekness of the lower body, and that greenhouse that almost seemed to float on thin pillars. Beautiful. —*JL*

315/1   1935

Back in 1935, the car industry, particularly the German car industry, was going through something of a transformation. The idea of driving as a sporting activity had really begun to take off, and the sleekly styled, open-top BMW 315/1 was a landmark machine in that respect. Its press release at the time claimed the car was "for people who feel that strong yearning for wide open roads simply perfect for driving fast, for Alpine passes just begging to be conquered, and for competitors so easy to overtake." And if nothing else it was quick, the 315/1, thanks to its 40-horsepower straight six engine, which propelled the car to what BMW optimistically claimed to be "120 kmh and beyond." —SS

- The 315/1 was introduced to the world at the 1934 Berlin Motorshow.

- It was referred to as a Sports Roadster, and was different from most other cars at the time in that it had only two seats.

- The 315/1's first significant victory came at the International Alpine Rally of 1934.

- The car also won the first-ever race to be held at the famous Nürburgring, finishing some 17 km ahead of the next car.

Engine: 1.5-liter inline six	Top speed: 75 mph
Horsepower: 40	Price when new: N/A
0–60 mph: N/A	Value now: $120,000+

- Among the 328's other innovations were independent front suspension and headlights faired into the fenders for increased aerodynamic efficiency.

- Some consider the 328 to be the first modern sports car.

- A total of 463 328s were built.

- The body of the 328s is done in aluminum.

Engine: 2.0-liter ohv inline six	**Top speed:** 93 mph
Horsepower: 80	**Price when new:** $3,500
0–60 mph: N/A	**Value now:** $500,000

Before World War II, BMW built the 328 sports car, which was well-known for both its speed and handling. Among the car's innovations was its inline six-cylinder engine with side-mounted camshaft that opened both the intake and exhaust valves of the hemispherical combustion chamber. The pretty two-seater body credited to Fritz Fiedler shows the early form of BMW's now-traditional kidney grilles. BMW used the 328s in several competitions, winning the RAC Rally in 1939 and taking a class win in the 1938 Mille Miglia. But its finest hour came in 1940 when a special 328 with a coupe body created by the Milanese firm of Touring (the car shown here) won that year's version of the Italian classic. —*JL*

507   1956–1959

Max Hoffman was the American importer for many European automakers, a position that allowed him to influence the design and creation of several models from several automakers. In the mid-1950s, he convinced BMW to hire Count Albrecht Goertz to design a new sports car that would come to be known as the 507. The new model made its debut at the famed Waldorf Astoria Hotel in 1955, and later that year at the Frankfurt auto show, where the 507 roadster was joined by an elegant twin wearing a removable hardtop. Not that the 507 wasn't elegant without a top. Goertz had stretched the double-kidney grille nearly across the full width of the front of the car, and his design also included a long and low profile with vents behind the front wheels and a kink just ahead of the rear wheels. Stunning. . . —*LE*

- Goertz was born in Europe, moved to the United States in 1936, and served in the U.S. Army for five years during World War II.

- After the war, Goertz met famed industrial designer Raymond Loewy, who encouraged him to study design and hired him to work in the Studebaker styling studio.

- The 507's glamorous looks made it popular among Hollywood types, including Elvis Presley. The King of Rock and Roll later gave his 507 to Ursula Andress.

- The 507 was the inspiration for the Z8 model BMW put into production in 2000.

Engine: 3.2-liter 16-valve V-8   **Top speed:** Est. 137 mph
Horsepower: 150   **Price when new:** $9,000
0–60 mph: Est. 11 seconds   **Value now:** $850,000

- The B7 is produced on the same assembly line as the regular 7-series, but its V-8 engine is produced by Alpina in-house.

- Alpina was created in 1965 as a BMW tuning business, but nowadays it is a manufacturer in its own right.

- Alpina developed the legendary 3.0CSL profiled a few pages earlier in this book.

- The B7 is the only current Alpina to be offered for sale officially in the United States, which is a shame because the entire lineup is equally as excellent.

Engine: 4.4-liter twin turbo V-8
Horsepower: 500
0–60 mph: 4.5 seconds

Top speed: 174 mph
Price when new: $124,175
Value now: Same

Strange kind of car company, Alpina, for on the one hand it appears to offer stiff competition to BMW's own M Division, but on the other there is a subtle difference between a full-fat M car and its Alpina equivalent. And in the case of the B7, the result is good enough to produce a better car than the factory itself can make. Truth is, the V-12 760i is not as well resolved as the V-8 B7; the former lacks the crisp dynamic resolve of the Alpina and the subtle styling tweaks to match it. But then Alpina has always managed to combine extraordinarily good handling and steering characteristics with a ride that's as supple as it is smooth. Dial in the monstrous power and performance of that twin turbo V-8, enjoy the comforts of huge amounts of cabin space. . .you have here a car that can do just about anything you'd ever want. —SS

BMW

M1 — 1978–1981

In 1972, BMW impressed the automotive world when it showed the Paul Bracq–designed Turbo Concept at that year's Summer Olympics. Six years later, the Munich-based automaker revived the Turbo's basic shape with the mid-engine M1 supercar. Giorgetto Giugiaro designed this version, which was to be built by Lamborghini. However, Lambo's often-uncertain financial situation forced BMW to take the project back into its Motorsports division. Powering the M1 was one of BMW's famed inline sixes with 277 horsepower. BMW intended to race the M1 to take on German rival Porsche, but its timing was off and the car's main racing fame came in the ProCar series, which pitted Grand Prix drivers against each other. In their time, M1s were respected for both their speed and excellent road manners. —JL

- BMW built only 456 M1s from 1978 to 1981.
- The production M1 was unveiled at the 1978 Paris auto show.
- The M1 is BMW's only production mid-engine model.
- In 2008, BMW had Giugiaro create the M1 Homage to celebrate the 30th anniversary of the M1's debut.

Engine: 3.5-liter dohc 24-valve inline six
Horsepower: 277
0–60 mph: 5.4 seconds

Top speed: 160 mph
Price when new: $60,000
Value now: $150,000

- The V-8 engine in this car weighs 15 kg less than the smaller-capacity straight six it replaced.

- In 2008, the car was offered with BMW's first-ever dual clutch gearbox, known as M-DCT (M double clutch transmission).

- *Car and Driver* magazine timed the M-DCT M3 V-8 at 3.9 seconds to 60 mph in 2009, with a standing quarter-mile of 12.9 seconds.

- In 2010, BMW produced a limited edition GTS model that was 300 pounds lighter than standard and cost $115,000.

Engine: 4.0-liter V-8	**Top speed:** 155 mph
Horsepower: 414	**Price when new:** $58,900
0–60 mph: 3.9 seconds	**Value now:** Same

The V-8–powered M3 is the latest and, most assume, greatest version of BMW's legendary icon. But if the purists of this world claim this car lacks the dynamic clarity of the original E30, what's not in any doubt is that the V-8 is easily the fastest M3. And the most civilized. And let's face it, even if the E92 model isn't as sweet in its responses as some of its predecessors, as a machine for all seasons there are few sporting coupes that offer a broader repertoire. The V-8 engine revs to a howling 8,400 rpm, there's a snappy paddle shift gearbox, and the rear-drive chassis is a true tire smokers' delight. Heck, there's even a power bulge on the hood to remind you of how much raw energy this car can unleash. Plus it has four seats and a decent size trunk to boot. —SS

BMW

M6 | 2005–2010

The M6 might not appeal to all tastes, all of the time—either visually or on the road—but then it was never designed to be all things to all men in the first place. At its core the M6 is a hot rod, pure and simple, with a snarling 5.0-liter V-10 engine and a seven-speed paddle shift gearbox that can deliver shifts faster (and occasionally with rather less delicacy) than the human hand ever could. And its styling was quite clearly intended to scare other road users out of its way whenever possible, especially around the nose, which looks unashamedly like that of a shark. Commercially it didn't do as well as BMW had hoped, but in 20 years' time this car will be remembered as one of the greats. —SS

- The M6 features a heads-up display that can be tailored to suit each individual driver's needs.

- On the steering wheel is a button marked "M" that allows you to alter the traction, diff, and even the engine's power setting at a stroke.

- The car will be remembered for having perhaps the least refined paddle shift gear change in history, ever.

- Untethered from its electronic limiter, the M6 is said to be capable of some 202 mph.

Engine: 5.0-liter V-10	Top speed: 155 mph (limited)
Horsepower: 500	Price when new: $96,000
0–60 mph: 4.2 seconds	Value now: $50,000–90,000

- BMW built 8,000 Z1s from 1989 to 1991.

- The Z1 never sold as well as BMW's expectations, mostly likely due to its high price, coupled with poor reviews of its performance.

- Because the body panels were not stressed members of the chassis, the car could be driven sans body panels.

- If you don't recognize this car, it might be because BMW never sold the Z1 in the United States.

Engine: 2.5-liter sohc inline six	**Top speed:** 140 mph
Horsepower: 170	**Price when new:** $46,000
0–60 mph: 8 seconds	**Value now:** $35,000

We all know BMW's Z sports cars today, but in 1989 when the first, the Z1, was launched, it was a breakthrough. The "Z" stands for *Zukunft*, which is German for "future." The handsome roadster has a body made of removable plastic and fiberglass panels; its most prominent feature is its electrically operated doors that drop down into the body. You can drive it doors up or down. BMW claimed that you could easily change the color of your Z1 by swapping body panels. BMW lifted the driveline from the 325i, but the chassis under the plastic body panels is unique. The front suspension uses MacPherson struts, while the multi-link rear design is called, appropriately, the Z axle. —JL

Z3   1995–2002

Mazda's Miata made two-seat roadsters popular again; then German automakers took the concept to a new plateau of dynamics and luxury with vehicles such as the Mercedes-Benz SLK, Audi TT, Porsche Boxster, and this car, the BMW Z3. The Z3 was the first of the Europeans to hit the street—or rather the screen: It made its debut in the 1995 James Bond film *GoldenEye*. The Z3 was remarkable in many ways, most significantly, perhaps, because it wasn't built in Germany or even Europe, but rather in a new BMW plant in Spartanburg, South Carolina.

Though its four-cylinder engine was rated at only 140 horsepower, the Z3 can be a fun car to drive, with acceptable acceleration and reasonably taut handling. It was not, however, what many expected from BMW. For 1997, things got much more exciting when BMW offered a 2.8-liter six-cylinder powerplant, and then came an M version with even more power and enhanced handling. —*LE*

- The designer of the Z3 was Tokyo-born Joji Nagashima, who also did exterior designs of BMW's 3 and 5 Series cars.

- The high-performance Z3—the 1999 M Roadster and a hatchback-style M Coupe—packed a 240-horsepower six-cylinder engine.

- Aftermarket tuners in Germany have crammed V-8 engines under the Z3 hood.

- The Spartanburg plant at first produced 3 Series and Z3 cars and now focuses on BMW sports activity vehicles (X3, X5, and X6 coupe).

Engine: 2.8-liter inline dohc 24-valve six
Horsepower: 192
0–60 mph: Est. 6.4 seconds

Top speed: Est. 140 mph
Price when new: $35,900
Value now: $4,500

- Why is the car called the Z4 instead of the Z3? BMW changed its naming system, assigning odd numbers to sedans and even numbers to coupes and convertibles.

- With more responsive handling and a better powerplant, the Z4 is the car many had hoped the Z3 would be.

- The Z4's styling was a reflection of the radical (and controversial) design philosophy of Chris Bangle, BMW's chief designer at the time.

- With demand increasing for BMW sport "activity" vehicles, production of the Z4 moved from South Carolina to Germany.

Tech specs (2011 Z4 sDrive35is model):	**0–60 mph:** Est. 4.8 seconds
Engine: 3.0-liter twin-turbocharged dohc inline six	**Top speed:** Est. 150 mph
	Price when new: $62,500
Horsepower: 335	**Value now:** Same

What would have been the next generation of the BMW Z3 roadster came to market in 2002 as the Z4, featuring more angular and even sharklike styling features. For the 2010 model year, the Z4 entered a new generation with a retractable hardtop roof system. By going to a retractable hardtop, BMW could replace the former Z4 roadster and coupe with a single vehicle, an all-weather sports car that can be driven with the top open or closed.

The Z4 is available in the United States with the buyer's choice of a 255-horsepower, normally aspirated 3.0-liter six-cylinder engine or a twin-turbocharged 300-horsepower version. Six-speed manual or paddle-shifted, double-clutch seven-speed automatic gearboxes are available. —LE

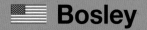

Bosley

Mk1 1953

Most likely you've never heard of Richard Bosley and his car. That's because he only built two machines, and this was the first. So why is it here? There are two stories: First comes Bosley, who, at 21, decided to build his own car. A true homebuilt machine, Bosley fabricated the frame and used Ford, Mercury, and Lincoln components in the chassis. The windshield was the rear window of a 1950 Ford. For power, Bosley went to Chrysler and its famous Hemi V-8. Building your own car is enough of a story, but here's the other. Bosley shaped the body and laid it up in fiberglass. What he created, the Bosley Mk I, became a landmark design used for reference by automotive designers. Instead of looking to Europe for influence, they could draw on an American design. —JL

- The gearbox was a Borg Warner five-speed truck transmission.
- Bosley installed a huge 55-gallon gas tank.
- Richard Bosley drove his Mk I some 100,000 miles.
- Bosley built a second car, the Interstate Mk II, which was not as attractive.

Engine: 5.4-liter ohv V-8	Top speed: Est. 160 mph
Horsepower: 180	Price when new: $9,000
0–60 mph: N/A	Value now: N/A

- SV-1 stands for "Safety Vehicle 1."

- Bricklin built just 2,854 SV-1s.

- Bricklin went into receivership in September 1975.

- Malcolm Bricklin's next adventure? Import the Yugo. . . .

Engine: 5.8-liter ohv V-8	**Top speed:** 111 mph
Horsepower: 175	**Price when new:** $7,490
0–60 mph: 9.9 seconds	**Value now:** $17,900

Malcolm Bricklin's adventure into building automobiles is more soap opera than engineering and production. The man who got Subaru started in the United States, Bricklin wanted to build a safety car. There was a big push to do such cars in the early 1970s, and the SV-1 had a built-in safety cage and 5-mph bumpers, and only came in bright safety colors. The gullwing cars are rather blunt and stubby-looking, and those of us who drove the SV-1s can attest to their minimal quality. The early cars had American Motors 5.9-liter V-8s, while the later versions used 5.8-liter Fords. The chassis was conventional, but the financing of the corporation was not. Richard Hatfield, premier of New Brunswick, Canada, bought into the Bricklin story and provided funding, but it was all a pipe dream. —JL

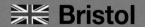

Bristol

400 — 1947–1950

The 400 was Bristol's first-ever foray into the world of cars, and it rumbled its way somewhat eccentrically into the world in 1947, sporting a straight-six engine and styling that made obvious the company's previous vocation as the British Bristol Aeroplane Company. It was, in many ways, a fairly outrageous copy of the BMW 328, featuring very similar styling and a mechanical makeup that was almost a dead ringer for the BMW's. Just 487 400s were built before the 401 took its place. —SS

- The 400 was one of the first cars to feature fully independent front suspension.

- Its gearbox was a four-speed manual featuring synchromesh on all of the last three ratios, plus a freewheel on first gear.

- The 400's straight-six engine was considered to be cutting edge in its time due to its hemispherical combustion chambers and very short inlet/exhaust ports.

- It's not surprising the 400 looked like a BMW 328, given that Bristol bought the licence from Frazer Nash to build BMWs.

Engine: 2.0-liter inline six	Top speed: 95 mph
Horsepower: 80	Price when new: $6,995
0–60mph: N/A	Value now: $150,000–$200,000

Bristol

Beaufighter — 1982–1993

Although it was yet another revision of the continuously evolving model line, the Beaufighter had rather more (undisclosed) power than the 412 on which it was based. The secret was, of course, turbocharging, and by the time the Beaufighter appeared in 1980, everyone was doing it. Although Bristol was as coy as ever about its power figures, the car's claimed performance was deeply impressive—0–60 miles per hour in 5.9 seconds with a top speed of 150. And, of course, it was a far less predictable choice of wheels than the two-a-penny Bentley Turbos of the same era. . . . —SS

- Bristol was famous for not letting the press drive its cars, and the Beaufighter was no exception. . . .

- The only way a magazine could test one, therefore, was to go out and buy one for itself, which is something that few magazines chose to do.

- That said, it's estimated that the Beaufighter had well over 300 horsepower from its turbocharged V-8 engine.

- The title Beaufighter came from the Type 156 plane of the same name, made by the Bristol Aeroplane Company in 1939.

Engine: 6-liter V-8 straight six	Top speed: 150 mph
Horsepower: 80	Price when new: $80,000
0–60 mph: 5.9 seconds	Value now: $40,000

2004–   Fighter

- The torque of the Fighter T is a whopping 1,036 lb-ft.

- Bristol claims the T has a potential top speed of 270 mph, but they limit it to a "more than sufficient" 225.

- Inside are light racing seats and a lot of handwork detailing.

- After World War II, Bristol cars grew from the famous Bristol Aeroplane Company.

(T version):
Engine: 8-liter twin turbo V-10
Horsepower: 1,012
0–60 mph: 3.5 seconds

Top speed: 225 mph
Price when new: $557,445
Value now: Same

The Fighter's gullwing-door styling is quite nice from the rear 3/4 perspective, but those headlights spoil the front view. Looks aside, its acceleration will take your breath away. The Fighter has been built in three forms, and as with every Bristol since 1961 it has a Chrysler engine. Here it's the 8-liter all-aluminum V-10, which is done as the Fighter at 525 horsepower, the Fighter S with 628 horsepower, and the big honker, the Fighter T, which has a pair of turbos and 1,012 horsepower. This in a car that weighs roughly 3,500 pounds, so you can understand why all three models get to 60 miles per hour in 4.0 seconds or less. —JL

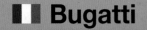

EB110   1991–1995

Romano Artioli revived the Bugatti name and in 1991 began to produce the EB110 in a factory just outside of Modena, Italy, home also to Ferrari. Paolo Stanzani, who was involved with the Lamborghini Miura, was responsible for much of the design of the mid-engine, all-wheel-drive supercar. Marcello Gandini, designer of the Lamborghini Countach, also did the EB110 with its typical swing-up Gandini doors. Up front is a tiny outline of the original Bugatti grille. The monocoque chassis of the EB110 was made of exotic composites by Aerospatiale, with aluminum body panels bonded to the chassis. There was a Super Sport version that boasted 650 horsepower. Unfortunately, Artioli's ambitious plans came to fruition just as the world economy softened, and after only five years of production the company was insolvent. —JL

- Why the name EB110? It comes from the initials of Bugatti founder Ettore Bugatti; the car was unveiled on the 110th anniversary of his birth.

- Volkswagen bought the rights to the Bugatti name in 1998.

- Each cylinder in the V-12 has five valves.

- The suspension featured racing-type upper and lower A-arms.

Engine: 3.5-liter quad-turbo V-12	**Top speed:** 213 mph
Horsepower: 560	**Price when new:** $350,000
0–60 mph: 4.0 seconds	**Value now:** $310,000

- The Type 32 "Tank" used hydraulic front brakes, a rear-mounted transmission, suspension designed to lower the car's center of gravity at speed, and engine architecture that featured overhead cams and three valves per cylinder.

- Ernest Friedrich drove one of the "Tank" Bugattis to a third-place finish in the 1923 Grand Prix at Lyon, but was 25 minutes behind the runner-up.

- The "Tank's" shape reportedly provided inspiration for the modern Bugatti Veyron.

- The five cars included a prototype and four racers.

Engine: 2.0-liter inline four	**Price when new:** N/A; never sold to general public
Horsepower: 80	
0–60 mph: N/A	**Value now:** Priceless
Top speed: 117 mph	

Benefiting from wartime airplane development, automotive designers and engineers experimented extensively with aerodynamic enhancements after World War I. Teardrop-shaped fenders—indeed, teardrop-shaped cars—and long, tapering tails and tall tail fins were tested as ways to cheat the wind and to boost top speeds while using less fuel.

In 1923 Ettore Bugatti created a Type 32 racer that became well known not because of its success, but because of its shape. The car was nicknamed the "Tank" because of its short, wide body with bullet-shaped nose, tall hood, and tapering tail.

Five examples were built, but because of their ill-handling characteristics—due to the car's stance, which was wide in track but with a very short wheelbase—and the car's shape, air making its away around the car's big nose section would, basically, lift the back end, thus limiting traction as speed increased. The cars raced only in 1923. For 1924, Bugatti would design the far more successful Type 35. —*LE*

■ Bugatti

After a short-lived experiment with the Type 32 "Tank" racer, Ettore Bugatti developed a much more conventional Grand Prix racer for the 1924 season, the Type 35. Over the course of the next seven years, Bugatti would produce more than 300 Type 35s for the road and for the track; those cars would win more than 1,000 races.

The Type 35 made its debut at the Grand Prix of Lyon, France. A year later, a less expensive and detuned Type 35A was offered. Although Bugatti didn't like superchargers, he used them on the Type 35C. The blower boosted horsepower to 128, and the car won the French Grand Prix in 1928 and 1930.

The engine grew from 2.0 to 2.3 liters in 1926, and Bugatti offered the Type 35T, though only 13 were produced because rules returned to the 2.0-liter limit. But before that rule change, Bugatti also produced the Type 35B, a supercharged version of the 35T, and won the 1929 French Grand Prix. —LE

- The Type 35 won the Targa Florio Italian road race five years in a row—1925, 1926, 1927, 1928, and 1929.

- At one point, Type 35s were winning a dozen or more races each week at various venues around Europe.

- The Type 35 chassis also would be the basis for the Type 37 and Type 39 Bugattis.

- The first Monaco Grand Prix in 1929 was won by British driver William Grover-Williams in a 35C painted a dark shade of green that would become known as British Racing Green.

Engine: 2-liter inline eight	Top speed: 100 mph
Horsepower: 90	Price when new: N/A
0–60 mph: N/A	Value now: $2 million

- It's estimated that only 10 Type 54s were built.

- The Type 54 matched the twin-cam Type 50 engine with a Type 45 chassis.

- A robust three-speed transmission was used.

- Type 54s weighed just shy of 2,100 pounds.

Engine: 4.9-liter dohc inline eight	**Top speed:** 124 mph
Horsepower: 300	**Price when new:** N/A
0–60 mph: N/A	**Value now:** N/A

Bugatti replaced the Type 35 racer with the Type 51 and its successors, the Type 53, 54, and 59, though victories were few, as Alfa-Romeo was dominant in this era. Then the German automakers began flexing their muscles in significant ways. . . Bugatti built exactly 10 Type 54s for the 1931–1934 racing seasons. They were powered by a 4.9-liter twin-overhead cam inline eight-cylinder engine that provided 300 horsepower. The Type 54 made its competitive debut at the Italian Grand Prix at Monza in 1931, where Achille Varza finished third. Teammate Louis Chiron won two weeks later at Bruno in the season-ending race. Type 54s were very difficult to drive; in fact, they were lethal to some drivers, including Czech Prince Jiri von Lobkowicz and Polish Count Stanislav Czaykowski, both of whom died driving them. A few 54s were rebuilt as roadsters. —LE

■■ Bugatti

Type 55   1931–1935

The Bugattis were an artistic family. Carlo was a famous 19th-century Italian furniture maker. He had two sons, Rembrandt and Ettore. Rembrandt became an acclaimed sculptor, known especially for his animal figures. Ettore became famous for another sort of sculpture, rolling sculpture powered by marvelous engines.

Ettore's son, Jean, also was a gifted artist, designing some of the most beautiful bodywork ever placed on an automobile. Unfortunately, Jean died in 1939 at age 30, when he veered off a road testing the newest high-speed version of the Bugatti Type 57. Jean had crashed rather than strike a drunken bicyclist who had somehow gotten onto the road that had been closed for the test.

The Bugatti Type 55 was the road car based on the Type 54 Grand Prix racer. It had a wider and stronger chassis and carried bodywork designed by Jean, who was barely in his 20s at the time. Some 38 Bugatti Type 55s were built between 1932 and 1935. —LE

- Some say the Bugatti twin-cam design mirrors that of the American Miller race car engines.

- The chassis has live axles at both ends.

- Type 55s have a four-speed gearbox.

- One reason the Type 55s were so quick was the fact they weighed some 1,800 pounds.

Engine: 2.2-liter supercharged dohc inline eight
Horsepower: 130
0–60 mph: N/A

Top speed: Est. 115 mph
Price when new: N/A
Value now: $1 million +

- Two years after his victory at Le Mans in the 57G "Tank," Jean-Pierre Wimille won again in the last pre-war 24-hour race, this time co-driving a Bugatti 57C with Pierre Veyron.

- If Veyron's name seems familiar, it's probably because Bugatti's contemporary supercar is called the Veyron.

- Rivets were needed to join the 57SC Atlantics' body panels because the magnesium alloy used for the bodywork would have melted had they been welded together.

- Fashion designer Ralph Lauren owns one Type 57SC Atlantic (the black car shown here). The other sold for more than $30 million in 2010 and resides at the Mullin Automotive Museum in Southern California.

Engine: 3.2-liter dohc inline eight	**Top speed:** 160 mph
Horsepower: 135 (or 160 when supercharged)	**Price when new:** N/A
0–60 mph: N/A	**Value now:** $1–$35 million depending on letter designation

Bugatti built 685 of its Type 57 (*below left and right*) models for various duties on the road and on the racetrack. Power was provided by a new 3.3-liter straight-eight engine inspired by those built by American racer Harry Miller.

For the track, Bugatti resurrected but updated its aerodynamic "Tank" (*bottom*) design for the 57G, and the car duly won the 1936 French Grand Prix with Jean-Pierre Wimille and Raymond Sommer driving. The following year, Wimille and Robert Benoist drove the car to victory in the 24 Hours of Le Mans, where they lapped the field and broke every race record.

Though winning races is impressive, the most memorable of the 57s were elegant Jean Bugatti–designed coupes, the 57SC Atlantics. The cars were lowered—the rear axles ran through the frame—and wore aerodynamic magnesium alloy bodies that were riveted together along the car's centerline. Only four of the Type 57 cars were SC Atlantics, and only two are known still to exist. —*LE*

■ Bugatti

Veyron 16.4   2005–

Just as the original Bugattis were among the world's most acclaimed automobiles, so too is the current Veyron 16.4. Now owned by Volkswagen, the firm is again located in Molsheim, France, though engineering takes place in VW's home in Wolfsburg, Germany. Dramatically styled with high-speed aerodynamics in mind, the Veyron is powered by an 8.0-liter W-16 fitted with four turbochargers. The transmission is a seven-speed DSG, and the Veyron has all-wheel drive. The interior is as fitting to the Bugatti—rich materials, fine detailing—as the exterior. Most recently Bugatti has produced the $2,400,000 16.4 Super Sport. Horsepower has been taken to 1,200 and torque to 1,106 lb-ft. The tires force the Super Sport to be limited to 257 miles per hour, though the car reached 268 at VW's German test track. —JL

- Torque of the "base" W-16 is 923 lb-ft.

- The Veyron is capable of reaching speeds that would literally lift a car off the ground like an aircraft, but it sticks to the ground via aerodynamic downforce.

- Each Veyron is hand-built over a period of three weeks by eight highly skilled craftspersons.

- Bugatti builds no more than one or two Veyrons per week.

Engine: 8.0-liter quad-turbo dohc W-16
Horsepower: 1001
0–60 mph: 2.4 seconds

Top speed: 268 mph
Price when new: $2,000,000
Value now: Not much less

- Torque of the 170-horsepower V-6 was 220 lb-ft.

- Buick had hoped to sell 20,000 Reatta per year, but. . .

- The automaker built 21,751 Reattas during the 1988–1991 model years.

- After making just coupes in 1988–1989, a Reatta convertible was added for 1990.

Engine: 3.8-liter ohv V-6	Top speed: 125 mph
Horsepower: 170	Price when new: $28,885
0–60 mph: 9.2 seconds	Value now: $5,000–$10,000

Just as Cadillac felt the need to create a sports car and designed the Allanté (see next profile), Buick concieved the Reatta. Like the Caddy, the front-drive Reatta was based on General Motors' cut-down E platform. It wasn't so much a sports car in the traditional sense as a sports car seen through the eyes of the golf-playing country club set. That's not a put-down, but the Reatta was known more for its luxury equipment—e.g., automatic transmission, touch screen controls for the radio and climate control—than for its refined handling. This was a time when GM had finally understood that its quality was suspect, so the Reatta was built in a "Craft Centre," which had assembly stations. The 3.8-liter V-6 started at 165 horsepower in 1988 and went to 170 in 1991. —JL

Cadillac

Allanté 1987–1993

It probably seemed like a good idea within General Motors, but the idea of doing a world-class sports car from Cadillac in the early 1980s was an impossible dream—sorta like Republicans humming hip-hop. It was an ambitious program, the sports car's body designed and built by Pininfarina in Italy, then flown via 747s to Detroit to mate it to the chassis. But there were fundamental problems trying to build a Caddy to compete with Mercedes-Benz and Jaguar. The main one was front-wheel drive, which made the Allanté a monument to torque steer and understeer. There were three engines in the Allanté's seven-year career, a 4.1- then 4.5-liter version of the HT pushrod V-8, and then one year with the very nice 295-horsepower, 4.6-liter Northstar V-8. —JL

- Cadillac built some 21,000 Allantés, half as many as it planned to sell.
- It was 3,300 miles from Pininfarina to Detroit, giving the Allanté the "world's longest production line."
- At Pininfarina, Allanté bodies were assembled next to those of Ferrari.
- Aluminum was used for the Allanté's removable hardtop.

Tech specs (1989 model):
Engine: 4.5-liter ohv V-8
Horsepower: 200
0–60 mph: 7.9 seconds

Top speed: 125 mph
Price when new: $54,700
Value now: $9,000

- The first car to exceed 60 mph was a pure electric (1899), a torpedo-shaped machine driven by Camille Jenatzy.

- The Converj has a front-engine, front-drive layout.

- Inside is a 2+2 configuration.

- Torque output of the drivetrain is 273 lb-ft.

Engine: 120-kW electric motor/ gas engine-generator	**Top speed:** 100 mph
Horsepower: N/A	**Price when new:** N/A
0–60 mph: N/A	**Value now:** N/A

Will they? Or won't they? When Cadillac revealed the Converj concept at the 2009 Detroit auto show, the crowd cheered. Here was a Cadillac sports car looking quite contemporary and powered by the extended-range powerplant of the Chevrolet Volt. Range? About 40 miles in pure electric power with a four-cylinder gas engine kicking in to power a generator and extend the range of the battery pack to several hundred miles. The batteries could also be rather quickly recharged by a 240-volt outlet. An electric sports car? Don't forget that electric motors provide max torque from 0 rpm. Jaguar is on the same track with its C-X75 supercar. Reports of the Converj's future say it's dead, but at some point this electric/gas combo will find its way into a GM sports car. —JL

CTS-V coupe   2009–

Okay, some might think we're stretching the sports car theme with this largish coupe, but there are many sports cars that would have trouble keeping up with the CTS-V on a road circuit. This is part of the lineup that includes a four-door sedan and a slick station wagon, all of them powered by a 6.2-liter supercharged V-8 and backed by a six-speed transmission. . .manual or automatic. Remember, the sedan version was the first production four-door on street tires to break the eight-minute barrier on the Nürburgring's Nordschleife circuit. If there's one problem with the coupe it is that its calm, around-city demeanor needs only an inch more on the gas pedal to turn it into a cop-catching ground pounder. —JL

- Torque? How about 551 lb-ft? That should be enough.

- The CTS-V features Magnetic Ride Control, which employs sensors, as well as steering wheel and braking inputs from the driver, to reduce noise, vibration, and harshness.

- Cadillac markets the CTS-V coupe as a direct competitor to BMW's M3 and M6 and the Audi S5.

- Jalopnik.com described the CTS-V's engine as "a monster, a near-silent ball of seemingly endless fury and white light that lives under that sharply angled hood."

Engine: 6.2-liter supercharged V-8

Horsepower: 556

0–60 mph: 3.9 seconds

Top speed: 189 mph (manual gearbox)

Price when new: $62,990

Value now: Same

- The XLR-V features an innovative system that veers the headlights as the car turns, increasing visibility on winding roads.

- The XLR-V's supercharger and intercoolers are neatly integrated into the intake manifold.

- The 2009 XLR-V was one of the first GM cars priced above $100,000.

- In 2004, Neiman Marcus offered 101 special edition XLRs; they sold out in 14 minutes.

Engine: 4.4-liter supercharged dohc V-8
Horsepower: 443
0–60 mph: 4.6 seconds

Top speed: 155 mph
Price when new: $98,000
Value now: $85,000

While the front-drive Allanté didn't deserve much respect, Cadillac's XLR never got the respect it deserved. Based on the Corvette and built in the 'Vette's Kentucky factory, the XLR had a front-engine, rear-drive layout powered by the 320-horsepower 4.6-liter Northstar V-8. To some, the XLR's hard-edge styling was a bit much, but it had an undeniable presence on the road. And it featured a folding aluminum hardtop. Driving the XLR was, not surprisingly, like driving a Corvette: quick, dependable, and stable. Cadillac kicked it up a notch and faced off the European on performance when, in 2005, it created the XLR-V, cutting the V-8's displacement to 4.4 liters, but integrating a supercharger, taking horsepower to 443—the performance level of supercars. Like Rodney Dangerfield, however, the XLR just couldn't get any respect. —JL

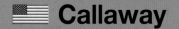

C16 and C16 Speedster — 2007–

At the top of Reeves Callaway's line of supertuned Corvettes are the C16 (coupe and cabriolet) (*inset*) and C16 Speedster (*below*). The former have just enough exterior changes to differentiate them from the Corvette underneath. Up front the engine is tuned to 650 horsepower (compared to the ZR1's 638), and, being a Callaway, this is not a fussy grenade motor, but reliable with a three-year/36,000-mile warranty. To match the power is a Callaway/Eibach Coil-Over Damper suspension system and huge disc brakes.

Now, if the Callaway C16 isn't individual enough for you, try the C16 Speedster. Start with the C16 bodywork, which is nicely smoothed by Paul Deutschman, and then lop off the top. Yup, the whole thing, including the windshield. That's right. . .if you want a car with a top, get something more pedestrian. There is a pair of wind deflectors for driver and passenger, plus small headrests aft of their seats. Lift the panel that has the rests and you'll find a pair of carbon fiber helmets that match the car's paint color. —*JL*

- The Callaway C16s have no external door handles. Instead, the door openings are triggered by an area of the bodywork that is touch-sensitive. Touching the spot pops the door open.

- Chances are you wouldn't buy one of these cars for the fuel mileage, but the Speedster's is pretty good: 18 mpg city/28 mpg highway with the manual transmission.

- All C16s feature Callaway/Dymag Carbon wheels that weigh approximately 40 percent less than the lightest aluminum wheels.

- The "base" C16s have tested an impressive 0.95g on the skid pad.

(Speedster):	
Engine: 6.2-liter supercharged ohv V-8	0–60 mph: 3.2 seconds
	Top speed: 210 mph
Horsepower: 700	Price when new: $305,000
	Value now: Same

- Reeves Callaway is the son of Ely Callaway of golf club fame.
- Canadian Paul Deutschman did the design for the Callaways.
- Where's the top? There isn't one.
- The Speedster's blue upholstery was done in Germany.

Engine: 5.7-liter twin-turbo V-8	**Top speed:** 190 mph
Horsepower: 450	**Price when new:** $150,000
0–60 mph: 4.2 seconds	**Value now:** $200,000

In 1991, Reeves Callaway's Speedster stopped everyone in their tracks at the Los Angeles auto show. Here was a Corvette ZR-1 hopped up with twin turbos to the tune of 450 horsepower and 613 lb-ft of torque. It's a true roadster with its cut-down windscreen and unique carbon fiber body pieces. Callaway's Corvettes were so quick and emissions-clean that Chevrolet sold them through their dealers, which is very rare for General Motors. Besides the blueprinted turbo V-8, the Speedster had a coil-over suspension, Brembo brakes, and three-piece Oz wheels. The tires are run flats. Callaway planned a production run of 50 Speedsters, though only 12 were assembled. —JL

T1   2007–

Think of the Caparo T1 as a (somewhat) civilized Formula 1 car. The mid-engine, rear-drive sports car is powered by a 575-horsepower Menard V-8, but weighs only 1,000 pounds, so that 0–60 time of 2.5 seconds is quite believable. Ditto with the 205-mph top speed. It is a dramatic-looking machine to say the least; you can basically see through that low-drag carbon fiber bodywork to find a lot of Formula 1 thinking lurking underneath. That would be a carbon fiber and aluminum honeycomb monocoque structure with a space frame in back to hold the V-8, the six-speed sequential gearbox, and the rear suspension. There is actually room for two in the cockpit, with the passenger sitting slightly aft of the driver. And the instrumentation is pure race car. —JL

- Some of the engineers behind the project also worked on the McLaren F1.

- The T1 corners at more than 3g, thanks to diffusers to generate almost all its downforce from the flow of air under the car.

- The T1's front and rear wings are adjustable to tune balance aerodynamically.

- The transmission needs a mere 60 milliseconds for upshifts, and downshifts in 30 milliseconds.

Engine: 3.5-liter 40-valve V-8	Top speed: 205 mph
Horsepower: 575	Price when new: $480,000
0–60 mph: 2.5 seconds	Value now: Same

- Get this: 850 lb-ft of torque.
- Each lightweight wheel weighs 24.6 pounds.
- One option is a 24-karat gold exterior.
- Tires: 265/30-20 front, 325/25-20 rear.

Engine: 6.0-liter twin-turbo dohc V-12	**Top speed:** 218 mph
Horsepower: 753	**Price when new:** $700,000
0–60 mph: 3.6 seconds	**Value now:** Same

You may have never heard of Carlsson, but the German firm has been around since 1989, modifying Mercedes-Benz models for the street and successfully racing them. At the 2010 Geneva auto show, Carlsson revealed its dramatically upgraded version of the Mercedes SL. C25s are exclusive, not just for their $700,000 price but also for the fact that only 25 were built, one for each country in which the company sells cars. Carlsson squeezes 753 horsepower from the V-12, but says this is with no loss of control or comfort. Despite the engine modifications, a C25 can be serviced at any Mercedes dealership. Carlsson certainly modified the Mercedes to look faster, and the new body has been wind tunnel tuned. The interior features carbon fiber, ultrasuede, and buffalo leather. —JL

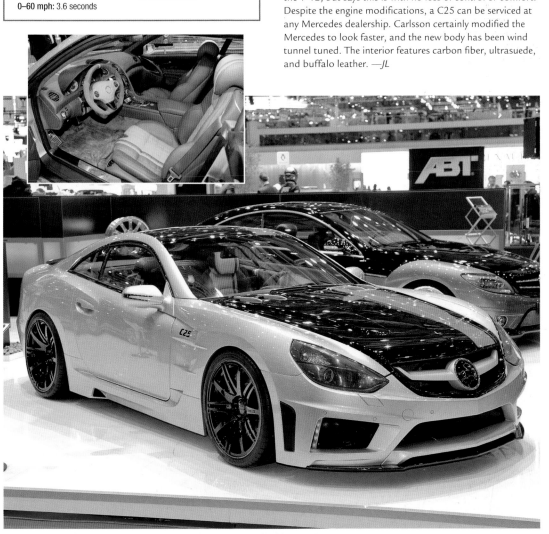

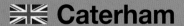

Seven   1973–

When Lotus ended production of its famous Seven sports car in the early 1970s, a company called Caterham, headed by Englishman Graham Nearn, bought the licence to carry on making it. And since then Caterham has never looked back, expanding the Seven range in numerous directions, often at the same time, but always remaining faithful to the car's simple, lightweight design philosophy—pioneered by legendary Lotus founder Colin Chapman himself. Most Sevens use a four-cylinder engine, some with little more than 100 horsepower; some pack a lump that pushes 250. But with a curb weight of little more than 1,100 pounds and a rear-wheel-drive chassis that behaves like a go-kart, the Seven remains unique in its appeal. As such, it is truly one of *the* sports cars you should drive before you you-know-what. . . . —SS

- The original Seven was designed by Colin Chapman, who went on to achieve even greater things in F1 and Indy car racing with Team Lotus.

- Even today, you can have your Seven delivered as a kit to be built at home.

- The fastest model is the R500, which gets its name from its power-to-weight ratio of 500 horsepower per tonne.

- A Seven finished 11th outright at the famous Nürburgring 24 Hours in 2002, much to the annoyance of the organizers; since then the car has been banned from the race.

Tech specs (Superlight R500):
Engine: 2.0-liter inline four
Horsepower: 263
0–60 mph: 3.2 seconds

Top speed: 150 mph
Price when new: $61,057
Value now: Same

- The original Z/28 option added $400 to the Camaro's price.

- During the 1968 and 1969 Trans-Am seasons, Roger Penske's Z/28 Camaros won 18 of 25 races. Mark Donohue won 16 times and Ronnie Bucknum twice.

- From 1975 through 1988, the Z28 replaced a Porsche as the basis for the International Race of Champions series. In 1985, Chevrolet changed the Z28's designation to IROC-Z, and that designation remained through the 1989 model year.

- Camaro enthusiasts are still waiting for a Z28 version of the new fifth-generation Camaro; as of 2011, Chevrolet is only offering base, RS, SS, and ZL1 versions.

Engine: 302-cubic-inch V-8	Top speed: 135 mph
Horsepower: 290	Price when new: $3,500
0–60 mph: Est. 7 seconds	Value now: $65,000

When Chevrolet launched the Camaro—its "challenger" to Ford's Mustang for the SCCA Trans-Am racing series—for the 1967 model year, it offered buyers a choice of two six-cylinder engines and V-8s with 327, 350, and 396 cubic inches of displacement. But the Trans-Am rules restricted V-8s to 305 cubic inches, so Camaro product promotion manager Vince Piggins and his team devised the Z/28 package. In addition to a modified suspension, quicker steering gear, upgraded rear axle, and installation of the same rear disc brakes used on the Corvette, Piggins and pals took a 327-cubic-inch V-8, changed the crank, pistons, cam, intake manifold, exhaust, and carburetion and—*voila!*—a new Camaro, the Z/28 was ready to go racing.

Tweaked by Henry "Smokey" Yunick, campaigned by Roger Penske, and driven by Mark Donohue, the Camaro Z28 would win 10 of 13 SCCA Trans-Am races in 1968. While other Camaros might boast more horsepower, the Z/28 would become the car of choice for mainstream Chevy enthusiasts. —*LE*

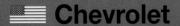
Corvette (first generation, part 1)
1953–1960

Chevrolet finally gave the United States its own sports car in 1953 with the introduction of the Corvette. The fiberglass-bodied machine inherited many of its mechanical components from other Chevrolet models—a money-saving move—and featured the Blue Flame Special inline-six engine and two-speed automatic transmission. Reflecting the sports car thinking of the time, it was a basic car with a live rear axle. Come 1955, the 'Vette got its first V-8, the now-fabled small-block at 265 cubic inches, 195 horsepower, and a manual transmission. Corvette got its first exterior design update in 1956 and as of 1958 went to quad headlights. Each year brought new iterations of the V-8: more displacement, added fuel injection, and higher horsepower each year. —JL

- Only 300 Corvettes were built in 1953. All of them were painted polo white.
- The early V-8 Corvettes got to 60 mph in under 9 seconds.
- By 1957, the 0–60 time had dropped to 6.6 seconds.
- The Corvette's godfather was Zora Arkus-Duntov.

Engine: 3.8-liter ohv inline six
Horsepower: 150
0–60 mph: 11 seconds
Top speed: 105 mph
Price when new: $3,498
Value now: As much as $400,000 (1953 models)

1961–1962 Corvette (first generation, part 2)

- In 1961, five versions of the 283 V-8 were offered.

- Chevrolet built 10,939 Corvettes in 1961 and 14,531 in 1962.

- The 1962 fuel-injected, 360-horsepower engine propelled the Corvette from 0 to 60 in 5.9 seconds.

- The last year for the first-generation Corvette was 1962.

Engine: 283-cubic-inch ohv V-8	Top speed: 120 mph
Horsepower: 230	Price when new: $3,934
0–60 mph: 7.0 seconds	Value now: As much as $140,000

The 1961 model year brought a major design refreshing for the 'vette; the rear end shape of the Stingray race car and GM Design's XP-700 show car was grafted to the quad-headlamp front end. With that change, the Corvette got the two round taillights layout still used today. By this time, the Corvette had become a very serious sports car, which it demonstrated through racing. In the United States, it proved equal to the exotic Ferraris, and also raced in Europe at the 24 Hours of Le Mans, where one finished eighth overall in 1960. Engines continued to be refined, and in 1962 the small-block was opened up to what would become a famous Corvette displacement: 327. Horsepower that year ranged from 250 on the basic carbureted version to 360 with fuel injection. —JL

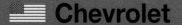
Corvette (C2) Sting Ray 1963–1967

Chevrolet's second-generation Corvette was called the Sting Ray, and it was a landmark design, setting an American standard for sports cars. Larry Shinoda designed the production car based on Peter Brock's Sting Ray race car. Not only did the fiberglass car have dramatic styling, but it finally put an independent rear suspension under the 'Vette. Chevrolet employed a variety of pushrod V-8s in the "Gen 2" Corvettes, from 327 to 427 cubic inches, with horsepower ranging from 360 to 435. Both coupe and convertible versions were available, and options included fuel injection, side exhaust pipes, and aluminum wheels. Sting Rays were raced successfully, and the most desirable of all Corvettes are the five lightweight Grand Sports built in 1963 before GM clamped down in racing. —JL

- Some 118,964 Corvette Sting Rays were built.
- The split-window rear treatment was dropped after 1963.
- Four-wheel disc brakes were offered as of 1965.
- Chevrolet called the second-gen Corvettes Sting Rays. The C3s are called Stingrays.

Engine: 427-cubic-inch V-8
Horsepower: 250–360
0–60 mph: 5.4 seconds
Top speed: 152 mph
Price when new: $4,037 (1963)
Value now: $40,000–50,000

1968–1982   Corvette (C3) Stingray

- In 1981, Corvette production moved to a new factory in Bowling Green, Kentucky.

- In 1978, the Corvette made its debut as the pace car for the Indianapolis 500.

- After 1975, Chevrolet stopped producing convertibles.

- Despite some quality-control problems with the fiberglass bodies, Chevrolet sold a best-yet 28,566 units in the C3's first year of 1968.

Engine: 350-cubic-inch ohv V-8	**Top speed:** 135 mph
Horsepower: 330	**Price when new:** $5,259
0–60 mph: 6 seconds	**Value now:** $15,000–$45,000

While the second-generation Corvette was based on the Stingray race car, the next iteration took its design cues from a concept called the *Mako Shark II*. It was an exciting update, which was fortunate, as the model was built from 1968 through 1982. Through those years the Corvette had to be adapted to the many changing federal safety and emissions rules. The original metal front bumpers and rear Kamm tail gave way to 5mph urethane-faced bumpers. Being 'Vettes, the engines were important, but emissions equipment hurt. The 327 V-8 gave way to the 350 small-block, while the big engine was opened up from 427 to 454 cubic inches. Horsepower ranged from as much as a rumored 550 in the rare aluminum ZL1 427 to as little as 180 from the LG4 305. —*JL*

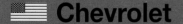
Corvette C4   1984–1996

Where the Generation 3 Corvette was in many ways a rebody of the 1963 chassis, the Generation 4 was a truly new Corvette. Not as new as the oft-rumored mid-engine 'Vette would have been, but still classic front-engine stuff. The new shape, built from 1984 to 1996, nicely integrated all the necessary safety features and boasted a removable Targa-style top. In 1986, the convertible body style returned. Underneath was a stiffer chassis and lightweight aluminum suspension components. Again, engines were the thing, starting in 1984 with the Cross-Fire V-8, horsepower climbing a bit over the years for the base engine. There were horsepower spikes, with the 1987 Chevy-authorized Callaway Twin Turbo at 345 horsepower and a top speed of 177.9 miles per hour and then the 1990 Lotus-developed ZR-1 twin cam V-8 at 375 horsepower. —JL

- Owing to production problems, only one true 1983 Corvette exists.
- In 1991, all Corvettes had the bodywork of the 1990 ZR-1.
- The ZR-1 got to 60 mph in 4.9 seconds.
- In 1990, the Callaway turbo option cost $26,895, the ZR-1 package $27,016.

Engine: 5.7-liter ohv V-8	**Top speed:** 140 mph
Horsepower: 205	**Price when new:** $21,800
0–60 mph: 7.0 seconds	**Value now:** $10,000–$20,000

- C5 Z06s with 405 horsepower get to 60 mph in 3.9 seconds.

- The C5 racers, the Corvette C5-Rs, were solid class winners in the 24 Hours of Le Mans and the 12 Hours of Sebring.

- In 2001, a C5-R took the overall win in the 24 Hours of Daytona.

- Torque of the 405-horspower Z06 was 400 lb-ft.

Engine: 5.7-liter ohv V-8 (LS1)	**Top speed:** 181 mph
Horsepower: 345	**Price when new:** $37,495
0–60 mph: 4.7 seconds	**Value now:** $16,000–$23,000

With the new, fifth-generation Corvette came a new engine, the all-aluminum LS1 with 345 horsepower. First out was the coupe, followed by a convertible—first 'Vette ragtop to have a trunk—and then a fixed-roof coupe. Styling was smoothed out once again, (some argue the best yet) and would serve the car through 2004. Corvette made the move to modern suspension systems with the Active Handling System. The base V-8 received a modest boost to 350 horsepower and 375 lb-ft of torque, but as of 2001, the top dog C5, as they are known, was the Z06. Chevy used the stiffer fixed-roof body style to improve handling and added the 385-horsepower LS6 V-8, later upping the horsepower to 405. Price of the 2001 Z06 was $47,500. —JL

🇺🇸 Chevrolet

Corvette Grand Sport — 1963

The Chevrolet Corvette Grand Sport project so enraged General Motors chairman Frederic Donner that he reportedly ordered that the five factory race cars be "burnt to the ground." In December 1961, the major American automobile manufacturers had mutually agreed not to participate in factory-supported motorsports efforts, but Zora Arkus-Duntov, chief engineer for the Chevrolet Corvette, couldn't stand being beaten by Carroll Shelby's Ford-powered Cobras. So, with a nod of support from Chevrolet general manager Bunkie Knudsen, Duntov defied the ban and built five Grand Sport racers with the 550-horsepower, 377-cubic-inch aluminum V-8 engines. Duntov divvied the ultra-lightweight Corvette racers among private racing teams, and people such as Roger Penske, Jim Hall, Dick Thompson, Augie Pabst, Grady Davis, John Mecom, A. J. Foyt, Dick Guldstrand, and others took them to legendary status. Happily, Duntov found a way to hide the cars from destruction, and they all remain in private collections. —JL

- Knudsen and Duntov hoped to build at least 125 Grand Sports for racing homologation purposes.

- Of the five Grand Sports built, three were coupes and two were roadsters.

- Several GM engineers took vacations in December 1963 and flew to Nassau for Speed Weeks to support the Grand Sport racing teams.

- There were supposedly six Grand Sport Corvettes, but one reportedly was destroyed before the other five were dispersed or hidden away.

Engine: 377-cubic-inch V-8	Top speed: 140 mph
Horsepower: 550	Price when new: N/A
0–60 mph: 5.9 seconds	Value now: $10 million

86

2011   **Corvette Grand Sport (C6)**

- The V-8's torque is 428 lb-ft.

- Manual gearbox Corvettes have launch control.

- The skid pad test for the GS comes in at 0.96g.

- You can watch your Corvette being assembled. . .and help build the engine.

Engine: 6.2-liter ohv V-8	Top speed: 190 mph
Horsepower: 436	Price when new: $54,770
0–60 mph: 4.1 seconds	Value now: Same

Grand Sport is a legendary name to Corvette lovers, taking them back to that handful of special Sting Rays built in 1963 (see previous profile). Now the name applies to a model that takes a $6,000 bump up from the base Corvette, but brings a great deal with it. Much of the bumping comes from the Z06 parts bin: wheels and tires, brakes, front clip, fenders, hood, and anti-roll bars. The springs and shocks are specific to the steel-frame GS (Z06s have an aluminum frame). The Grand Sport may lack the Z06 engine, but the power of the dry-sump 6.2 still gets you to 60 in 4.1 seconds and through a quarter-mile in 12.4 seconds at 116.5 miles per hour. And get this: The EPA mileage is 16 mpg city/26 mph highway. . . in case you need that to soothe your conscience. —JL

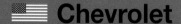

Chevrolet

Corvette *Stingray* concept 2009

When is a car a robot? When it is one of the five vehicles created by GM Design for the 2009 movie *Transformers: Revenge of the Fallen*. In this case, the car played the part of Sideswipe. More importantly for car fans is the fact that the concept pays homage to the original Stingray race car and the coupes from the car's Generation 3. From the aggressive front end to the fender tops to the angle of the rear window, the concept brings that original shape into the 21st century. The *Stingray* concept could be a look at the future of Corvette, though GM design chief, Ed Welburn, only says, "By giving the creative team the freedom to design no-holds-barred-vision concepts, it helps them push boundaries and look at projects from different perspectives." —*JL*

- The *Stingray* concept was first shown at the 2009 Chicago auto show.

- In case you're keeping track, Sideswipe is an Autobot—one of the good guys in the Transformers universe.

- Among Sideswipe's Autobot teammates is Bumblebee, a yellow and black fifth-generation Camaro.

- There is a long heritage of Corvette concepts from GM, including the *Mako Shark* (1961), *Mako Shark II* (1965), and the *Aerovette* (1977).

Engine: N/A	Price when new: N/A
Horsepower: N/A	Value now: You can't buy the
0–60 mph: N/A	actual car. But you can buy the
Top speed: N/A	Transformers toy for about $15.

- The racer was originally equipped with a 283-cubic-inch, 315-horsepower V-8. This was later swapped out for a 427-cubic-inch big-block V-8.

- GM still owns the Stingray and often displays it at car shows.

- The Stingray has a DeDion rear suspension.

- Mitchell had the Stingray done in secrecy to avoid any GM corporate meddling.

Engine: 283-cubic-inch V-8	Top speed: N/A
Horsepower: 315	Price when new: N/A
0–60 mph: N/A	Value now: N/A

When U.S. automakers banned their participation in racing, it killed the Corvette SS racing program. Bill Mitchell, the flamboyant chief of design at GM, bought a mule SS chassis to create a race car. The shape of the car was penned by Peter Brock, who later designed the Shelby Daytona coupe, and was used as the basis for the Larry Shinoda–designed 1963 production Corvette Sting Ray. Mitchell convinced Corvette driver Dr. Dick Thompson to race the Stingray, which he drove to an SCCA racing title in 1960. Mitchell then retired the car, had it civilized a bit, and drove it on the street. —JL

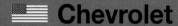

Corvette SS 1957

During one of the periods when it thought racing was a good idea, General Motors allowed Chevrolet to develop an all-out Corvette race car. Called the SS, it was created by famed Corvette engineer Zora Arkus-Duntov. GM Design was also quite involved, giving the SS a beautiful shape that was formed in magnesium, which helped the car tip the scales at just 1,850 pounds. GM raced the SS at Sebring in 1957 with an eye on bringing it to the 24 Hours of Le Mans. The car proved very quick in the hands of Juan Manuel Fangio and Stirling Moss in testing. Raced by John Fitch and Piero Taruffi, the SS fell victim to a failed rear bushing early in the race, and soon the SS project fell victim to Detroit's racing ban. —JL

- The SS has a De Dion rear suspension.
- You can see the Corvette SS at the Indianapolis Motor Speedway Hall of Fame Museum.
- The chassis of the second "mule" SS was used under Bill Mitchell's 1959 Corvette Stingray race car.
- Inspirations for the SS were Mercedes-Benz' 300SL and Jaguar's D-Type.

Engine: 4.6-liter ohv V-8
Horsepower: 310
0–60 mph: N/A

Top speed: 183 mph
Price when new: N/A
Value now: Priceless

Chevrolet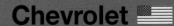

2006– **Corvette Z06 (C6)**

- Torque of the Z06 engine is 470 lb-ft.

- Tick off all the great options and the Z06 closes up on $100,000.

- Both the engine's block and heads are aluminum.

- Despite its horsepower, the Z06's estimated highway mileage is 24 mpg.

Engine: 7.0-liter ohv LS7 V-8	**Top speed:** 193 mph
Horsepower: 505	**Price when new:** $74,305
0–60 mph: 3.6 seconds	**Value now:** Same

The term *Z06* is not a new one for Corvettes. It began in 1963 when Zora Arkus-Duntov created the RPO Z06 high-performance package for customers who wanted to race their 'Vettes. The option cost $1,818, and many of the customers used their Sting Ray Z06s for the street. Chevrolet resurrected the Z06 name for 2001 with a 385-horsepower LS6 V-8, bumping it up to 405 horsepower in 2002, a model built until 2004. With the Generation 6 Corvette, the Z06 was back as of 2006 with a unique aluminum body structure and carbon fiber bonded to the structure. Other lightweight components include a magnesium engine cradle. What makes the Z06 such a stormer is the LS7 V-8, with its forged steel crankshaft, dry-sump oiling system, and hydroformed exhaust headers. —JL

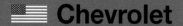

Corvette ZR1 (C6)   2009–

You can get snobby about exotic cars, but that might leave Corvette's ZR1 off your list, and that would be a big mistake. Okay, it's half the price of a Lamborghini Gallardo, but it is just as much fun. Much of the excitement comes from its hand-built 6.2-liter Roots-blown aluminum LS9 V-8 that cranks out 638 horsepower, and—just as important—604 lb-ft of torque. You can hear that supercharger ever so slightly up front as you chop through the gears, whistling past 100 miles per hour in 7.4 seconds and through the quarter-mile in 11.4 seconds at 125 miles per hour. And this car isn't just a straight-ahead racer; the Nürburgring-proven ZR1 will generate l.12g on the skid pad. Some might feel the interior could be a bit more uptown, but, again, remember the price. —JL

- In case you're into details: The high-performance version of the C4 Corvette was called the ZR-1. The C6 version is called the ZR1.
- Both front and rear suspensions use a transverse leaf spring.
- The gearbox is a six-speed.
- Carbon-ceramic discs are used for the brakes.

Engine: 6.2-liter supercharged ohv LS9 V-8
Horsepower: 638
0–60 mph: 3.3 seconds
Top speed: 205 mph
Price when new: $112,050
Value now: Same

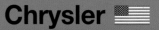

- Crossfires were built by Karmann in Germany.

- The torque of the normally aspirated 3.2 V-6 is 229 lb-ft.

- Manual and automatic transmissions were available.

- The interior room was arguably a bit tight.

Engine: 3.2-liter sohc V-6 (normally aspirated version)	**Top speed:** Est. 150 mph
Horsepower: 215	**Price when new:** $33,620
0–60 mph: 6.7	**Value now:** $14,000

It certainly seemed like a good idea. With the marriage of Chrysler and Mercedes-Benz, the U.S. manufacturer inherited the one-generation-old platform of several German cars. That included Mercedes' SLK320 sports car, which was morphed into the Chrysler Crossfire. The styling was done as a coupe or roadster; it's exciting and did an excellent job of separating the Chrysler from the Mercedes, despite the fact that the Crossfire used about 80 percent Mercedes parts, from platform to engines to all the crucial equipment in the dashboard area. For 2005, Chrysler created the Crossfire SRT-6, which was equipped with a 3.2-liter V-6 supercharged to 330 horsepower and 310 lb-ft of torque. Crossfires sold rather well their first two years (2003: 35,700; 2004: 28,000), but then sales began to slide and the Crossfire was never replaced. —JL

ME Four-Twelve   2004

Oh, we came so close on this one. Mercedes-Benz and Chrysler were still together in 2004, and at that year's Detroit auto show they unveiled an exotic sports car called the ME Four-Twelve. The name meant *Mid-Engine Four*-turbo *Twelve*-cylinder engine. The car looked terrific, and the sense we had at the time was that this might be more than just a show car. Turns out Chrysler had a program to make the car a production reality, via Chrysler's Street & Racing Technology (SRT) department. SRT's version had a carbon fiber and aluminum honeycomb tub, with a steel rear subframe for the Mercedes-based four-turbo V-12. Credibility of the program skyrocketed in August 2004 when media were invited to Mazda Raceway Laguna Seca to take rides in a developed ME Four-Twelve. Alas, the program was later killed. —*JL*

- Torque came in at 850 lb-ft.
- If built, the ME Four-Twelve would have cost $500,000.
- The gearbox was a seven-speed sequential automatic.
- Weight of the supercar was 2,880 pounds.

Engine: 6.0-liter quad-turbo dohc V-12
Horsepower: 850
0–60 mph: 2.9 seconds
Top speed: 240 mph
Price when new: N/A
Value now: N/A

Cisitalia

- Cisitalia built just 170 units of the 202 GT.
- Cisitalia 202s had Fiat-based engines and Fiat chassis components.
- Dusio hired Ferdinand Porsche to design a four-wheel-drive Grand Prix car.
- Pinin Farina hand-formed the GT's aluminum body over wooden body bucks.

(SMM Nuvolari):	
Engine: 1.1-liter ohv inline four	Top speed: 100 mph
Horsepower: 60 horsepower	Price when new: N/A
0–60 mph: N/A	Value now: $500,000

Piero Dusio was a rich Italian industrialist who loved automobiles. He created Compagnia Industriale Sportive Italia, or Cisitalia. In addition to race cars, Dusio commissioned a GT car (*inset*) from Pinin Farina that became one of the most honored post–World War II designs. First presented in 1947, the sublime shape of the 202 was an early example of creating an automobile as one flowing form. New York's Museum of Modern Art has a 202 in its permanent collection. And that wasn't the only beautiful Cisitalia. For the 1947 Mille Miglia, Giovanni Savonuzzi built a superb open sports car body for a Cisitalia race car (*bottom*) that the great Tazio Nuvolari drove to second place against much more powerful opposition. Since then, the cars have been called 202 SMM Nuvolari. —*JL*

Corvette replica   2011

- Conversion takes about three months.

- Owners can follow the progress of their car on CRC's website.

- The first CRC Corvette took six years and 5,000 hours to create.

- SPRINT CBS (SPRINT is a trademarked brand; CBS stands for "car body sheet") has been used in Aston Martin and Mercedes-Benz cars.

Okay, so it looks like a 1962 Corvette, but in fact it is a new car. . .kind of. CRC is an outfit in Lakewood, Washington, that will rebody a Corvette C5 (1998–2004) with new reworked panels that stretch the vintage look onto the "new" chassis. Sounds odd, but it looks great and puts the modern engine and chassis under the 1962 shape. And they aren't just some cheap knock-off panels, but tough SPRINT CBS composite bodywork made off a set of computer-generated forms that were developed with help from Boeing's computers. A new owner provides a "donor" Corvette, and its panels are removed and the chassis is checked to factory specs. Then the new panels are carefully fitted—and the result is impressive. —JL

Engine: 5.7-liter ohv V-8
Horsepower: 350
0–60 mph: 4.8 seconds
Top speed: Est. 150 mph

Price when new: $100,000 plus a donor C5 Corvette
Value now: Same

1949–1951 — Hotshot

- The Hotshot was launched on July 14, 1949.

- Crosley built 2,498 Hotshots before production ended in 1952.

- The transmission was a three-speed manual.

- Powel Crosley purchased the Cincinnati Reds baseball team in 1934 and owned the team until his death in 1961.

Engine: 725cc inline four	Top speed: 75 mph
Horsepower: 26	Price when new: $849
0–60 mph: 28.1 seconds	Value now: $15,500

Powel Crosley Jr. of Cincinnati, Ohio, was the picture of the American entrepreneur. He had earned his fortune in the radio and appliance businesses, but his first dream had been to build an automobile company. After several failed attempts, Crosley chased that dream again and had sold some 55,000 cars by 1949. But those models had a questionable reputation, so he developed the Hotshot. It was a tiny, 80-inch-wheelbase basic car with a homely-but-lovable exterior, a 26.5-horsepower engine, and a curb weight of 1,175 pounds. It was cheap and turned out to be a good race car. Seems unlikely, but in 1950 a Hotshot won the Index of Performance at the inaugural endurance race at Sebring (each entrant was handicapped according to engine size, and the Hotshot ran its required number of laps in the shortest amount time.) In fact, Hotshots would dominate the SCCA's 750cc sports car racing class throughout the 1950s. —JL

C-3   1953

- About 30 Cunningham C-3s were built as coupes or roadsters.

- Cunninghams were considered the Ferraris of the United States.

- This was the street version of the successful C-2R race cars, which had scored top-5 finishes at Le Mans from 1952 to 1954.

- It took two months to make each Vignale body.

Engine: 331-cubic-inch Chrysler "hemi" V-8	**Top speed:** 130 mph
Horsepower: 310	**Price when new:** $12,000
0–60 mph: 7.0 seconds	**Value now:** Est. $400,000

Wealthy American sportsman Briggs Cunningham wanted to build street machines that were as strong and powerful as his now-legendary race cars (see next profile). For 1951, he offered the C-3, which had a Chrysler V-8 engine and a Carrozzeria Vignale body made in Turin, Italy. Cunningham rolling chassis were done in West Palm Beach, Florida, shipped to Italy to be bodied, then back to the United States for final detailing. —JL

🇺🇸 Cunningham

Le Monstre   1950

- Cunningham and Phil Walters drove *Le Monstre* at Le Mans. The Collier brothers—Miles and Sam—drove the other Caddy.

- Cunningham had met the Colliers in college, where they founded the Automobile Racing Club of America, a forerunner to the Sports Car Club of America.

- *Le Monstre* raced with five carburetors feeding fuel to its engine.

- Cunningham was a sportsman with many talents. In 1958 he won the America's Cup sailing championship in his yacht, Columbia.

Engine: 329-cubic-inch V-8	**Price when new:** One-off prototype
Horsepower: N/A	
0–60 mph: N/A	**Value now:** Priceless
Top speed: 130 mph	

Briggs Cunningham wanted to win the 24 Hours of Le Mans in an American car with American drivers. For his first attempt, in 1950, he purchased a pair of 1950 Cadillac Series 61 Coupe de Villes. One car appeared pretty stock, but the other carried much modified bodywork to enhance its aerodynamics. It was dubbed *Le Monstre* by French racing fans, and although it went off course early in the race, it came back and finished 11th, one place behind its more conventional teammate. —LE

Datsun

- Datsun Zs were renowned in racing circles, the most famous Z driver being the late Paul Newman.

- At the time, a Corvette cost some $5,000, a Jaguar E-type almost $6,000.

- Datsun was rebranded as Nissan in the United States in the early 1980s.

- In Japan, the 240Z was named the Fairlady.

Engine: 2.4-liter sohc inline six	Top speed: 125 mph
Horsepower: 151	Price when new: $3,526
0–60 mph: 8.0 seconds	Value now: $12,000

Datsun's 240Z (*below*) was so greatly anticipated in 1969 that *Road & Track* magazine broke all the rules and ran a black-and-white photo on the cover just to show the car. British sports cars were beginning to show their age when along came this great-looking sports car with an inline six engine, independent front and rear suspension, and a price tag of just $3,526. Americans, who were just learning that the Japanese could build sound, reliable, and fun cars, snapped up the Z cars in droves. The car's performance was good, but very quickly there was an aftermarket for performance parts for the engine, suspension, and wheels. The two-seater was supplemented with a 2+2 model in 1974, while the 2.4-liter engine was replaced with a 2.6, creating the 260Z, which was followed by the 2.8-liter 280Z (*bottom*) in 1975. —JL

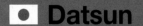 Datsun

Sports 1500   1963–1965

- Datsun produced the Sports/Fairlady line from 1959 to 1970.

- The rear axle of the car was also to be found in the somewhat less incisive Cedric.

- The Sports was a well-equipped car for its day, and had a transistor radio, map lights, and a clock.

- A mere 300 examples were equipped with single carburetors; in 1964 Datsun began offering dual SU carbs.

Engine: 1.5-liter inline four	**Top speed:** Est. 95 mph
Horsepower: 85	**Price when new:** $1,200
0–60 mph: Est. 12 seconds	**Value now:** $8,000–$10,000

The Datsun Sports 1500, also known as the Fairlady 1500 in certain markets, was one of Japan's first committed attempts to produce a genuine open-top sports car. The key advantage it had over its predecessors was that it was based on a saloon, rather than a truck, and this endowed it with crisp(ish) handling and a decent turn of speed thanks to its 85-horsepower 1.5-liter engine and four-speed manual gearbox. It was also notable for its third "sideways" rear seat. —*SS*

▬ Dauer

962   1993

- Dauer developed a hydraulic ride height system that allowed the 962 to be raised for speed humps.

- In 1994, the rules at Le Mans were altered to favor road cars rather than prototypes, and the Dauer 962 promptly cleaned up.

- A small but perfectly functional luggage compartment was engineered into the front of the car. . .

- . . .As was a DVD system that would allow owners to record their on-track antics if and when required.

Engine: Water-cooled 3-liter twin turbo flat six	**Top speed:** More than 250 mph
Horsepower: 730	**Price when new:** $600,000
0–60 mph: 3.0 seconds	**Value now:** More than $1 million

Very possibly the most thinly disguised racing car that has ever been legalized for the road, the Dauer 962 was effectively a road-going version of the Porsche 962 that had dominated Le Mans for several years. Launched in 1993, it had a 730-horsepower turbocharged flat-six engine with a five-speed gearbox, and it looked just like the racing car but with a set of number plates fitted to its nose. Rumor has it that its creator, Jochen Dauer, did over 250 miles per hour in his 962 on the Autobahn. . .regularly. . .on his way to work. —*SS*

- DeLorean convinced wealthy celebrities such as Johnny Carson to invest in DMC.

- DMC went bankrupt in 1982 after DeLorean's arrest for drug trafficking. He was later found not guilty.

- The most famous DMC-12 was the car used in the *Back to the Future* movies.

- Two DeLoreans were gold-plated by American Express.

Engine: 2.8-liter sohc V-6	Top speed: 110 mph
Horsepower: 130	Price when new: $25,000
0–60 mph: 10.5 seconds	Value now: $20,000–$25,000

You could write a book about the rise and fall of John DeLorean's car company. . .and I did. It was titled *The Stainless Steel Illusion,* and that about wraps up the story of the short-lived gullwing sports car. There's no denying the Giorgetto Giugiaro–designed body was exciting, and the final engineering of the car by Lotus was interesting. A center backbone chassis held a plastic resin underbody to which the stainless-steel body panels were attached. Out back was a V-6 jointly developed by Peugeot-Renault-Volvo—a nice package but underpowered. Looming over the technical side of the project was the funding and the decision to build the car in Northern Ireland. In the end it was all for naught after some 8,000 cars were built. —JL

1300WD   1953–1959

When you see a Denzel from a distance, your first thought might be, "Well, that's an odd-looking Porsche." It's not, of course, but Austrian Wolfgang Denzel had the same idea as Porsche: Build lightweight sports cars with engines based on the Volkswagen flat-4. These eventually came in three versions: two at 1.3 liters (54 or 65 horsepower) and another at 1.5 liters and 85 horsepower. The cars also had VW suspensions, and it's said the earliest cars were based on war surplus Kübelwagen chassis, though soon Denzel was making his own chassis and bodies. Being shorter and lighter than Porsches, Denzels were able to beat them, taking an overall win (and great publicity) at the 1954 Coupe des Alpes rally. —JL

- These days the Denzel company is a major car dealer in Austria.
- Denzel built his aluminum bodies over a steel tube frame.
- Estimates are that 300 Denzels were made, many of which were exported to the United States.
- The car shown here is a 1300 (1.3-liter) model.

Engine: 1.3-liter ohv flat-four	**Top speed:** 105 mph
Horsepower: 65	**Price when new:** N/A
0–60 mph: 13.7 seconds	**Value now:** N/A

- Virgil Exner tried but failed to convince Chrysler to put the original Adventurer into production; it would have been America's first four-seat sports car.

- Exner's other collaborations with Ghia include the Chrysler K-310 and Dodge Firearrow concepts.

- DeSoto did put the Adventurer name on a series of high-performance, V-8–powered cars from 1956 to 1960.

- Later, the Adventurer name went on a line of Dodge pickup trucks.

Engine: 276-cubic-inch Hemi V-8	**Top speed:** N/A
Horsepower: 170	**Price when new:** N/A
0–60 mph: N/A	**Value now:** Priceless

In the early 1950s, Chrysler commissioned the building of a pair of sports car concepts as a response to the new Chevrolet Corvette. They were badged for Chrysler's mid-price DeSoto division and given the name *Adventurer*. The first car, designed by legendary stylist Virgil Exner, was a four-seater with DeSoto's version of the Hemi V-8 engine and side-mounted exhausts. The second, *Adventurer II* (shown here), was a much more dramatic concept. Its Ghia bodywork featured a low nose, no front bumper, and jet-style cone taillamps. The plastic rear window could be retracted into the trunk. —*LE*

De Tomaso

Mangusta   1967–1971

Alejandro De Tomaso was an Argentine-born racer who drove for the Maserati brothers. He founded De Tomaso Automobili to build racing cars, and later added street cars to his lineup, starting with the Vallelunga in 1963. His next act was the Mangusta, Italian for "mongoose," the snake-hunting mammal. Legend has it De Tomaso had been promised Ford engines that ended up going into Shelby Cobras instead. Giorgetto Giugiaro (working at Ghia) designed the body with its gullwing-style engine covers. In a sense this was a super-Vallelunga, for it had a similar central backbone chassis, but this machine was powered (the U.S. versions, at least) by Ford's Boss 302 V-8. Therein lay the problem, as the engine was too much for the chassis, which led to problematic handling. And then there was De Tomaso's questionable quality control. Still, a Mangusta would be worth owning, just to be able to look at it. —JL

- Just over 400 Mangustas were built.
- The Mangusta was first shown at the 1966 Turin auto show.
- The transmission is a five-speed.
- One Mangusta problem was a heavy rearward weight bias.

Engine: Ford 5.0-liter ohv V-8	**Top speed:** 155 mph
Horsepower: 230	**Price when new:** $11,500
0–60 mph: 7.1 seconds	**Value now:** $85,000

- Alejandro De Tomaso's wife was a wealthy granddaughter of General Motors founder William C. Durant.

- At $9,995, the Pantera cost about half as much as a Maserati Ghibli and a third as much as a Ferrari Daytona.

- In 1981, *Popular Mechanics* magazine did a comparison test involving 16 sports cars. The winner was a Pantera GTS.

- U.S. sales of the Pantera ended after the 1974 model year, but sales continued in Europe and other markets.

- In the early 1980s, De Tomaso was Italy's fifth-largest automaker in terms of annual volume.

Engine: 351-cubic-inch Ford Cleveland V-8
Horsepower: 310
0–60 mph: 5.5 seconds

Top speed: Est. 150 mph
Price when new: $9,995
Value now: $52,000

By 1970 Ford had taken an ownership stake in De Tomaso and would provide its 310-horsepower 351-cubic-inch Cleveland V-8 to the mid-engine Pantera. More than 6,000 of these supercars were sold at selected Lincoln-Mercury dealerships from 1971 to 1974. The last and final Pantera was delivered to its lucky if somewhat bold owner in 1992, the first car having rolled out of De Tomaso's Modenese factory 21 years earlier. Designed by a Dutchman (Tom Tjaarda) while he was in Italy (working for Ghia), the Pantera ("panther" in Italian) was the supercar-world equivalent of a spaghetti western. And it shared its transaxle and most of its gearbox with none other than the Maserati Bora. The Pantera's muscular styling had the performance to go with it. *Car and Driver* recorded a 0–60 time of 5.5 seconds, which, in 1971, was just about as quick as it got. —SS

De Tomaso

Vallelunga   1964–1968

Before he created the Mangusta or Pantera, Alessandro De Tomaso did the Vallelunga. While the other two had big Ford V-8s, the little Vallelunga was powered by a 1.5-liter Ford Kent four, which worked through a modified VW gearbox. This midmounted driveline was in a central backbone chassis with independent suspension at both ends. But what makes the Vallelunga special is its beautiful exterior design. This is a vest-pocket car you could almost pick up and carry. Of course, it does weigh 1,600 pounds, but that's impressively light for an automobile. The first few cars had aluminum bodies, though the rest of the run was in fiberglass. Part of the problem was, like many De Tomaso projects, the talented man was distracted before the car was fully developed. Still, the result is beautiful. —JL

- Among Vallelunga owners is Tom Mitano, co-designer of the first Mazda Miata.
- The car was named for the Vallelunga racetrack near Rome.
- An estimated 50–58 Vallelungas were built.
- The first Vallelunga was a spyder shown at the 1964 Turin Show.

Engine: 1.5-liter inline four	Top speed: 128 mph
Horsepower: 104	Price when new: N/A
0–60 mph: 7.4 seconds	Value now: $100,000

2008–   **Challenger SRT8**

Dodge launched the high-performance SRT8 version of its new Challenger modern muscle car for the 2008 model year with a 425-horsepower, 6.1-liter Hemi V-8 engine. A year later the car was offered with a six-speed manual instead of only an automatic transmission, and with revised shock tuning to improve ride and handling. For the 2011 model year, Dodge offered the SRT8 392, bringing back a famous engine moniker and backing it up with 470 horsepower and 470 lb-ft of torque. —*LE*

- Only 1,492 copies of the SRT8 392 were scheduled for the 2011 model year—1,100 for the United States and 392 for Canadian customers.

- The SRT8 392 was available in Deep Water Blue with Stone White stripes or Bright White Clear Coat with Viper Blue stripes.

- The original 392-cubic-inch Hemi V-8 was introduced for the 1957 model year and would become the mill of choice for most drag racers for many years after.

- In stock guise, the new SRT8 392 should be a 12-second drag racer.

Engine: 392-cubic-inch Hemi V-8	Top speed: 180 mph
Horsepower: 470	Price when new: $46,000
0–60 mph: Est. 4 seconds	Value now: Same

1990–2001   **Stealth**

The Stealth was Dodge's version of the Mitsubishi 3000GT, a sports car produced from 1990 to 2001. Dodge and Mitsubishi had several joint-venture projects during that period, and, as a result, Dodge dealers got the Stealth from 1991 to 1996 as a coupe, and as a convertible with a retractable hardtop in 1995–1996. Initially, the Stealth was offered with a 160-horsepower normally aspirated or 296-horsepower twin turbocharged V-6 (Stealth R/T). Later the twin turbo was boosted to nearly 320 horsepower. —*LE*

- The Stealth was scheduled to be the pace car for the 1991 Indianapolis 500, but was replaced at the last minute by a Dodge Viper prototype.

- Mitsubishi sold the 3000GT as the GTO in Japan, but not in export markets.

- Mitsubish offered four-wheel drive, four-wheel steering, active aerodynamics and electronically controlled suspension.

- Despite its sporty appearance, nonturbo Stealths had front-wheel drive.

Engine: 3.0-liter twin turbocharged V-6	Top speed: Est. 160 mph
Horsepower: 296	Price when new: $25,000
0–60 mph: Est. 5.3 seconds	Value now: $2,500

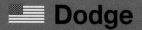 # Dodge

Viper RT/10 (first generation)

1992–1995

The Dodge Viper concept car was the stunning star of the 1989 Detroit auto show. Little more than a year earlier, Chrysler president Bob Lutz added a kit-car version of the Shelby Cobra to his car collection and wondered if a Chrysler V-8 might fit into the engine bay. This got him to thinking about the new V-10 truck engine Dodge had in development. Why not build a modern-day Cobra? Lutz suggested the idea to Chrysler design director Tom Gale, whose studio was already working on such a project. Lutz brought Carroll Shelby into the discussion, and a concept car was unveiled. The concept proved so popular that Chrysler eagerly assigned an engineering team to take it into production. At the time, Chrysler owned Lamborghini, and tasked the Italian firm with creating an aluminum version of the cast-iron truck engine. The Viper RT/10 went into

- The Viper—in prototype form—was the pace car for the 1991 Indianapolis 500-mile race. It paced the race again—this time in double-bubble roofed GTS production guise—in 1996.
- The Viper was available only with a six-speed manual transmission.
- The Viper design included side-mounted exhaust pipes.
- The car's body was made of composite panels attached to a steel-tube, racing-style space-frame chassis.

Engine: 8.0-liter V-10
Horsepower: 400
0–60 mph: Est. 4.6 seconds

Top speed: Est. 168 mph
Price when new: $50,000
Value now: $30,000

series production for the 1992 model year as a two-seat roadster with a cloth top that could span the gap between its windshield header and its integral roll bar structure. —*LE*

1996–2002
Viper GTS (second generation)

- The GTS made its debut as the pace car for the 1996 Indianapolis 500.

- In 2000, a Viper GTS-R was the overall winner of the 24 Hours of Daytona race.

- After years of complaints about the Viper's braking performance, Dodge added ABS in 2001.

- With its more powerful engine and aerodynamic bodywork, the new Viper coupe's top speed was more than 10 mph faster than the original roadster's.

Engine: 488-cubic-inch V-10	**Top speed:** 180 mph
Horsepower: 415	**Price when new:** $66,700
0–60 mph: Est. 4.0 seconds	**Value now:** $16,000

A second-generation Dodge Viper was introduced for the 1996 model year, and this one came in two versions—open roadster and closed coupe. The coupe, designated the GTS, had a "double-bubble" roof, presumably to provide additional room for occupants to wear racing helmets (or maybe it was just that Chrysler president Bob Lutz was a tall man and the cockpit needed to be large enough for him to be comfortable). In addition to a redesign of the car's bodywork—in both roadster and coupe form—the new Viper had a lighter but more rigid chassis, revised suspension and brakes, and a more powerful V-10 engine. The car also was equipped with dual front airbags. The coupe provided the basis for the GTS-R, a racing version of the Viper that posted three GT-class victories in the 24 Hours of Le Mans and also claimed three FIA GT world championships. —*LE*

 **Dodge**

Viper SRT-10 and Viper ACR 2008
(fourth generation)

The Viper began its third generation in 2003 and in 2008 received a facelift and other modifications significant enough to be considered a fourth-generation version. Now known as the Viper SRT10 (*below*), it came equipped with a new 8.4-liter V-10 engine that pumped out 600 horsepower, yet met low-emission vehicle regulations. This new Viper could accelerate to 60 miles per hour in less than four seconds and then return to a complete stop within less than 100 feet. In fact, the car could start, accelerate to 100 miles per hour, and then return to a stop within a span of 11 seconds.

The Viper SRT10 was available as a roadster or a coupe, and in 2009 an ACR (American Club Racer, inset) version—a street-legal car ready for track-day events—was added to the lineup. The racing version was more than 40 pounds lighter and featured tunable aerodynamics and suspension. —*LE*

- Brembo was the supplier of the Viper's stunning new braking hardware.
- The ACR version of the Viper had a carbon fiber "fanged" front splitter with rub strips and a carbon fiber rear wing that could be adjusted to seven different positions depending on track conditions.
- Chrysler twice unveiled Viper-based concept cars equipped with smaller engines. In 1998, it was the Dodge Copperhead with a V-6, and in 2006 it was the 6.1-liter Hemi V-8–powered Chrysler Firepower.
- Although production of the Viper was expected to end with the fourth generation—and 50 Final Edition cars were built—Chrysler's partnership with Fiat portends a fifth-generation Viper for 2012.

Engine: 8.4-liter V-10
Horsepower: 600
0–60 mph: Est. 3.9 seconds
Top speed: Nearly 200 mph
Price when new: $86,000
Value now: $75,000

- Frank Sinatra, Dean Martin, Desi Arnaz, Ronald Reagan, and Richard Nixon owned Dual-Ghias.

- Reagan reportedly lost his car in a poker game to President Lyndon Johnson.

- Design inspiration for the Dual-Ghia came from the Virgil Exner's Dodge Firearrow concept car.

- More than 30 of the 117 Dual-Ghias are believed to be extant.

Engine: 315-cubic-inch Dodge FirePower Hemi V-8	**Top speed:** N/A
Horsepower: 230	**Price when new:** $7,700
0–60 mph: N/A	**Value now:** $250,000

Eugene Casaroll's Dual Motors Corp. took its name from the two-engined vehicles it built for military use in World War II. After the war, Casaroll was fascinated by Chrysler's concept cars and, with designer and engineer Paul Farago, obtained V-8–powered Dodge chassis that were shipped to Italy, where Ghia-crafted bodywork was installed. Only 117 Dual-Ghia convertibles were built, and they were very popular with celebrities. —LE

Courier   1958–1969

First, the name: Elva. It is a shortened version of "elle va," French for "she goes." This specialized British car was the brainchild of Frank J. Nichols, and the production side of a company that built many winning race cars. During its run of 11 years, the Courier was done in four series, from Mk I through Mk IV. What established the Courier as desirable was its light weight, a fiberglass body on a ladder frame with an MG powerplant set back in the chassis to create a 50/50 weight distribution. Various components came from several British sports cars. The engines varied from 1.5 to 1.8 liters over the years, and this weight advantage made the Couriers quicker than the MGs, though at some sacrifice in creature comforts. —JL

- Some 500 Elva Couriers were built in 1958–1969.

- Mark Donohue began his career racing in a Courier.

- Elva Couriers were sold either fully manufactured or in kit form; the fully trimmed and wired kits could be assembled in about 18 hours.

- The vast majority of Elva Couriers were exported to the United States.

Engine: 1.6-liter ohv inline four (Mk II)
Horsepower: 72
0–60 mph: 11.8 seconds

Top speed: 100 mph
Price when new: $2,895
Value now: $15,000

- Production is predicted to begin in 2012.

- Seating will be a 2+2 layout.

- Expect a price of at least $200,000.

- The electric-only range is said to be 130 miles.

Engine: Two Siemens electric motors	**Top speed:** 155 mph
Horsepower: 340	**Price when new:** Est. $200,000
0–60 mph: 3.4 seconds	**Value now:** N/A

Between emissions rules and fuel prices, it would appear the future will include many electric cars. If so, the Exagon Furtive eGT is a pioneer. To begin with, the French machine is quite attractive—somewhat conventional perhaps, but not the oddball shape of some electric cars. And yet the drivetrain is made up of a pair of liquid-cooled Siemens motors that produce the equivalent of 340 horsepower. Being electric motors, their max torque starts at 0 rpm. And being an electric car, the eGT needs batteries, which are lithium-ion with a life cycle said to be some 10 years, with 3,000 charging cycles. Like the Chevrolet Volt, the car can be had with a gasoline engine that extends its range well beyond the nearest electrical outlet. —*JL*

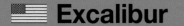

Excalibur

Hawk   1961

This car so wonderfully represents the sort of sports car-thinking that could bubble up in the 1950s. Brooks Stevens was an internationally regarded industrial designer who loved cars. Based near Milwaukee, he created a number of cars, including the Excalibur, an elegant classic with many similarities to the great pre-war Mercedes-Benz coachbuilt cars, but with many Studebaker mechanicals underneath. In 1961, Stevens built the Excalibur Hawk coupe shown here in an attempt to entice Studebaker into building something more interesting than the Avanti. The prototype was originally equipped with a supercharged Studebaker R-2 engine. The four-speed gearbox was also from the South Bend company; the front suspension was an independent design, the rear a live axle. The body was done in fiberglass. This car was kept in storage for many years and has only recently been appearing at classic car functions. —JL

- Stevens' Excalibur cars were often called "Mercebakers."

- The car had a brief racing career from 1963 to 1965.

- This one-and-only Excalibur Hawk coupe is still owned by the Stevens family.

- Stevens had also drawn up plans to build a Hawk roadster. In the 1990s, a friend of Brooks Stevens commissioned the building of a one-off Hawk roadster.

Engine: 4.7-liter supercharged ohv V-8
Horsepower: 289
0–60 mph: N/A

Top speed: N/A
Price when new: N/A
Value now: N/A

1947   **125 S**

- Atop the V-12 were three Weber carburetors.

- The gearbox was a five-speed manual.

- Colombo also designed the engine of the famed Alfa Romeo Alfetta Grand Prix cars.

- Ferrari was inspired to use a V-12 because of the American Packard V-12.

Engine: 1.5-liter sohc V-12	Top speed: 130 mph
Horsepower: 118	Price when new: N/A
0–60 mph: N/A	Value now: N/A

While Ferrari built two cars before World War II—the 1940 Auto Avio Costruzioni 815s—the first true Ferrari is the 125 S. Where the 815s had an engine made up of Fiat powerplants, the 125 used the first Ferrari V-12, which was designed by Gioacchino Colombo. While the 125 S failed in its first race, Franco Cortese won with its second time out; this was the initial win in Ferrari's long racing history. Many elements of this car, such as the V-12 and oval tube frame, provided the basis for Ferraris to come. The chassis had an independent front suspension and live rear axle. It's thought the original pair of 125s were cannibalized to build later Ferraris, and the car seen here was later built by Ferrari to honor its history. —JL

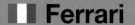
166 Barchetta   1948–1953

In 1948, Ferrari's original 125S evolved into the new 166 model. A variety of Italian coachbuilders, including Vignale, Allemano, Bertone, Ghia, Pinin Farina, Stabilimenti Farina, and Touring created bodywork, though all cars carried Gioachino Colombo's compact new V-12 engine, which displaced two liters rather than the 1,500 cc that propelled the 125.

Touring's roadster body was designed with racing competition in mind. It made its debut in Turin in the fall of 1948 and reportedly moved one of Italy's leading automotive journalists to remark, "This is not a car. It is absolutely new. That is a little boat—a barchetta!" The boat proved fast and maneuverable, winning many races, including the famed Mille Miglia. The 166 was built in various configurations—coupes and roadsters, even single seaters for Formula 2 racing—and with engines topped by single or even a trio of carburetors. —LE

- The model shown here has bodywork by Touring.

- The 166S made its racing debut with Clemente Biondetti winning the Targa Florio.

- A month later, Biondetti and co-driver Giuseppe Navone won the Mille Miglia by nearly an hour and a half.

- The first Ferrari brought to the United States is believed to be a 166 Spider imported by Briggs Cunningham.

Engine: 2-liter V-12
Horsepower: 110–155 depending on carburetion
0–60 mph: N/A

Top speed: 135 mph
Price when new: N/A
Value now: $1.87 million

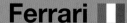

1962–1964   **250 GT Lusso**

- The 250 moniker comes from the displacement (in cubic centimeters) of each of the engine's 12 cylinders.

- Lusso production reached around 350.

- Most Lussos have four-speed transmissions.

- Steve McQueen owned a Lusso.

Engine: 2.0-liter sohc V-12	**Top speed:** 150 mph
Horsepower: 250	**Price when new:** $13,375
0–60 mph: 8.0 seconds	**Value now:** $500,000

Ferrari's famed 250 GT SWB (short wheelbase—*see page 119*) was done as a steel-bodied street machine or aluminum race car. Its track successor was the 250 GTO, while its street follow-up was the Lusso (Luxury). You'll find that 250 designation on many Ferraris, as it represents the company's famous 3.0-liter V-12. Again Pininfarina shaped the body, which was just as pretty and even more curvaceous than the SWB. While the Scaglietti-built body is steel, the doors, hoods, and trunk lids are lightweight aluminum. Interiors were more luxurious and better finished than many earlier Ferraris, and the gauge layout is classic, the main emphasis being on the tachometer. The rear suspension has a live axle, but Ferrari was soon to make the transition to an independent rear design. —*JL*

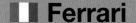

Ferrari

250 GTO 1962–1964

Many experts will argue that Ferrari's 250 GTO takes the title as the greatest Grand Touring car—maybe the greatest sports car—ever. When the group that governed international racing demanded GT cars compete for the manufacturer's title as of 1962, Ferrari was ready. Much of what had made the Scuderia's prototype sports cars— the famed 250 Testa Rossas—so successful was already available and fit perfectly inside the GTO's flowing Scaglietti bodywork. From the start the GTO was a success, with Phil Hill and Olivier Gendebien winning the car's first outing, the 1962 12 Hours of Sebring. Thanks to the GTO, Ferrari took the championship in 1962, 1963, and 1964. These beautiful GT cars are now among the most treasured—and most expensive—automobiles in the world. —JL

- Giotto Bizzarrini led the development of the GTO, which included wind tunnel testing at the University of Pisa.
- Ferrari built 36 3.0-liter 250 GTO versions and three 4.0-liter GTO versions.
- GTO stands for Gran Turismo Omologato—grand tourer, homologated for racing.
- GTO owners include Ralph Lauren and Pink Floyd drummer Nick Mason.

Engine: 3.0-liter sohc V-12	Top speed: 170 mph
Horsepower: 300	Price when new: $18,000
0–60 mph: 6.1 seconds	Value now: $27,000,000

- The 250 GT SWB was designed by Pininfarina and built by Scaglietti.

- Nineteen specially prepared 250 GT SWB competition Berlinettas became known as the SEFAC (Scuderia Enzo Ferrari Auto Corse) "Hot Rods." Officially Comp/61 cars, they were built on lighter but more rigid frames, they had very thin aluminum bodies, and their engines were topped by six carburetors to pump out 300 horsepower.

- SWB Ferraris won GT category honors at Le Mans in 1960 and 1961 and at the Tour de France in 1960, 1961, and 1962.

- Some 165 250 GT SWBs were produced between 1959 and 1962.

Engine: 3.0-liter sohc V-12	Top speed: 145 mph
Horsepower: 165	Price when new: $12,500
0–60 mph: Est. 8 seconds	Value now: $3.3 million

Ferrari introduced a new engine and a new car to carry it at the 1952 Mille Miglia. The car, the 250 S, would go on to be produced in various versions—250 MM, 250 Europa, 250 Monza, 250 GT, and 250 Testa Rossa. In 1959, a short wheelbase model was unveiled at the Paris auto show. The shorter wheelbase—trimmed from 102.4 inches to 94.5—improved the car's dexterity. But a shortening of the wheelbase wasn't the only change for a car produced as a racy coupe, a luxury Lusso (*see page 117*), and a California Spyder roadster. The new 250 GT series also was outfitted with disc brakes at each corner. This new Ferrari quickly became a terror on the track or the street, especially the early models, which carried lightweight aluminum bodies. —*LE*

250 GT Zagato · 1956

In 1956, two of Enzo Ferrari's best customers came with a special request: They wanted to buy Ferrari 250 GTs, but instead of bodywork by the usual coachbuilders (a group that included Touring, Ghia, and Pininfarina) Vladimiro Galluzzi and Camillo Luglio wanted their cars skinned by the Zagato *carrozzeria*. Among the distinguishing features of these beautiful and extremely rare cars is a "double-bubble" roof that left room for the driver and passenger to wear helmets while keeping the rest of the roof low for reduced wind resistance.

Galluzzi wanted his car for use on the road and the racetrack. Luglio was interested only in racing. So while the cars were similar, they differed in some details. For example, Luglio's was sheetmetal gray and lacked anything that might be considered a frill that would add unwanted weight on the track. Luglio won the 1956 Italian sports car championship in his car while Galluzzi's car not only competed on the track but won honors at concours d'elegance. —*LE*

- The success of the Galluzzi and Luglio cars led to three more being commissioned.

- Luglio took his new car to the Mille Miglia with sponsorship from paint-producer Idriz, which thus became one of the first European companies to pay to put its name on a racing car.

- Galluzzi also ordered a second car—this time for the road—and Vittorio De Milcheli commissioned the fifth 250 GT Zagato, which didn't have a double-bubble roof but did have a pair of tail fins.

- The car pictured here is one of the 1956 models, chassis number 0515GT.

Engine: 3.0-liter sohc V-12	**Top speed:** 135 mph
Horsepower: 240	**Price when new:** Est. $17,000
0–60 mph: 6.9 seconds	**Value now:** $5 million

- In 1964, the 250 LM won 10 major races (in 35 starts) and was second in six others.

- In 1965, Maston Gregory and Jochen Rindt drove a privately entered 250 Le Mans equipped with a larger 3.3-liter engine to a startling overall victory in the 24 Hours of Le Mans.

- The winning car at Le Mans was entered by NART—the North American Racing Team.

- Pininfarina later built berlinetta speciales, a road car based on the 250 LM.

Engine: 3.0-liter V-12	Top speed: 180 mph
Horsepower: 320	Price when new: N/A
0–60 mph: 6.5 seconds	Value now: $5.5 million

The *LM* stands for "Le Mans," site of the historic 24-hour sports car race in France. The Ferrari 250 LM made its debut at the 1963 Paris auto show, and its Pininfarina design looked more like an exotic concept car than a racer or a road car. The car was built around the 250P Le Mans racer's wheelbase and V-12 engine. Its distinctive low nose, raked windshield, roll bar that was integrated into the engine cover, and chopped tail harkened to prototype racers. Somehow, all of those elements were blended together into a smooth, gorgeous, and fast form. The plan was to homologate the car for GT-category racing, but with only 33 built (of the 100 required), the car had to compete against the all-out prototypes in racing, and it more than held its own. —*LE*

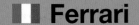

Ferrari

275 GTB/S/4   1964–1967

Production of Ferrari's famed 250 models ended in the fall of 1964, just as the company was unveiling their successor at the Paris auto show. The new car, the 275 (275cc per cylinder; 3.3 liters total), was displayed in GTB *(gran turismo berlinetta)* coupe and GTS *(spyder)* open roadster versions. However, instead of merely chopping off the car's roof, the GTS gained its own unique Pininfarina-designed rear bodywork. Whether as berlinetta or spyder, the 275 GTB and 275 GTS are cherished as among the Italian design house's finest works. Not only was the car new, but so was its V-12 engine. To enhance dynamic balance, the five-speed transmission was moved from just behind the engine into unity with the rear differential. To make the most of this enhanced balance, the 275 GTB and 275 GTS were the first Ferrari road cars to ride on fully independent suspension. —*LE*

- A racing version of the car was known as the 275 GTC (*C* stands for "corsa," or racer).

- In 1966, the 275 GTB/GTS were updated with six instead of three carburetors and with four overhead camshafts, bringing a boost to 300 horsepower. . .

- . . .New, bulging hoods were needed to cover the reconfigured engines.

- 275 GTB/4 coupes are million-dollar cars at classic car auctions.

Engine: 3.3-liter V-12	Top speed: 155 mph
Horsepower: 280	Price when new: $13,900
0–60 mph: 6.0 seconds	Value now: $625,000

1984–1985   288 GTO

- The engine in the GTO originally was developed for use in Lancias competing in the World Rally Championship.

- The 288 GTO made its debut at the Geneva auto show in the late winter of 1984.

- Ferrari planned to build only 200 of its 288 GTOs, but there was so much demand from customers that 272 were built.

- All of the 272, the 288 GTOs were sold to order before the car went into production.

Engine: 2.9-liter twin-turbocharged V-8
Horsepower: 400
0–60 mph: 5.0 seconds

Top speed: 189 mph
Price when new: $83,400
Value now: $650,000

Ferrari brought back two historic nameplates for the 1984 model year—Testa Rossa (though now spelled as one word instead of two) and GTO (the abbreviation for *Gran Turismo Omologato*). While the 288 GTO (*below*) may have looked like the Ferrari 308/328 coupe (*bottom*), its wheelbase had been stretched by four inches so its midmounted engine could be positioned longitudinally rather than transversely. That engine was a V-8 displacing only 2.9 liters, but boosted by two turbochargers it pumped out 400 horsepower through a five-speed manual gearbox. To keep such power under control, the 288 GTO rode on wide tires beneath blistered fenders, and featured air spoilers both front and rear. The 288 GTO was designed to meet international Group B racing regulations. Though the category didn't succeed, Ferrari went ahead with production of its new supercar, which had composite bodywork made from Kevlar, Nomex, aluminum, fiberglass, and carbon fiber. —*LE*

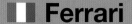
340 Mexico   1952

The 4.1-liter V-12 engine that had powered Ferrari's 340 F1 racer in the Grand Prix of Nations in 1950 found its way to the Paris auto show that fall, installed in a sports car with a coupe body by Touring. The following spring, the combination was back for the Turin auto show as the Ferrari 340 America model, this time with bodywork by Touring and Vignale. Three 340 Americas would go on to compete in the Mille Miglia, with one of them winning. Ferrari gave the car its name in hopes of increasing its exports to the United States. In 1952, Ferrari built and Sinclair oil sponsored a quartet of special versions of the car for the Carrera Panamericana road race. Three of these 340 Mexico models were coupes and one was a roadster (the car shown here), all with bodywork by Vignale. Power came from the 340 America's engine, though it was now equipped with new Weber carburetors. —*LE*

- The original Paris Show Car had black bodywork and dark green leather interior.

- Of the four 340 Mexico models entered in the Carrera Panamericana in 1952, only one finished. . .

- . . .Luigi Chinetti and Jean Lucas took third behind a pair of gullwinged Mercedes-Benz 300SLs.

- Only 22 Ferrari 340 Americas were built between 1951 and 1955 with bodies by Touring, Vignale, and Ghia.

Tech specs (340 Mexico):
Engine: 4.0-liter V-12
Horsepower: 220
0–60 mph: Est. 7.5 seconds

Top speed: 145 mph
Price when new: $16,000
Value now: $2 million

Ferrari 🇮🇹

- The nickname Daytona comes from Ferrari's 1–2–3 win at Daytona in early 1967.

- Dan Gurney and Brock Yates won the first Cannonball Trophy Dash in a Daytona.

- Around 1,400 Daytonas were built; about 100 of those were built as spyder convertibles.

- The spyder version has proven so popular that many people have taken to having their coupes "converted" into convertibles.

Engine: 4.4-liter dohc V-12	Top speed: 174 mph
Horsepower: 350	Price when new: $19,500
0–60 mph: 5.9 seconds	Value now: $290,000

Odd as it might sound today, the now-venerated Ferrari 275 GTB/4 wasn't a great seller. Seeking a replacement, Ferrari shipped a GTB chassis to Pininfarina, where 26-year-old Leonardo Fioravanti was given the task of quickly creating a successor. In a remarkably short time, Fioravanti shaped what would become the 365 GTB; it was a hit from the moment it was unveiled at the 1968 Paris auto show, the classic round headlamp and oval eggcrate grille updated with a sharper-edge design. Ferrari offered both spyder and coupe versions, with the famed V-12 engine and rear-mounted five-speed transmission. There were a few Daytona race cars, their main competition successes being in the 24 Hours of Le Mans and a memorable second overall in the 24 Hours of Daytona in 1973. —JL

▮▮ Ferrari

456 GT 2+2   1992–2003

Ferrari revived its tradition of grand touring cars with seating for four when it introduced the 456 GT 2+2 in Paris in 1992. The introductory car was particularly stunning; not just because of its elegant and sculptural Pininfarina bodywork, but because of the very un-Ferrari-like metallic blue hue in which it was presented. The profile was low, despite the fact that the hood had to cover a 5.5-liter V-12. The greenhouse arced smoothly back into a short rear deck that showed the hint of a spoiler. Though elegant, and with a luxurious interior, the 456 GT and GTA (automatic transmission) not only looked fast but was fast; indeed, it was so quick that Ferrari equipped it with a rear spoiler that deployed from beneath the rear bumper when the car exceeded 75 miles per hour to enhance high-speed stability. —*LE*

- The 456 designation comes from each of the 12 cylinders having a displacement volume of 456 cubic centimeters.

- The 456 was the last Ferrari to take its name from the displacement of each of the engine's cylinders.

- In 1998, the 456 GT became the 456 M GT (as in Modificata, Italian for "modification") with improved aerodynamics, better cooling, and a new interior.

- 456 GT 2+2s were reconfigured as four-door sedans, station wagons (called the Venice), convertibles for various members of royalty, and as a Targa top.

Engine: 5.4-liter V-12	**Top speed:** 190 mph
Horsepower: 442	**Price when new:** $224,800
0–60 mph: N/A	**Value now:** $40,000

- Racing seats cost $7,555, carbon fiber trim $15,267.

- Torque is 398 lb-ft.

- Ferrari uses carbon-ceramic brake discs.

- Gas guzzler tax? $2,600.

Engine: 4.5-liter dohc V-8	**Top speed:** 202 mph
Horsepower: 570	**Price when new:** $225,325
0–60 mph: 3.0	**Value now:** Same

For many years, Ferrari went to its history for design cues for its new cars. Not so with the 458 Italia, which brings the famed Italian exotic carmaker into the 21st century. Inside and out, the mid-engine 458 reflects the sort of beauty and attention to details we love in these supercars. The instrument panel includes the sort of speed-related information one would get from a race engineer. Aft of that cockpit is a 4.5-liter V-8 matched to a seven-speed paddle-shifter gearbox that lets you pop from gear to gear in milliseconds as you swallow up road. In just 6.7 seconds you can be at 100 miles per hour. Knifing down a winding road, the 458 remains stable, its suspension adapting to the conditions. —*JL*

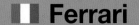 # Ferrari

512 BB   1976–1984

It wasn't until the 1971 Turin auto show that Ferrari finally unveiled a mid-engine grand touring sports coupe. That car went into production for 1973 as the 365 GT/4 BB; the *BB* was short for "Berlinetta Boxer," with *Boxer* indicating the installation of what might be considered a 180-degree, or flat, engine; the 12 cylinders were arrayed along the same axis. Such engines were called boxers because their pistons pumped back and forth like a boxer's jab. In 1976, the 365 GT/4 BB evolved into the 512 BB. The car itself had changed very little, but the engine had grown from 4.4 to 5.0 liters, and Ferrari had changed its naming style—from cubic centimeters of displacement to 5 (as in liters) and 12 (as in cylinders). The engine was not only larger, but more powerful, with horsepower climbing from 344 to 360. —LE

- Karl Benz patented the design of a "boxer" engine with horizontally opposed pistons in 1896. Subaru and Porsche build images with similar architecture.

- Changes from the 365 GT/4 BB to the 512 included a front lip spoiler and revised taillights.

- In 1981, fuel injectors replaced the boxer 12's quartet of carburetors.

- The 512 BB was replaced in 1984 by the stunning Testarossa.

Engine: 5.0-liter flat 12
Horsepower: 360
0–60 mph: 7.2 seconds

Top speed: 185 mph
Price when new: $85,000
Value now: $110,000

- Maranello is a small industrial suburb of Modena.

- The 550 Maranello's long hood was interrupted by a large, single air-intake nostril.

- In 2000, a roadster version—only 500 were produced—of the car was introduced as the 550 Barchetta Pininfarina.

- In 2002, the 550 Maranello was replaced by the 575 M Maranello model.

Engine: 5.5-liter V-12   **Top speed:** 183 mph
Horsepower: 485   **Price when new:** $204,000
0–60 mph: 4.2 seconds   **Value now:** $90,000

Even a Ferrari would have to be very special to wear the name of the company's hometown. Introduced in 1996, the 550 Maranello was Ferrari's replacement for the famed and beloved 365 GTB/4 Daytona, whose production had ended in some 22 years earlier, in 1974. Like the Daytona, the 550 Maranello was a two-seat coupe with a powerful V-12 mounted up front, a luxurious grand tourer with supercar capability.

In the 550 Maranello, that engine was a 5.5-liter that provided 485 horsepower, thrusting the car from a standing start to 60 miles per hour in barely more than four seconds and on to a top speed in excess of 180 miles per hour. The car also featured the latest technology and a design that used cues from several classic Ferrari models while appearing totally contemporary and modern. —LE

599 GTB Fiorano and 599 GTO

2006–

To replace its 575 M Maranello Super GT, Ferrari developed the 599 GTB Fiorano (*below*). Pininfarina again shaped the new Ferrari, from its eggcrate grille back to the flying buttress greenhouse. Being a classic Ferrari GT, the 599 has a front-mounted V-12, now backed by a six-speed manual or F1-type paddle-shifted "automatic." The interior is also classic Ferrari, with beautiful gauges and superb leather. There have been several variations on the 599 theme since the car was introduced in 2006. First came the Handling GT Evoluzione—a bit lower, a bit stiffer suspension, more aggressive shift points. Next came the 599 FXX, a lighter, racetrack-only version, with the V-12's horsepower urged up to 720. Then Ferrari civilized the FXX for the street— horsepower at 661—to create the 599 GTO (*right*). And finally a convertible version, the SA Aptera. —*JL*

- Ferrari unveiled the 599 GTB at the 2006 Geneva auto show.
- Ferrari built a hybrid 599 fitted with a KERS energy recovering system.
- Fiorano in the name refers to Ferrari's famous test track.
- The 599 GTB's V-12 is related to the Enzo's engine.

Engine: 6.0-liter dohc V-12	Top speed: 205 mph
Horsepower: 611	Price when new: $280,000
0–60 mph: 3.7 seconds	Value now: $210,000

- The car is produced (where else?) at Ferrari's Carrozzeria Scaglietti plant in Modena.

- You can have your 612 with either a manual or a six-speed F1-style automatic with paddle shifters.

- The 612 is equipped with the same 5.7-liter engine as the 575M Maranello.

- The space-frame chassis is made from aluminium, and the body (also aluminium) is then welded to it.

Engine: 5.7-liter V-12	Top speed: 196 mph
Horsepower: 530	Price when new: $263,519
0–60 mph: 4.3 seconds	Value now: $200,000–$250,000

Ferrari has a long and dramatic history when it comes to producing genuine, world-beating grand touring cars, and the four-seater 612 Scaglietti is, despite its slightly awkward styling, without question one of its very best. Visually, its scallop-sided body is intended to pay homage to the 375 MM that film director Roberto Rossellini had Ferrari custom-build for his wife, Ingrid Bergman, in 1954. But it's how the 196-mile-per-hour, V-12–engined 612 drives that's more important, because on the road there are few, if any, cars that combine this much luxury with this much speed, or that sound as good as a Scaglietti in full flight. —SS

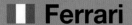
California   2011–

We don't often think of Ferraris as being controversial, but when the California was launched in Paris in 2008, some critics wondered if the Italians had made a misstep. Here was a Ferrari with a V-8 in the front (a first), and with a dual-clutch automatic transmission. The layout is 2+2, allowing room for small children, and the top is metal and folds behind the rear seat. Some argue this hurts the rear styling, though the front is classic Ferrari, as is the name, California, derived from a Ferrari classic from the 1950s. And yet when you drive the California there's no mistaking its heritage; it's quick, lithe, and forgiving. Since its introduction, the California has changed the minds of many would-be critics and brought a new set of owners into the Ferrari stable. —JL

- The torque of the Ferrari V-8 is 358 lb-ft.
- Californias have carbon-ceramic brakes.
- A California can get to 100 mph in 8.6 seconds.
- You can raise or lower the folding hardtop in 20 seconds.

Engine: 4.3-liter dohc V-8
Horsepower: 453
0–60 mph: 3.5 seconds

Top speed: 193 mph
Price when new: $210,000
Value now: Same

Ferrari

Year — Enzo

- The Enzo Ferrari is, of course, named in honor of the company founder.
- Race car heritage aside, the Enzo has ABS, traction control, and airbags.
- The Enzo has a Formula 1–derived launch control system.
- Ken Okuyama designed the Enzo while at Pininfarina.

Engine: 6.0-liter dohc V-12
Horsepower: 650
0–60 mph: 3.3 seconds
Top speed: 218 mph
Price when new: $643,330
Value now: $1,200,000

First of all, the official name of this car is the Enzo Ferrari, not the other way around. When the Enzo came out, some loved its radical shape. Others thought it odd. But no one was indifferent. Meant to capture the spirit of a Formula 1 car in a street machine, the Enzo is based on a lightweight monocoque of carbon fiber and carbon fiber/aluminum honeycomb. In back is a 650-horsepower Ferrari V-12 that sounds as cool as it drives. Open the Enzo's butterfly doors and drop down into the carbon fiber seats. Ahead of you is a gauge display that shouts "race car." Pop the six-speed paddle shifter into first and off you go. Simple as that you're past 100 miles per hour in 6.6 seconds and into jailable speeds. Been there, done that. —*JL*

F40   1987–1992

Enzo Ferrari wanted a special automobile to celebrate the 40th anniversary of his now-famous firm. Engineers began with the 288GTO that had been developed for the FIA's later-abandoned Group B class and developed the F40. The twin-turbo V-8 was opened up to 2.9 liters and upped to 471 horsepower. Much of the GTO chassis thinking remained—such as upper and lower A-arm suspensions— and there was a lot of then-current Formula 1 thinking in evidence. The body was all-new from the studios of Pininfarina. This was a true high-tech car in its era, combining aluminum, carbon fiber and Kevlar to keep the weight to around 2,400 pounds. Wind tunnel testing helped create a car with a low coefficient of drag and yet impressive downforce. . .and a classic Ferrari look. —JL

- The engine cranked out 426 lb-ft of torque.
- Ferrari built 1,315 F40s from 1987 to 1992.
- Though not intended to be raced initially, F40s were successful on the track.
- Unlike modern supercars, the F40 has no electronic suspension aids . . . just a pure driving experience.

Engine: 3-liter twin-turbo quattrovalvole V-8
Horsepower: 471
0–60 mph: Less than 4 seconds

Top speed: 201 mph
Price when new: $400,000
Value now: $1,300,000

- Ferrari considered the F50 to be an F1 car "dressed" for the road.

- Among the racing components applied to the F50 were its suspension, carbon fiber body-panel technology, underbody panel and rear wing designs, fuel cell-style gasoline tank, and—thanks to a removable roof panel—open cockpit.

- The F50 had a larger engine than the Ferrari F1 car, but the racer had more horsepower, thanks to its 17,000 rpm rev limit.

- Ferrari's research determined the worldwide market for the F50 to be 350 potential buyers, but only 349 were built. Why? A Ferrari spokesman explained that Ferraris should be hard to find, and therefore the decision was made to build one car less than the market capacity.

Engine: 4.7-liter V-12
Horsepower: 513
0–60 mph: 3.7 seconds

Top speed: 202 mph
Price when new: $487,000
Value now: $700,000

Although it was unveiled in 1995, a few years before the actual anniversary date, the F50 was designed to celebrate Ferrari's 50th birthday as an automaker and as a replacement for the F40 that marked the company's 40th year in business. The new car was basically a road-going Ferrari F1 racer with seats and fenders. At the time, Ferrari president Luca di Montezemolo said that because of increasingly stringent emission legislation, the F50 would be the last Ferrari road car based on an F1 racing engine. But while F1 racers were restricted to 3.5-liter engines, supercars had no such restrictions, so the F50 got a 4.7-liter V-12 version of the engine. Combined with the car's slick aerodynamics and lightweight construction, the F50 could exceed 200 miles per hour. —*LE*

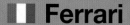
F355 — 1994

The F355 was so much better sorted (read: less hairy to drive) than its immediate predecessor, the 348; it was almost as if an entire model generation had gone missing somewhere in between. Like the 348, the F355 used a midmounted V-8 engine that produced most of its stunning performance at stratospheric revs but, unlike the 348, it also had a chassis that could be exploited and enjoyed by drivers who knew what they were doing. And its steering and brakes were in a different league from those of its predecessor. The 355 is also notable for being the very first road-going Ferrari to feature F1-style paddle shifters, albeit only as an option. To begin with the F1 shift wasn't too popular; nowadays it has become de rigeur pretty much across the breed. —SS

- The 355 comes from its 3.5-liter V-8 engine featuring five valves per cylinder.
- At launch there were two models available, a Berlinetta and GTS. The Spider arrived a year later.
- The F1 model was officially called the Ferrari 355 F1, meaning the F in F355 was dropped.
- The first-ever Ferrari racing car to feature paddle shifters was the Formula 1 car from 1989.

Engine: 3.5-liter V-8
Horsepower: 380
0–60 mph: 4.6 seconds
Top speed: 185 mph
Price when new: $105,000
Value now: $70,000–100,000

2011–   FF

- As of spring 2011, Ferrari has already sold out the initial 800 orders for the car.

- The seven-speed gearbox is a dual-clutch F1-style transmission.

- Carbon-ceramic brakes are standard.

- There's even a rear-seat twin-TV screen infotainment system.

Engine: 6.3-liter dohc V-12	Top speed: 208 mph
Horsepower: 660	Price when new: $395,000
0–60 mph: 3.6 seconds	Value now: Same

That would be FF as in "Ferrari Four," signifying two things. *Four* as in this hatchback has room to seat four adults. Plus luggage. The rear seat's split seat backs can be folded separately to increase that room. *Four* also as in four-wheel drive. This was the first production Ferrari that delivers power to all corners. While basically a rear-drive system, the Power Transfer Unit can route power to the front wheels when needed. And not just the front pair but to an individual front wheel. Naturally this top-line Ferrari has the latest V-12, now at 660 horsepower. With all the expected dynamic vehicle controls onboard, the FF is said to be as quick around Ferrari's Fiorano test track as the 599 GTB. . . is that with four aboard? Will twice as many people get to enjoy the fun? —JL

FXX   2006

Ferrari promised to build a fixed number of Enzos—400—but then came back with two vehicles based on that car, the Maserati MC12 and the FXX. Only 30 of the latter were built and sold to special customers, who snapped them up quickly, even though they couldn't drive them on the street. Ferrari maintains the vehicles and owners can only drive them on special track days, sharing the information learned with Ferrari. The Enzo V-12 was upped from 6.0 liters to 6.3 for the FXX, horsepower from 696 to 800, and torque to 509 lb-ft. The FXX features a carbon fiber tub and body, which helps keep its weight down to a svelte 2,546 pounds. Aerodynamics were changed from the Enzo to increase downforce. —JL

- Ferrari's five-time F1 world champion Michael Schumacher was given an FXX when he retired in 2006.
- Brembo carbon-ceramic brakes are fitted.
- The six-speed gearbox shifts in 100 milliseconds.
- Ferrari's FXX V-12 produces 127.75 horsepower per liter.

Engine: 6.3-liter dohc V-12	Top speed: 243 mph
Horsepower: 800	Price when new: $2,100,000
0–60 mph: 2.8 seconds	Value now: $2,500,000

2009   Scuderia Spyder 16M

- Ferrari never did an open version of the 360 CS, which makes the 16M a stand-alone model, with no specific predecessor.

- Ferrari has said that the 16M is faster than an Enzo around its own test track at Fiorano.

- Gear change speed is 60 milliseconds for the 16M, faster than the blink of a human eye.

- The 16M features Ferrari's E-Diff, which allows drivers the choice between numerous different traction control settings.

Engine: 4.3-liter V-8	Top speed: 196 mph
Horsepower: 500	Price when new: $277,000
0–60 mph: 3.7 seconds	Value now: Same

As if the 430 Scuderia wasn't enough on its own to remove the hairs from the back of your neck, Ferrari went one better in 2009 and produced the Scuderia Spider 16M, which was effectively an open-top version of the 430 Scuderia and created to commemorate Ferrari's 16th Formula One Constructor's World Championship in 2008. There are all sorts of extraordinary things about the 16M, but the standout feature is the way it sounds. In a tunnel, with the roof not there, you may even need ear-defenders if you value your long-term hearing. This car is that loud and that exciting to be in when its V-8 engine is rotating at close to 9,000 rpm. And like the fixed top version, it's searingly rapid as well. Maybe it's a good thing overall that only 499 ever got made. —SS

■ Ferrari

Testarossa   1984–1996

There are two Ferraris with this name. First came the Testa Rossa race cars from the 1950s and early 1960s. . .great front-engine V-12 machines that won many, many races. Then came the Testarossa (one word), successor to the automaker's famed mid-engine Berlinetta Boxer. Bigger than the BB, the Pininfarina design of the Testarossa is best remembered for its side strake grilles over the rear-mounted radiators. "TRs," as they are often called, were made in three forms, all with the 4.9-liter flat-12: the first (1984–1991) at 390 horsepower; the 512 TR (1991–1994) at 428 horsepower; and the F512M (1994–1996) 440 horsepower. Driving a TR is enormous fun, but you must be aware of its width. . .not difficult to do in its wide, leather-upholstered interior. —JL

- Testa Rossa means "red head" in Italian and refers to the color of the cylinder heads.
- Just shy of 10,000 Testarossas were built.
- TRs needed their side strakes due to laws demanding that large intakes must be covered.
- The car pictured here is a 390-horsepower 1989 model.

Engine: 4.9-liter dohc flat 12	Top speed: 180 mph
Horsepower: 390	Price when new: $180,000
0–60 mph: 5.2 seconds	Value now: $85,000

1952–1954   **8V Rapi Berlinetta**

- Fiat used the 1952 Geneva auto show to unveil the 8V.

- The V-8 design was based on a pair of inline fours in a common crankcase.

- Fiat built 114 8V automobiles.

- Reportedly Fiat called it the 8V instead of V-8 to avoid problems with Ford.

Engine: 2.0-liter ohv V-8	**Top speed:** 124 mph
Horsepower: 115	**Price when new:** $3,100
0–60 mph: 10.5 seconds	**Value now:** $400,000

Famed for its small, economical cars, Fiat opted in 1952 to launch a V-8–powered automobile. While V-8 means big displacement to an American, Fiat did this one at just 2.0 liters to compete in races for cars of that size. To keep the engine narrow, they created an unusual V-8 with 70 degrees between cylinder banks. Well-known engineer Dante Giacosa directed the car's development, dipping into Fiat's extensive parts bin for such components as the suspensions. Several design houses were commissioned to create bodies, which vary from the pretty Zagato coupes to the amazing Ghia 8V Supersonics. The Rapi cars came in two series, named for Fabio Luigi Rapi, the head of Fiat's design department. Not well known by many sports car fans, the 8Vs are treasured by collectors. —JL

Fiat

As it got older, the Fiat 124 Coupe got less attractive somehow, but on the other hand it did become more reliable and was much better to drive in its latter years, so you pays your money. . . . The very first cars had a distinct whiff of Italian elegance in the way their curvaceous, lightly chromed bodyshells adorned such a long wheelbase. But beneath the skin there wasn't much to offer to support such effortless good looks. To begin with there was a 1.4-liter twin cam engine, although this was eventually replaced by a more potent 1.8 lump attached to a five-speed gearbox. On the road, the 124 Coupe was a good rather than great car to drive. —SS

- The 1971 Fiat Coupe shared its taillight design with the Lamborghini Jarama.

- It featured a speedometer that read to a somewhat ambitious 140 miles.

- Options included green tinted windows and chromed alloy wheels.

- Fiat eventually managed to offer air conditioning in the coupe.

(1.4-liter):	Top speed: N/A
Engine: 1.4-liter inline four	Price when new: $1,800
Horsepower: 89	Value now: $5,000
0–60 mph: N/A	

- Fiat and Pininfarina built approximately 130,000 of these cars during its 17-year run...

- ...and every single one was left-hand drive.

- A supercharged "Volumex" variant was briefly offered in the U.S. market.

- The car pictured is a Pininfarina model.

Engine: 2.0-liter dohc inline four	**Top speed:** 102 mph
Horsepower: 102 horsepower	**Price when new:** $8,100
0-60 mph: 10.6 seconds	**Value now:** $12,000

It isn't often you hear a sports car called a sweetheart, but this one is. Fiat built 124 Spiders from 1979 until 1982, then handing sales off to Pininfarina, which had designed and built the cars. They weren't super quick, but once 124s were at 2.0 liters they were fast enough. Drop the top in seconds, row your way through the five-speed manual gearbox, and have a ball. —JL

508S Balilla — 1932–1937

So what's this little guy doing here? Just as the Fiat 500 put Italy back on wheels after World War II, Fiat 508s did much to put the country on wheels in the first place. And, being Italy, there were sport versions. Again being Italy, they were raced. The two best-known sports car Balillas were the 508 Spider Sport and the rare Coppa d'Oro Corsa MM. Ghia designed the neat little body, and the truly trick versions had a Siata-modified engine and a four-speed transmission. Though little-known in the United States, in the mid-1930s these Fiats were quite competitive in the 1,000cc racing classes in Europe. It is now common to see Balillas being used on classic car rallies like the historic Mille Miglia. —JL

- 508 Balillas were built from 1932 to 1937.
- There is a rare coupe version, the Berlinetta, with a beautiful aero body.
- These cars tipped the scales at less than 1,400 pounds.
- Fiat 508s could also be bought as a sedan or light truck.

Engine: 1.0-liter ohv inline four
Horsepower: 43
0–60 mph: N/A
Top speed: 75 mph
Price when new: N/A
Value now: $120,000

The original Fiat Abarth was based on the small but perfectly formed Fiat 600, also known as the Seicento, and it was designed primarily for racing and rallying. Carlo Abarth began hopping up these nifty little cars in 1956, with many iterations following over the next fifteen years. The ultimate versions were the 1000 Radiales of the late 1960s, which squeezed 85–112 horsepower from a mere 982 cc and won many a race in the tiny-displacement classes. —SS

- The car pictured is a 1000 Radiale.
- Radiale was the termed used to describe Abarth's hemispherical heads.
- In its heyday Abarth was managed by famed ex–Ferrari engine designer, Aurelio Lampredi.
- The scorpion depicted in the Abarth logo reflects the birth sign of its founder.

Engine: 982cc hemispherical head inline four
Horsepower: 85
0–60 mph: N/A

Top speed: 117
Price when new: 1,525,000 (lire)
Value now: $20,000–$35,000

Not content to just revive the famous 500 name, in 2008 Fiat came up with another masterstroke in the form of the all-new Fiat 500 Abarth. One look at the car was enough to tell you most of what you need to know about the way it drove—namely, very well indeed. But nothing could prepare you for the raw and rapid acceleration of the new Abarth, especially when fitted with the juiciest of its engine options and in Esseesse specification—a 1.4 turbo with 160 horsepower. This is one of the most entertaining front-wheel-drive cars that money can buy. —SS

- There is also an Assetto Corse version with 200 horsepower and its own one-make race series.
- The 500 Esseesse option is sold as a conversion kit, and must be installed on the standard Abarth within the first 12,000 miles of the vehicle's life.
- The 500 Abarth was unveiled exactly one year after Fiat's rebirth of the Abarth brand.
- This car's underpinnings are shared with those of the all-new Ford Ka.

(Esseesse):
Engine: 1.4-liter turbocharged inline four
Horsepower: 160

0–60 mph: 7.4 seconds
Top speed: 131 mph
Price when new: $22,000
Value now: Same

Chrysler

Barchetta
1995–2005

Fiat had lost its way creatively somewhat when the Barchetta appeared toward the end of 1994, but the so-called "little boat"—which was pronounced "Bar-Ketta"—helped change our opinion on that pretty much overnight. And the really clever thing about the Barchetta is that although it may have looked like a traditional, rear-drive rival for the likes of the MX5, beneath the skin it was actually front-wheel drive. Which meant it worked for Fiat commercially, every bit as well as dynamically. In short it was a scream to drive, with a vivacious 1.8-liter engine and tidy handling and steering to match. And it was remarkably reliable for a Fiat, too, being based on sound, established underpinnings that didn't fall to pieces if they were pushed. —SS

- The Barchetta was jointly designed by Andreas Zapatinas, Alessandro Cavazza, and American Pete Davis.

- It was based on the Mk 1 Fiat Punto beneath its handsome two-seater bodyshell.

- It was the first-ever Fiat to use an engine fitted with variable camshaft timing.

- Despite its worldwide popularity, the Barchetta was only ever built in left-hand drive.

Engine: 1.8-liter inline four	**Top speed:** 118 mph
Horsepower: 129	**Price when new:** $20,000
0–60 mph: 8.9 seconds	**Value now:** $5,000

1993–2000   Coupe

- The interior was every bit as bold as the exterior, and was designed by Pininfarina.

- To begin with, the engine was a four-cylinder turbo, but the five-cylinder 20-valve was the one to have.

- For the more powerful models, Fiat developed a complex limited slip differential for the front axle.

- Fiat made over 70,000 coupes in total, meaning it is one of its most successful coupes ever.

Engine: 2.0-liter turbocharged 20-valve inline five
Horsepower: 220
0–60 mph: 6.5 seconds

Top speed: 155 mph
Price when new: $33,000
Value now: $10,000–$15,000

You can almost tell as much just from looking at the Fiat Coupe's striking good looks that it was created by someone with a touch of genius (or perhaps madness) at their core. That someone was a gent named Chris Bangle, who would later go on to completely restyle the whole of BMW's passenger car range; and in the flesh the Fiat Coupe is arguably one of his finest hours. It was a pretty stonking beast to drive, too, never more so than when it had the turbocharged 20-valve engine installed, which provided the front-wheel-drive Coupe with supercar levels of straight line performance and a propensity to understeer that was almost as manic as the car's chief designer. What was never in doubt was the Coupe's VFM factor because, for the money, it was almost unbeatably exciting in every way. —SS

Fiat

X1/9 — 1972–1982

The idea for Fiat's engineering project X1/9, a codename that would stick with the car even in production, was to create a successor to the popular Fiat 850 sports coupe and roadster of the 1960s. Like the 850, this new sports car would be affordable because it would use readily available components. For the Fiat X1/9, those components would come from the Fiat 128, a mundane, front-wheel-drive sedan. But when the engine was moved to the rear to drive the back wheels, and when disc brakes were installed at all four corners, mundane became fun to drive, especially after 1979 when a new, more powerful engine and five-speed transmission were added to the package. The X1/9 was a wedge-shaped two-seater with a short wheelbase and a Targa-style roof that could be stowed under the front hood. With the engine tucked behind the seats, there was room for a second trunk at the back of the car. —LE

- The forerunner for the X1/9 was a 1969 Bertone concept car, the topless, dune buggy–styled Autobianchi A112, which had a long, wedge-shaped nose and an integrated roll bar behind just aft of the cockpit.

- The A112's "headlights" were mounted just ahead of the rear wheels and hung outboard off the roll bar.

- The Autobianchi A112 was the work of Marcello Gandini and was presented as a "mini-Miura," a reference to the first true supercar, a Bertone design by Gandini for Lamborghini.

- Fiat produced the X1/9 until 1982; Bertone then took over until 1989.

Engine: 1.3-liter sohc inline four
Horsepower: 62
0–60 mph: 11 seconds plus
Top speed: 110 mph
Price when new: $6,300
Value now: $7,800

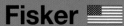
2011–   **Karma**

- Fisker says the Karma can accelerate to 60 mph in less than eight seconds in "stealth" (electric) mode. . .

- . . .or in less than six seconds in "Sport" mode, with the ICE engine providing extra electrical punch.

- Karma also has solar panels on its roof that, according to Fisker, can provide as much as 200 miles of emission-free voltaic driving on an annual basis.

- Paint and leather surfaces also use the latest in environmentally friendly technologies, Fisker says.

Engine: 200kW electric battery with Q Drive (ICE range extending 2.0-liter generator)
Horsepower: 403
0–60 mph: Est. 5.9 seconds
Top speed: 125 mph
Price when new: Est. $90,000
Value now: Same

You may not recognize Henrik Fisker's name, but you likely know his work, which includes the BMW Z8 and the Aston Martin DB9 and V8 Vantage. Having achieved one career goal—designing a car that would be featured in a James Bond movie—Fisker set out to achieve another, creating his own car company, Fisker Coachbuild, with former BMW and Ford manager Bernhard Koehler. At first, Fisker did what might be termed custom cars based on BMW and Mercedes-Benz products, but then Fisker joined with Quantum Technologies to create Fisker Automotive to build plug-in electric luxury vehicles with an onboard gasoline engine extending range by acting as a generator to resupply energy to the battery pack. Fisker Automotive's first vehicle, the Karma sports sedan, is designed to be driven up to 50 miles on battery power, then another 250 miles with the generator motor supplying power to the lithium-ion batteries. —JL

Fisker

Latigo CS and Tramanto   2005–

So what do you think of the Mercedes-Benz SL and BMW 6-Series seen here? Don't recognize them? Well, they are the SL and 6-Series transformed into a Fisker Tramonto (*inset*) (Mercedes) and Latigo CS (*bottom*) (BMW). After he set up his independent design firm and before starting on his hybrid sports car, former BMW designer Henrik Fisker created this pair of special-bodied cars, proposing to build only 150 of each. Not that many finally hit the roads, but those that did are truly unique. The original body panels were replaced with Fisker-penned replacements, which were fashioned from aluminum, stainless steel, and magnesium. Note the grille is similar to that on the hybrid Karma. The interiors were scrumptious, done in fine Italian leather and very carefully detailed. It was also possible for owners to custom-order interior detailing. —*JL*

- Tramontos had Mercedes-Benz AMG V-8 or V-12 engines.
- Latigo CS BMW engines were supertuned by RDsport.
- Henrik Fisker designed BMW's Z8 sports car.
- A Latigo CS will clip to 60 in just 3.9 seconds.

Engine: 5.4-liter supercharged dohc V-8
Horsepower: 610
0–60 mph: 3.6 seconds

Top speed: 202 mph
Price when new: $296,775
Value now: $150,000

- Ford produced 4,038 GTs in Wixom, Michigan.

- Ford's GT is about 10 percent larger than the GT40.

- Initial plans were laid out in the Saleen factory in California.

- Former Microsoft exec Jon Shirley bought the first Ford GT at a charity auction for $557,000.

Engine: 5.4-liter supercharged V-8	**Top speed:** 205 mph
Horsepower: 550	**Price when new:** $150,000
0–60 mph: 3.6 seconds	**Value now:** $160,000

When Ford decided to do a modern version of its iconic GT40 race car, we rather expected a modern styling update. Instead, Ford Living Legends design chief Camilo Pardo penned an only slightly revised shape of the original. And it works perfectly, looking as good as ever. It helps, of course, that Ford stuck a supercharged 5.4-liter V-8 with 500 horsepower and 550 lb-ft of torque out back. It goes without saying that V-8 dropped in a 3,390-pound, aero-trimmed sports car created a GT that will go head-to-head with its equivalents from Ferrari, Lamborghini, and Porsche. Inside the retro-but-modern theme continues, from the manner in which the gauges are laid out to the row of toggle switches. Everything old is new again. . . and even better. —JL

 # Ford

GT40   1964–1969

Henry Ford II wanted very badly to beat Enzo Ferrari after the Italian had spurned Ford's attempt to buy Ferrari. Ford began with the mid-engine Lola GT and developed it into the GT40, which first raced in May 1964. Early attempts yielded mixed results with the small-block V-8 Mark Is, but when Ford went to the big 7.0-liter Mark IIs, they began to close the gap. There was also a Mark III, which is the rare small V-8 road-going GT40. Ford created a new, larger J car–based GT40, the Mark IV, which won both times it was raced, at Sebring and Le Mans in 1967. When the 7.0-liter engines were banned for 1968, teams racing the GT40 reverted to the small 5.0-liter V-8 and continued to win. —*JL*

- GT40 #1075 won the 24 Hours of Le Mans twice (1968 and 1969).
- GT stands for Grand Touring, "40" standing for the car's height of 40 inches.
- There have been numerous recreations of the GT40.
- Rarest of the GT40s is the roofless X-1.

Engine: 7.0-liter ohv V-8 (Mk II)	**Top speed:** 205 mph
Horsepower: 485	**Price when new:** $16,500
0–60 mph: 4.2 seconds	**Value now:** $1.4 million

- Before starting a T (with a handle), the spark had to be manually retarded to prevent the engine from kicking back.

- The center pedal within a T's footwell is used to engage reverse gear.

- The earliest Ts had a brass radiator and headlights.

- The word Fordism was invented to describe the way in which the T was so efficiently produced.

Engine: 177-cubic-inch inline four
Horsepower: 20
0–60 mph: N/A

Top speed: 45 mph
Price when new: $290
Value now: $30,000+

The Tin Lizzie, as it was known at the time, first appeared in 1908 and represented the beginning of time for the automobile in the United States. It mobilized the country, providing a relatively cheap, eminently available method of transport that allowed the middle classes, at least, to travel from coast to coast without requiring the services of a train, or a horse. And the way in which it was assembled, on a line and not individually by hand, set the template for the whole industry. On May 26, 1927, founder Henry Ford watched the 15 millionth Model T roll off his production line in Michigan, and although, in all honesty, the T was never that amazing to drive, its historical significance should never, ever be underestimated. —SS

 # Ford

Mustang Boss 302   1969–1970

There were Shelby Mustangs and even the factory-built Mustang Mach I with its 351-cubic-inch V-8 engine, and a bunch of Bonneville speed records set by Mickey Thompson, but Ford also needed a Mustang that qualified for the Sports Car Club of America's Trans-Am racing series and also could compete on the street with Chevrolet's Z28 Camaro. Thus the Mustang Boss 302 was born. Power came from Ford's 302-cubic-inch V-8, which was tweaked to provide 290 horsepower. But the most significant tweaks were to the car's suspension, wheels and tires, which caused *Car and Driver* magazine to call the Boss 302 "the best-handling Ford ever to come out of Dearborn," and proclaiming that this new pony "may just be the new standard by which everything from Detroit must be judged." The Boss 302 also got a front chin spoiler, rear wing, metal slats over the rear fastback window, and special racing stripes. —*LE*

- There also was a Boss 429 version of the Mustang for drag racing.

- Ford planned to put an SR badge, short for "Sports Racing," on the car, but designer Larry Shinoda (who also had done the Z28 Camaro when he worked at General Motors) suggested the Boss moniker.

- SCCA rules required a homologation run of 1,100 cars to qualify for the Trans-Am series. But demand was so high that Ford built more than 1,900 Boss 302 Mustangs for the 1969 model year.

- The Boss 302 took the Trans-Am championship in 1970.

Engine: 302-cubic-inch V-8	Top speed: Est. 130 mph
Horsepower: 290	Price when new: $3,500
0–60 mph: Est. 6.9 seconds	Value now: $83,000

Ford

- Torque rating: 390 lb-ft.
- Even the Mustang V-6 has 305 horsepower, more than the original Boss 302.
- Both automatic and manual six-speed transmissions are available.
- An important option: Brembo disc brakes.

Engine: 5.0-liter dohc V-8
Horsepower: 412
0–60 mph: 4.8 seconds
Top speed: 155 mph
Price when new: $30,495
Value now: Same

Plenty of Mustangs have carried the "GT" suffix. While some might wonder why it is in a sports car book, consider that this GT will outrun and outcorner many sports cars. We'll start with the standard aluminum 5.0-liter V-8 version, which comes as a coupe or convertible. Though it's comfortable enough to be driven daily, the chassis is also quite competent on twisty mountain roads. Also important these days, the GT manages 17 mpg city/26 mpg highway. There are, of course, many variations on the Mustang GT, like the Shelby GT500 that caps its 5.4-liter V-8 with a supercharger for 550 horsepower and 0–60 mph in 4.4 seconds. Or the modern version of the classic Boss 302 with the 5.0-liter engine at 444 horsepower and 60 miles per hour flying past in 4.0 seconds. —JL

Ford

RS200   1984–1986

In the early 1980s, auto racing's new Group B category drew frenzied attention from the world's automakers, which needed to produce only 200 vehicles to achieve homologation. Those vehicles included the likes of the Audi Quattro, Peugeot 205 Turbo 16, Renault 5 Turbo, Lancia Delta S4, Rover Metro 6R4, and even the Porsche 959. Ford wanted to play, too, eventually coming up with the RS200, an Escort-inspired rally car with a midmounted Cosworth engine and four-wheel drive. Of the 200 cars needed for homologation, two dozen were upgraded to "Evolution" status with larger 2.1-liter engines rated at some 600 horsepower. For a dozen years, the 200RS Evolution was the world's fastest-accelerating car, sprinting to 60 miles per hour in less than three seconds! —LE

- One of the 24 RS200 Evolutions sold for $159,500 at a classic car auction early in 2011.

- The RS200's best performance in a World Rally Championship event was third in the 1986 Swedish Rally. Compared to its competitors, the RS200 lacked power, especially at low revs.

- Group B rallying ended after multiple crashes in which spectators as well as a rally driver were killed.

- If the car's top speed seems slow, remember that rally cars were geared for acceleration, not top speed.

Engine: 1.8-liter turbocharged inline four
Horsepower: 250
0–60 mph: 2.9 seconds (Evolution version)

Top speed: 120 mph
Price when new: N/A
Value now: $159,500 (Evolution version)

Ford 🇺🇸

- Jaguar's engine in the 11th-generation Thunderbirds had 252 or 280 horsepower.

- First-generation T-Birds had an optional supercharged 300-horsepower V-8.

- Ford debuted the 1955 Thunderbird at the 1954 Detroit auto show.

- The 1956 Thunderbird had a continental kit spare tire out back.

(1957 manual):	
Engine: 4.8-liter ohv V-8	**Top speed:** 115 mph
Horsepower: 212	**Price when new:** $3,408
0–60 mph: 10.1 seconds	**Value now:** $65,000

There have been all sorts of Thunderbirds, including rather hefty four-seaters, some forgettable coupes, and the exciting BMW-like supercharged 10th generation. What we care about are the pair of two-seater T-Birds. The first and easily most famous were built from 1955 to 1957. While Chevrolet had its sports car Corvette, the first-generation Thunderbirds were two-seat luxo cruisers. They are very pretty cars—arguably the 1957s are the best. Ford went back to the two-seat Thunderbird theme from 2002 to 2005. This version was based on a platform shared with the Lincoln LS and Jaguar S-type, even using a version of the Jaguar V-8. The exterior was reminiscent of the first T-Birds, but after an initial good response, sales fell off dramatically and the Thunderbird again faded away. —JL

 # Geely

Gleagle GS   2012

- Geely expects to sell the Gleagle in China only.
- The GS will have a six-speed manual or seven-speed automatic transmission.
- Geely owns Volvo.
- Gleagle is a mashing together of "global eagle."

Engine: 1.3-liter turbocharged dohc inline four	Top speed: N/A
Horsepower: 127	Price when new: N/A
0–60 mph: N/A	Value now: N/A

There are a lot of N/As in the specs below, but then again the Gleagle GS is not available. . .yet. It is, however, a peek at where China is going with its auto industry. Geely is a major factor in that market and will soon begin building this front-drive 2+2 coupe. The grille is a bit much, but the rest of the shape is rather. . .cute? —JL

Gemballa

Mirage   1990

The Gemballa Mirage, given that it was created in 1990 and was based loosely on a 911 Turbo of the same era, was a genuinely outrageous machine. Its roof was lower than normal, its engine was massaged to produce an eye-watering 490 horses, and its top speed rose to a vaguely hilarious 205 miles per hour as a result. Used by Pioneer as a promo car, it was also a deadly serious piece of engineering from Uwe Gemballa, who went on to produce a range of highly tuned Porsches. —SS

- Gemballa's latest 911-based creation is the GTR800 EVO-R, which has 800 horsepower.
- The original Mirage from 1990 was used as a promotional car by Pioneer.
- Formerly famous rap star Vanilla Ice once drove a Gemballa 911.
- Sadly, Uwe Gemballa was murdered in South Africa in 2010.

Engine: 3.3-liter turbocharged flat six	Top speed: 205 mph
Horsepower: 490	Price when new: Est. $80,000
0–60 mph: 4.1 seconds	Value now: $375,000

1951   LeSabre

In the early 1950s, one of the big automotive events was General Motors' Motorama. This car show often featured GM show cars, and the LeSabre is a classic example. GM's design guru, Harley Earl, had the car built, and among its many new ideas were hidden headlights, built-in jacks, and a top that went up when sensors detected rain. Also unusual for the time was a rear-mounted transmission. —JL

- Buick later adopted the LeSabre name for production cars.
- The LeSabre's aluminum V-8 ran on either gasoline or methanol.
- Harley Earl often drove the car to and from work.
- Design elements of the LeSabre were used on later GM production cars.

Engine: 3.5-liter supercharged V-8
Horsepower: N/A
0–60 mph: N/A
Top speed: N/A
Price when new: N/A
Value now: N/A

Gigliato

1997   Aerosa

- Though conceived in Japan, Gigliato would have been headquartered in Germany.
- Plans included a racing program.
- Torque would have been 300 lb-ft.
- The Aerosa would have had a five-speed transmission.

Engine: 4.6-liter dohc V-8
Horsepower: 309
0–60 mph: 4.9 seconds
Top speed: 162 mph
Price when new: $65,000 (proposed)
Value now: N/A

Ah, another sad story of one that got away from us. Come 1997, Nobou Nakamura announced plans to built an exotic car, the Aerosa. Not the purest exterior design, perhaps, but exciting, and with power from a Ford Mustang V-8, the price could be kept to $65,000. Lamborghini signed on to do the engineering, but the project died after the prototype was built. —JL

GTA Motors

Spano 2012–

- GTA Motor has said it will build just 99 Spanos.
- Torque is a wheelspinning 708 lb-ft.
- The Spano's monocoque weighs just 123 pounds.
- There is also a version with 780 horsepower.

Engine: 8.3-liter supercharged ohv V-10	**Top speed:** 217 mph
Horsepower: 820	**Price when new:** $670,000
0–60 mph: 2.8 seconds	**Value now:** Same

After years of racing cars, Domingo Ochoa decided to build one. It's not a subtle design, but the Spano looks the part of a car with the potential to go 217 miles per hour. Like all modern supercars, it starts with a monocoque; this one is of carbon fiber honeycomb, Kevlar, and titanium honeycomb. Over this is that very aggressive body in carbon fiber, which helps keep the curb weight to just under 3,000 pounds. The V-10 comes from Chrysler via the Viper and is offered with gas or gas/ethanol options.—JL

Gumpert

Tornante 2012–

- Gear shifts in the six-speed automatic transmission take only 40 milliseconds.
- Touring-bodied cars from the 1930s are highly prized.
- The doors are a gullwing design.
- This car joins the Gumpert Apollo.

Engine: 4.2-liter twin turbo dohc V-8	**Top speed:** N/A
Horsepower: 700	**Price when new:** $400,000
0–60 mph: N/A	**Value now:** Same

Gumpert is a well-known German supercar-maker. Touring Superleggera is one of the most famous design houses in Italy. They have combined to create the Tornante, a mid-engine supercar. The sleek design will be done in carbon fiber over a chrome-molybdenum space frame and carbon fiber monocoque. Audi will supply the engine, while a second version, with the German automaker's V-10, is in the works. —JL

- *CR-Z* is short for Compact Renaissance Zero.

- The CR-Z has three driving modes: sport, normal, and green.

- Among a dozen souped-up CR-Zs displayed at the 2010 SEMA Show was one tweaked to an astounding 533 horsepower.

- Like the CRX, the CR-Z is a two-seater.

Engine: 1.5-liter sohc inline four plus 10-kW electric motor	**Top speed:** 120 mph
Horsepower: 122	**Price when new:** $19,000 (base)
0–60 mph: Est. 8.4 seconds	**Value now:** Same

The Honda CRX Si of the mid-to-late 1980s was about as sporty as it got for front-drive Japanese cars of that era. But the CRX barely survived into the '90s, and its replacement, the Civic del Sol, was derided by car enthusiasts as the "dull Sol." Fast forward to the 2006 Los Angeles auto show and a Honda concept car that reminded those in attendance of the CRX. Except this car, the Remix, was built around a gasoline-electric hybrid powertrain. A hybrid sports car? You gotta be kiddin'.

Honda wasn't. For 2011 it launched the CR-Z, and while it may not be quite as fast or furious, push the Sport mode button and crank up the six-speed manual shifter—that's right, a manual in a hybrid—and it can be a lot of fun to drive. To make the CR-Z even more exciting, a variety of tuners, including Honda's in-house Mugen group, are designing all sorts of go-fast components and exotic body kits for this hybrid hottie. —*LE*

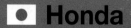

Curtiss 1924

In 1922, at the age of 15, Soichiro Honda joined Art Shokai, a Tokyo automobile and motorcycle repair shop, as an apprentice, working for Art Shokai owner Yuzo Sakakibara. Like Honda, Sakakibara had a passion for motorsports. In 1923, Art Shokai built its first race car around a Daimler engine. Then it built another, this time fitting an engine from an American Curtiss "Jenny" A1 biplane into the chassis of a Mitchell speedster. Honda was invited to serve as riding mechanic when Sakakibara's younger brother, Shin'ichi, drove the car in its first race—the fifth Japan Automobile Competition—on November 23, 1924. Sakakibara, Honda, and their Mitchell-Curtiss won the race and collected the first of many trophies. At the age of 21, Honda became the first of Sakakibara's apprentices to be granted permission to open his own Art Shokai. —LE

- Mitchell was an American company that started producing wagons in 1837 and built cars in Racine, Wisconsin, from 1903 to 1923.

- Honda's Art Shokai branch was at Hamamatsu, and the Mitchell-Curtiss racer would become known as "The Hamamatsu."

- The car now resides in the Honda corporate museum.

- Honda raced "The Hamamatsu" until 1936.

Engine: 502-cubic-inch V-8	Top speed: 100 mph
Horsepower: 90	Price when new: N/A
0–60 mph: N/A	Value now: N/A

- The S600 was preceded by the 531cc S500.

- Many S800s were imported to the U.S. by American servicemen.

- In its day, the Honda S sports cars were considered the fastest 1-liter cars in the world.

- Honda didn't build another S sports car until the S2000 in 1999.

Engine: 606cc dohc inline four	Top speed: 90 mph
Horsepower: 57	Price when new: $2,200
0–60 mph: N/A	Value now: $10,000

Back in the 1960s, Honda was earning worldwide publicity mainly for its motorcycles and its amazing transverse-engine Grand Prix car, but not production sports cars. Then in 1964 it launched the rear-drive S600 with a 606cc, 57-horsepower four-cylinder and a unique rear drive that featured chain drive to the rear wheels. Honda built the S600 as a roadster or coupe and upgraded the car as the S800 for 1966. While early S800s had the chain drive, the design was changed to a more conventional live rear axle layout. These little sports cars were known for being free-revving and reliable, with fuel mileage that would impress today. When you see one of these cute, diminutive sports cars it's difficult to imagine it as the beginnings of the huge Honda Corporation today. —JL

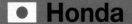 # Honda

S2000   1999–2009

To celebrate its 50th anniversary, the Honda Motor Company created the S2000, a modern throwback to the sports cars that had first brought the company into the automaking industry. Like the S500, S600, and S800s before it, the *S* stood for "sports," and the number stood for cc displacement (actually 1,997). The S2000 name was retained for the car's second generation, despite its larger 2,157cc power source. Like earlier Honda sports cars, the S2000 engine produced power with high revs. The original 2.0-liter four-banger spun its crankshaft 8,300 times per minute to pump out an amazing 240 horsepower. The engine was mounted behind the front axle, contributing to the car's sensational dynamic capabilities. —*LE*

- Honda previewed the S2000 with the SSM (Sports Study Model) concept car at the 1995 Tokyo auto show.
- Slotted between the less exotic Mazda Miata and priced less than roadsters from European luxury brands, the S2000 quickly found its own niche in the sports car marketplace.
- A Club Racer version of the car was unveiled in 2007 at the New York auto show. Among the changes was a tonneau cover instead of a power convertible top.
- S2000 production ended in 2009.

Engine: 2.0-liter inline four	**Top speed:** N/A
Horsepower: 240	**Price when new:** $32,000
0–60 mph: 5.2 seconds	**Value now:** $7,000

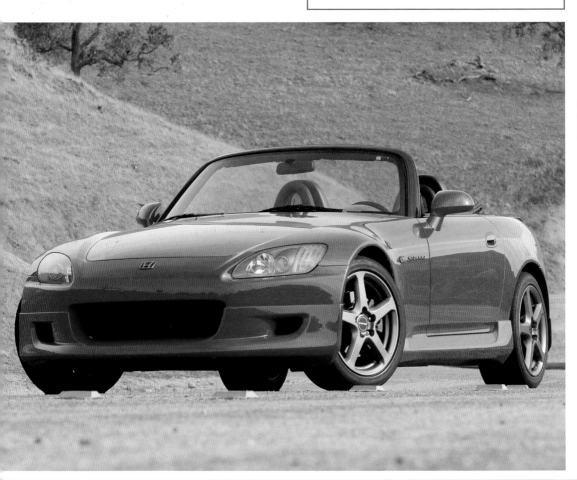

1955   **Stovebolt Special**

- Stirling Moss raced an HWM in Formula 2 in 1950.
- This is likely the first race car to use the famous small-block Chevy V-8.
- Bill Pollack drove the Stovebolt at the Pebble Beach Road races.
- Kirk Douglas drove the car in *The Racers*.

Engine: 5.0-liter ohv V-8	Top speed: N/A
Horsepower: N/A	Price when new: N/A
0–60 mph: N/A	Value now: $350,000

Okay, only one of these was built, but it needs mention as the sort of hot rod/sports car special that was often built and raced in the 1950s. Originally a Formula 2 car with an Alta engine, the car was used for the 1955 movie *The Racers*. Tom Carstens bought the HWM chassis and had one of the first small-block Chevrolet V-8s—tuned by Vic Edelbrock—fitted into it. —*JL*

Hyundai 🇰🇷

2008–   **Genesis coupe**

- Torque is 266 lb-ft.
- Six-speed manual or automatic transmissions are available.
- There's also a 210-horsepower turbo four version.
- At the rear is a five-link independent suspension.

Engine: 3.8-liter sohc V-6	Top speed: 149 mph
Horsepower: 306	Price when new: $31,600
0–60 mph: 5.5 seconds	Value now: Same

Whoa, a Korean car? You bet, because it's not only good-looking, but has the performance to back those looks. And it comes in up to nine models that range from $23,100 to $33,100, so, like the Mustang and Camaro, you have a good time without breaking the bank. The build quality is there, but so too is the driving quality on all types of roads. —*JL*

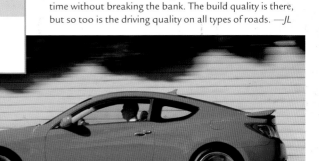

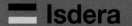

Isdera

Imperator | 1984–2001

By chance do you recall Mercedes-Benz's experimental C111 Wankel-powered supercar from the late 1960s? You'll find it later in this book. Or just look at the German-built mid-engine Isdera Imperator to see what it looked like. Built from 1984 to 2001, the mid-engine machine came with a variety of Mercedes-Benz V-8s. In production form it looked a bit chunky compared to the Mercedes, but the performance was impressive for the time. —JL

- About 30 Imperators were built.
- The gearbox was a five-speed manual.
- This Mercedes engine had 420 lb-ft of torque.
- Imperators had a fiberglass body over a tube frame.

Engine: 6.0-liter sohc V-8
Horsepower: 404
0–60 mph: 4.8 seconds
Top speed: 199 mph
Price when new: $135,000
Value now: Est. $100,000

Iso

Grifo | 1965–1974

After World War II, Italian motorcycle manufacturer Iso built the original "bubble car," the Isetta. It sold the rights to its design in 1955 to BMW and didn't produce another car until 1962, when it introduced the Rivolta, a four-door sedan powered by a Chevrolet V-8. In 1965, Iso shortened the Rivolta platform to produce a sports car, the Grifo. The Grifo could be equipped with Chevrolet engines producing 300, 365, or even a 7.0-liter, 400-horse powerplant that propelled the car to nearly 180 miles per hour. —LE

- The Grifo's engineering was by Giotto Bizzarrini, formerly of Ferrari.
- The bodywork was by Giorgetto Giugiaro and produced by Bertone.
- Bizzarrini produced an aluminum-bodied Corsa version of the Grifo for racing.
- Bizzarrini would go on to produce his own version of the Grifo, the 5300 GT Strada.

(7.0-liter model):
Engine: 7.0-liter Chevrolet V-8
Horsepower: 400
0–60 mph: N/A
Top speed: 180 mph
Price when new: $15,000
Value now: $140,000

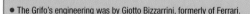

1991   Nazca M12

When a panel of more than 130 automotive journalists from around the globe was assembled to honor the car designer of the 20th century, their choice was Giorgetto Giugiaro, grandson of a painter of frescoes and son of an artist who worked in oils. Sent to Turin at age 14 to study art and technical drawing, Giorgetto began working for Fiat while still in his teens. He went on to draw beautiful creations for Bertone and Ghia before launching his own firm, Italdesign.

In 1990, Giugiaro created the Bugatti ID90 concept, and wanted to produce a running prototype, perhaps as a possible successor to his earlier BMW M1. However, Giugiaro's 26-year-old son, Fabrizio, suggested not just a running prototype, but a small production run, and oversaw construction, which was based on current Group C race car technology. A trio of such cars were produced—the M12, C2 coupe (with removable overhead panels), and C2 Spyder. —LE

- The Nazca's double-kidney grilles were designed to appeal to BMW. . .
- The compound curve of the glass greenhouse was unique. . .
- . . .and required the doors to be in two pieces.
- The Sultan of Brunei was the customer for the "production" version of the Nazca M12.

Engine: 5.0-liter BMW V-12	**Top speed:** 180 mph
Horsepower: 380	**Price when new:** N/A
0–60 mph: 4.5 seconds	**Value now:** N/A

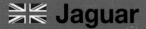 # Jaguar

C-Type   1951–1953

As his XK120 was winning on tracks and in the showroom, Jaguar founder William Lyons decided to bolster his brand with a pure race car. The C-type had the drivetrain of the XK120, but upped to 200 horsepower in a lightweight tube frame. Around this was a beautiful aerodynamic body shaped by Malcolm Sayer; the total package was almost 25 percent lighter than the stock XK120. Jaguar figured the best publicity in the racing world was France's 24 Hours of Le Mans, so it entered the 1951 event and won. While the following year was a disaster for Jaguar, it returned in 1953—now with disc brakes and more power—and finished 1st, 2nd, and 4th. C-types were also raced successfully in the United States by such drivers as Phil Hill (*below*) and John Fitch. —JL

- Dunlop's innovative disc brakes on the C-type brought the end of drum brakes in racing.

- Originally, the car was called the XK120C.

- Jaguar dedicated its 1953 Le Mans win to the newly crowned Queen Elizabeth II.

- Jaguar built 52 C-types.

Engine: 3.4-liter inline six	**Top speed:** 149 mph
Horsepower: 250	**Price when new:** $5,900
0–60 mph: 8.0 seconds	**Value now:** $3.7 million

Jaguar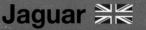

- Jaguar recently announced plans to build a production version.

- Coefficient of drag for the C-X75 is 0.32.

- The turbines spin at 80,000 rpm.

- Why C-X75? Jaguar is now 75 years old.

Engine: Turbine/electric hybrid	**Top speed:** 205 mph
Horsepower: 195 per wheel	**Price when new:** N/A
0–60 mph: 3.3 seconds	**Value now:** N/A

For a company with books full of history, Jaguar is pointed straight into the future. And doing it with a sleek, mid-engine prototype that features a hybrid turbine/electric drivetrain. Fitted inside the aerodynamic body is a pack of lithium-ion batteries that feed electricity to 195-horsepower motors mounted at each wheel. Total horsepower is 780 with what is essentially all-wheel drive. When the batteries are headed for empty, a pair of small turbine engines spool up to run generators that recharge the batteries. Jaguar estimates the C-X75's range to be 560 miles. The body was shaped to be like the trailing edge of an aircraft wing and is loaded with active aero devices. But you best beware when walking behind the C-X75 when it's running. . .a sign back there reads, "Beware of Blast" from the turbines. —JL

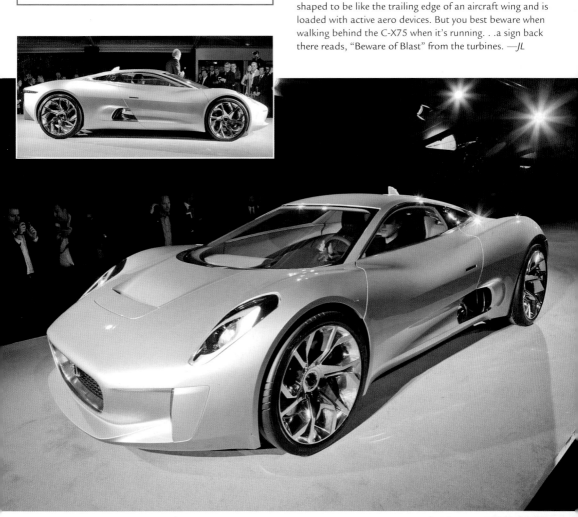

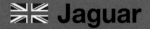 **Jaguar**

D-type

1954–1957

The D-type was Jaguar's follow-up to the C-type. Seeking to replicate the previous car's success at Le Mans, aerodynamicist Malcolm Sayer spent hours in the wind tunnel shaping the monocoque-chassis D. This might be one of the great examples of form following function, for not only is the D-type one of the most beautiful race cars ever created, but it carved through the air with ease. In early tests at Le Mans with the 3.4-liter engine used in the C-type—now with 250 horsepower—a D broke the lap record by five seconds. D-types went on to win the famous French round-the-clock race in 1955, 1956, and 1957. They also went on to win the hearts of many racing fans just for their outright beauty. —JL

- This is an early use of a monocoque race car chassis.
- In 1957, D-type took five of the top six places at Le Mans.
- About 87 D-types were built.
- D-types were done in both long- and short-nose versions.

Engine: 3.4-liter dohc inline six	**Top speed:** 179 mph
Horsepower: 250	**Price when new:** $10,250
0–60 mph: 4.7 seconds	**Value now:** $3.75 million

- A factory lightweight E-type was built for racing in 1963–1964.
- American Briggs Cunningham raced the E-type prototype called E2A.
- Enzo Ferrari called the E-type "the most beautiful car ever built."
- Jaguar sold a detachable hardtop for the roadsters.

Engine: 3.8-liter dohc inline six	**Top speed:** 150 mph
Horsepower: 265	**Price when new:** $5,595
0–60 mph: 7.0 seconds	**Value now:** $100,000

Just as Jaguar stunned the automotive world with the XK120 in 1948, it dropped their jaws again in 1961 with the E-type (known as the XK-E in the States). This now-classic Jaguar is just as beautiful as a coupe or roadster, thanks to that long, graceful nose. Under it is the classic Jaguar twin cam inline six, the first version of the Series 1 cars having 3.8 liters with 265 horsepower. And a great chassis with its independent rear suspension. A 2+2 body style came along in 1966, as did a 4.2-liter version of the six. Come 1969 the Series 2 was launched, with open headlights and bigger taillights and a bit less grace. The Series 3 E-types were built from 1971 to 1975 and featured a 5.3-liter V-12 in the convertible or 2+2 body. —JL

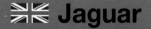

SS100 1936–1939

The *SS* in the SS100 name is said to stand for William Lyon's Swallow Sidecar firm, but this was the first open sports car to carry the Jaguar name. It was unveiled in 1935 and went into production the following year. The SS100 is a beautiful car that set the standard for the looks of British sports cars from the 1930s. The suspension used semi-elliptic springs front and rear. The first engine used in the SS100 was a 2.5-liter Standard Motor Company inline six converted from side to overhead valves by well-known engineer Harry Weslake, who later developed the famous engine in Dan Gurney's Eagle Formula 1 car in the 1960s. The SS100 proved to be very successful in European rallies, and to support the competition efforts the engine was enlarged to 3.5 liters and 125 horsepower for 1938. —JL

- Jaguar built 198 2.5-liter SS100s and 116 3.5s.
- Production of the SS100 was ended when World War II began.
- Jaguar founder William Lyons was knighted in 1956.
- The name SS was dropped after World War II because of the war implications.

Engine: 2.5-liter inline six	**Top speed:** 100 mph
Horsepower: 100	**Price when new:** $1,925
0–60 mph: 10 seconds (3.5-liter)	**Value now:** $250,000

- The shape of the XJ13 was an inspiration for Jaguar's C-X75 hybrid supercar.

- The V-12 is showcased "under glass."

- You can buy a street-ready replica of the XJ13.

- XJ13 stands for Experimental Jaguar number 13.

Engine: 5.0-liter dohc V-12	Top speed: 170 mph
Horsepower: 502	Price when new: N/A
0–60 mph: N/A	Value now: N/A

"For all sad words of tongue and pen, the saddest are these, 'It might have been.'" John Greenleaf Whittier's lament is perfect for Jaguar's XJ13. The company's aim was to return to Le Mans, so it created a 5.0-liter V-12 from a pair of its famous inline sixes. Malcolm Sayer penned a beautiful streamlined body for the mid-engine car's aluminum monocoque. Sadly, Jaguar's timing was off. When the XJ13 was ready for the 24-hour race, the rules had changed, and along came the 7.0-liter Ford GT40s. Jaguar put the car in storage, taking it out in 1971 to do a publicity film. During the filming, one of the XJ13's magnesium wheels collapsed and the car crashed heavily; thankfully its driver, Norman Dewis, was unhurt. Jaguar later restored the car and still uses it for publicity. —JL

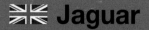

XJ-S and TWR XJ-S 1975–1996

Jaguar's 1975 XJ-S had an impossible task: replace the beloved E-type/XKE, and so do in the aftermath of the first fuel crisis. Ever tougher emissions and safety rules had made the XKE outdated, and Jaguar decided on a 2+2 replacement. From the start, the styling was controversial, especially the bug-eyed front end and, to some eyes, the flying buttress rear roofline. The initial engine was a fuel-injected V-12, which was joined in the early 1980s by a new 3.6-liter, twin cam straight six. Eventually the coupe was joined by a Targa-style XJ-SC and, later, a proper convertible. The six was opened up to 4.0 liters and the V-12 to 6.0 liters. Despite the early complaints about the XJ-S, it seemed to become more graceful as it aged. Jaguar's European racing arm, Tom Walkinshaw Racing (TWR), did a series with modified bodywork and added horsepower (the red car shown). —JL

- The XJ-S was in production from 1975 to 1996 after more than 115,000 were sold.

- Bob Tullius drove a racing XJ-S to Trans-Am titles in 1977 and 1978.

- Competition XJ-Ss were also successful in Europe and Australia.

- The first true factory XJ-S convertibles were done by Hess & Eisenhardt in the United States.

Engine: 5.3-liter OHC V-12	Top speed: 149 mph
Horsepower: 285	Price when new: $61,500
0–60 mph: 7.3 seconds	Value now: $8,000

- There was a competition version called the XJ220C.

- The XJ220 factory was a converted mill in Banbury, England.

- Austin's Metro 6R4 rally car was the source of the turbo V-6.

- A total of 281 XJ220s were assembled.

Engine: twin turbo 3.5-liter V-6	**Top speed:** 220 mph
Horsepower: 542	**Price when new:** $580,000
0–60 mph: 3.8 seconds	**Value now:** $190,000

The supercar world had gone nuts in the late 1980s, and many automakers were designing supercars. Jaguar's proposal was a sensational Keith Helfet–designed mid-engine machine with a V-12 and all-wheel drive. The production version, shown in late 1991, was different, the V-12 gone in favor of a foul-sounding twin turbo V-6 that drove through the rear wheels only. Still, it was quick, and Davy Jones drove one with me in the right seat to 220 miles per hour on Italy's circular Nardo race track. Jaguar set up production, but things went sour. The price was bumped up, and many of those who had put down deposits—a good number of them speculators—got cold feet as the world slipped into a recession. Law suits tarnished the reputation of this otherwise beautiful Jag. —*JL*

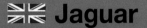

Jaguar

XK8   1997–2006

In 1996, Jaguar needed the XK8. Badly. Having been in the doldrums for too long design-wise, the XK8 was a blast of fresh air when it appeared in 1996, and its excellent homegrown V-8 engine and five-speed automatic gearbox provided it with more than enough muscle to justify its feline good looks. In the States the version to be seen driving was the brilliantly engineered convertible, whose electric top glided up and down with the silken precision of a senator who's been caught cavorting with the local barmaid. And the supercharged XKR was the best of the lot: super fast, even more aggressive to look at, and, yes, better to drive (if a tad thirsty when you opened its big taps). —SS

- First-gen XK8's shared their platform with the Aston Martin DB9.
- The entire XK8 project was codenamed X100, a famous name in Jaguar history.
- In 2000, Jaguar produced 107 limited edition Silverstone XK8s to celebrate Jag's entry into F1 racing.
- An even faster XKR-R model was created, but it was never actually launched by Jaguar.

(Original 4.0 model):
Engine: 4.0-liter V-8
Horsepower: 290
0-60 mph: 6.8 seconds

Top speed: 155 mph
Price when new: $65,000
Value now: $12,000

- Jaguar built 12,055 XK120s.

- XK120s were later sold with 180- or 210-horsepower engines.

- Jaguar was the first foreign carmaker to win a NASCAR race.

- The first 244 XK120s built have aluminum bodies; the rest have steel.

Engine: 3.4-liter dohc inline six	**Top speed:** 124 mph
Horsepower: 160	**Price when new:** $4,039
0–60 mph: 9.8 seconds	**Value now:** $75,000 and up

When World War II ended, William Lyons had his new sports car nearly ready. Its heart was a new twin cam inline six with overhead camshafts and 160 horsepower. This went into a flowing sports car body, and when the car was debuted at the 1948 British Motor Show it caused a sensation. XK120s were offered in roadster, drophead coupe, or hardtop coupe form. The "120" stood for the car's top speed, and in 1949 "Soapy" Sutton achieved that in a stock XK120. The car proved a winner both in sales and in racing, bringing in badly needed export funds from the United States. In 1950, Phil Hill did much to set the car's reputation in America when he won the first Pebble Beach road race main event. —JL

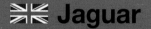 # Jaguar

XK Series   2007–

This is Jaguar's latest sports car, launched in 2007. Done as both a coupe and convertible, the Jag can be had with two engines, a normally aspirated 5.0-liter V-8 with 385 horsepower or a supercharged version of the same AJ-V8 GEN III engine with 510 horsepower. A six-speed transmission comes with each version, but arguably more important, so does leather upholstery and your choice of wood veneer or metallic trim. Jaguar sports cars always had a touch of luxury, and luxury is the XK's prime purpose. Nonetheless, its supercharged XK will hold its own when the road gets tight and twisty. Included are all the expected driving dynamics equipment, from ABS to adaptive dynamics and the ability to choose a comfort or sport mode. —JL

- Famed automotive designer Ian Callum gets credit for the XK shape.
- The Jaguar XKE's nose was the inspiration for the front of the XK.
- XKs have an all-aluminum monocoque bodyshell.
- Even the nonsupercharged XK gets to 60 mph in 5.2 seconds.

Engine: supercharged 5.0-liter dohc V-8
Horsepower: 510
0–60 mph: 4.6 seconds
Top speed: 155 mph
Price when new: $82,150
Value now: $38,000

- Only 16 XKSSs were finished.

- Twelve of the 16 were delivered to the United States.

- The car's production was halted by a fire in the factory.

- The XKSS was debuted at the 1957 New York auto show.

Engine: 3.4-liter twin-cam inline six
Horsepower: 250
0–60 mph: 5.5 seconds

Top speed: 145 mph
Price when new: $6,900
Value now: $4.5 million

When Jaguar withdrew from racing in 1956, it still had a stock of chassis built for the successful D-type racers. William Lyons hit on the idea of basing what we'd now call a supercar on those chassis. Called the XKSS (reviving the SS name), it was a thinly disguised race car. There was a full-width windscreen and a door added for the passenger. The trademark headrest and fin for the driver were removed and vestigial bumpers added. There were side screens and a top in case of bad weather, plus a luggage rack added at the back. The 3.4-liter twin cam six was tuned to 250 horsepower. Most famous of the XKSS was the car bought by actor Steve McQueen, which he later sold, but loved so much he bought it back. —*JL*

Jensen

Interceptor   1967–1976

Possibly one of the coolest cars of all time, and certainly one of the most technically ambitious, the Jensen Interceptor remains a car that can make grown men go weak at the knees. Styled by Carrozzeria Touring of Milan, Italy, and assembled in part by Vignale, the Interceptor was powered by a 6.3-liter Chrysler engine and had more sophistication in its ignition key than most rivals' ranges can summon over an entire lifetime. And when Jensen went one better by deciding to build the car in West Browmich, England, it also chose to endow the fantastically named Interceptor with an even bigger 7.2-liter Chrysler V-8 as well as four-wheel drive. What a car (and don't even dare mention its unreliability). —SS

- The Interceptor took its styling cues from the even rarer Brasinca Uirpuru.
- Jensen finally went bump as late as 1993, while working on an Mk 5 version of the Interceptor.
- The FF wasn't merely four-wheel drive, it also had ABS and traction control—in 1967!
- In 2011, the Interceptor R was unveiled, fitted with a Corvette LS3 engine and modern underpinnings. Sales are slow but steady, with prices starting at £107,000 (sterling).

(6.3-liter):
Engine: 6.3-liter V-8
Horsepower: 390
0–60 mph: 6.5 seconds

Top speed: 145 mph
Price when new: $10,000 (approximately)
Value now: $20,000–$50,000

Jensen-Healey

- Jensen toyed with engines from Vauxhall, Ford, and BMW before choosing the notoriously unreliable Lotus 907 twin cam.

- All Jensen-Healeys bound for the United States were fitted with rubber bumpers, not chrome ones.

- The interior design was intentionally stark, with a plastic center console and all black color schemes.

- A fastback model, called the Jensen GT, followed the Healey into production in 1976.

Engine: 2.0-liter Lotus twin cam inline four	**Top speed:** 119 mph
	Price when new: $1,500
Horsepower: 144	**Value now:** $5,000–$9,000
0–60 mph: 8.7 seconds	

One of the smoother-sounding cars ever to have been produced out of West Bromwich, England, the Jensen-Healey was, as its name suggests, a little bit of a hodgepodge kind of car. It actually replaced the famous Austin-Healey 3000 and was designed by a committee that included William Towns, Donald Healey himself, his son Geoff, and various staff at Jensen Motors. Powered by the same 2.0-liter Lotus twin cam lump that also did service in the Lotus Elite and Eclat, it was quick because it was light, and the handling was of the "don't get it wrong or else" variety. And when it was running properly (once or twice a month) the Jensen-Healey was a true delight to drive, with the hood down, and the smell of optimism in the air. And when it wasn't. . . . —SS

Kaiser

Darrin 1952–1954

The history of automaking in Jackson, Michigan, dates to 1905, when William Crapo Durant bought majority interest in Buick and had cars built in a buggy factory he owned in the town some 80 miles west of Detroit. Durant would eventually build an automotive empire known as General Motors, and Buick production would move to Flint, Michigan. But Jackson continued to produce cars, including the Jaxon, Briscoe, Carter, Earl, and Jackson, into the 1920s. And then, at last but certainly not least, again from 1952 to 1954 when Kaiser produced more than 400 fiberglass-bodied roadsters called the Darrin. Designed by the famed Howard A. "Dutch" Darrin, the design featured a three-position top and unusual doors that slid into hollow areas within the bodywork instead of using outward-swinging hinges. —LE

- The Darrin, not the Corvette, was the first fiberglass-bodied American production sports car.

- During World War II, Darrin trained pilots for the military.

- The sliding doors looked great, but they did not work very smoothly.

- With their unusual doors and with only some 485 built, Kaiser Darrins have become much prized by classic car collectors.

Engine: 161-cubic-inch Willys F-head inline four
Horsepower: 125
0–60 mph: N/A

Top speed: Not quite 100 mph
Price when new: $3,655
Value now: Up to $125,000

1990 — Competition

In 1990, German tuner Koenig got hold of a regular old Ferrari Testarossa and turned it into the Competition. The car had 1,000 horsepower thanks to a twin turbo version of the TR's flat-12 engine, and it looked a little bit like something they'd drive on Mars; virtually every body panel was new. And the result was an F40-munching machine that could, claimed Koenig, do 230 miles per hour. In 1990! —SS

- Boost could be turned down to a mere 600 horsepower for runs to the grocery store.
- A price of $650,000 was rather a lot in 1990, even in downtown Miami.
- The turbos were provided by IMSI and were each the size of a shoe.
- Koenig offered its customers bespoke interior specifications, which may or may not have included fresh underwear.

Engine: 4.9-liter Ferrari twin turbo flat 12
Horsepower: 1,000
0–60 mph: 3.5 seconds
Top speed: 230 mph
Price when new: $350,000
Value now: $500,000–$600,000

Koenigsegg

2006– — CCX

- The company produced just three examples of a model called the Trevita ("three whites"), made of diamond-coated carbon fiber, and boasting 1,018 horsepower!
- The CCXR biofuel model can run on any mix of regular gas or ethanol.
- In 2009, Koenigsegg pulled out of exhaustive negotiations to buy Saab from GM.
- CCX stands for "Competition Coupe X."

(CCX):
Engine: 4.7-liter twin supercharged V-8
Horsepower: 806
0–60 mph: 3.2 seconds
Top speed: 250 mph
Price when new: $545,568
Value now: $545,568

Christian von Koenigsegg, a Swede, launched his revolutionary "free-trade" supercar company in 1994. He and a small team of colleagues then spent eight years designing and testing various prototypes before delivering the first Koenigsegg (the CC 8S) to a customer in 2002. Since then, he has produced the even faster CCX (pictured, with 806 horsepower), the CCXR (a biofuel CCX with between 806 and 1,018 horsepower), and most recently the 910-horsepower Agera. —SS

X-Bow   2008–

- You pronounce the name "crossbow."

- Audi also produces the six-speed transmission.

- The competition version is called the X-Bow GT4.

- There is an X-Bow race series in Europe. . .it looks like a grid of very quick aliens.

Engine: 2.0-liter turbo dohc inline four	**Top speed:** 135 mph
Horsepower: 240	**Price when new:** $80,000
0–60 mph: 3.8 seconds	**Value now:** Same

It won't win any beauty contests, but it would be tough to beat to 60 mph. Austrian motorcycle maker KTM produces what it calls the X-Bow. A no-nonsense 1,500-pound mid-engine machine with very functional bodywork, the X-Bow's engine was developed by Audi, with Dallara doing the chassis and Brembo the brakes. Street legal in many countries, the X-Bow is based on a lightweight carbon fiber monocoque. Almost a motorcycle on four wheels, the X-Bow forsakes roof and doors with only a vestigial air deflector. —*JL*

Kurtis

500S   1953–1955

- Kurtis often drove his sports cars from Los Angeles to Indianapolis for the 500.

- Kurtis built his own midget racer in the early 1930s.

- The 500S was called "an Indy car with fenders."

- The 500S shown here was restored by Frank Kurtis' son, Arlen.

Engine: 331-cubic-inch Cadillac V8	**Top speed:** 150 mph
Horsepower: 325	**Price when new:** $5,800
0–60 mph: N/A	**Value now:** $350,000

Los Angeles–based Frank Kurtis made his name building race cars, especially for competition in the Indianapolis 500. He also built custom street cars for wealthy clients. After winning at Indy in 1950 and 1951, Kurtis built 50 sports car chassis based on his 1953 Indy car design. The 500KK was a fiberglass-bodied kit car for which the buyer supplied the powertrain. Kurtis also did some 20 turnkey cars, the 500M, with Cadillac V-8s as the standard engine. —*LE*

- Lamborghini's factory is in Sant'Agata, Italy, near Modena.

- An American, Bob Wallace, was instrumental in the 350 GT's development.

- ZF supplied the five-speed manual transmission.

- In 1966, Lamborghini increased the V-12 to 4.0 liters, creating the 400 GT.

Engine: 3.5-liter dohc V-12	**Top speed:** 156 mph
Horsepower: 320	**Price when new:** $13,900
0–60 mph: 6.6 seconds	**Value now:** $150,000

Not happy with his 350 GTV prototype (see next profile), Ferruccio Lamborghini proceeded with a redesign of what would be his first production car. Gian Paolo Dallara and Paolo Stanzani—two of Italy's most famous engineers—were given the job of revamping the car for production. The body was reworked to a rounder shape by Touring in Milan, and the Bizzarrini-designed V-12 was detuned to be more civilized. Dallara, whose company still makes Indy cars, developed the upper and lower A-arm suspension; the disc brakes were from Girling. Just months after the 350 GTV was shown, the 350 GT was debuted at the 1964 Geneva auto show to such acclaim its production was assured. After testing a 350 GT, *Road & Track* magazine declared, "Watch out, Ferrari." From 1964 to 1966, Lamborghini made 120 350 GTs. —JL

Lamborghini

350 GTV   1963

If you're not a Lamborghini fan, you might not recognize this one, but it's the first car from the fledgling Italian automaker. Trying to compete with Enzo Ferrari, Ferruccio Lamborghini commissioned famed designer Franco Scaglione to create the body. Another legendary Italian, Giotto Bizzarrini, prepared the 3.5-liter V-12. It turns out Lamborghini was not happy with the resulting car, particularly as when assembling it workers discovered they couldn't fit the V-12 in the engine bay. Lamborghini had his staff use bricks to get the correct ride height and used the GTV as a show car while what would become the production 350 GT (see previous page) was being developed. The factory later sold the car, and it was finally finished with an engine. The GTV is now on display in the Lamborghini factory museum. —JL

- The original color of the 350 GTV was pale blue.
- The show car also lacked pedals and windshield wipers.
- Carrozzeria Sargiotto of Turin built the body.
- Still another well-known Italian firm, Neri & Bonacini, assembled the frame.

Engine: 3.5-liter dohc V-12	Top speed: N/A
Horsepower: 342	Price when new: N/A
0–60 mph: N/A	Value now: N/A

- *Countach* is an expression an Italian man might say when a beautiful woman enters a room.
- The Countach was designed by the legendary Marcello Gandini.
- The 4.0-liter production version of the Countach was the LP400.
- In 1985 Lamborghini celebrated its 25th anniversary with a revamped Countach.

Engine: 4.0-liter. V-12	**Top speed:** 180 mph
Horsepower: 375	**Price when new:** $52,000
0–60 mph: Est. 6.5 seconds	**Value now:** $130,000

If Lamborghini's Miura (*see page 191*) was the first supercar, its ensuing creation, the Countach, was the first supermodel. For proof, you need look no farther than adolescent boys' bedroom walls in the mid-1970s, where right next to the poster of Charlie's Angel Farrah Fawcett in her red swimming suit there most likely was a poster of this car, usually in red or yellow and displaying doors that opened via scissors-style hinges like a beetle's wings.

Speaking of beetles, the Countach was previewed by the Bertone Carabo (*see page 44*) concept car at the 1968 Paris auto show, and in 1971 by the Countach LP500 concept at Geneva. While the Carabo was built around an Alfa Romeo Type 33 sports racer, the LP500 carried a 5.0-liter version of the Lamborghini 3.9-liter V-12 that powered the Miura. The LP stood for *longitudinale posteriore*, indicating the engine had been turned 90 degrees, the transmission protruding into the cockpit where the driver had direct shift control. —*LE*

▋▋ Lamborghini

The Diablo was the successor to Lamborghini's Countach. Design work was begun by Marcello Gandini, who had created the Miura and Countach, but was revised after Chrysler took control of the Italian sports car manufacturer in 1987. Compared to the Countach, the Diablo was wider, bigger, and heavier, but also more aerodynamic. Part of the engineering prospectus had been a top speed of more than 320 kilometers per hour (198 mph); the car met that goal and then some, with a top speed of 202 miles per hour in testing. At the heart of the Diablo was a 5.7-liter, 485-horsepower V-12. The car was designed for all-wheel drive, and in 1993 an even more powerful VT version—VT for Visco Traction—was introduced, which could send as much as 15 percent of the engine's power to the front wheels. —*LE*

- Like other Lamborghinis, the Diablo (devil) took its name from a famous fighting bull.

- Lamborghini built 2,097 of the first-gen Diablos and Diablo VTs.

- Diablo production ended in 2001, several years after Chrysler had sold Lamborghini to an Indonesian company.

- An early Diablo option was a $10,500 Breguet clock mounted on the dashboard.

Engine: 5.7-liter dohc 48-valve V-12
Horsepower: 500
0–60 mph: Less than four seconds
Top speed: 202 mph
Price when new: $240,000
Value now: $80,000

Lamborghini ▌▌

- This supercar gets a respectable EPA rating of 12 mpg city/ 20 mpg highway.

- Add $15,600 for carbon-ceramic brakes.

- The Gallardo will develop 0.95g on a skid pad.

- The quarter-mile passes in 11.5 seconds.

Engine: 5.2-liter V-10	**Top speed:** 199 mph
Horsepower: 550	**Price when new:** $222,795
0–60 mph: 3.5 seconds	**Value now:** Same

Lamborghini has created many different editions of its Gallardo in coupe and open-top spyder forms. For example, there's the lightweight LP570-4 Superleggera and the LP550-2 edition that honors the company's legendary test driver, Valentino Balboni. The *-2* after the name means a Gallardo has rear-drive only, while the *-4* signifies all-wheel drive. Power comes from a 5.2-liter V-10 that has a particularly nice snap to its growl. Lambos do that. Torque from the engine is a healthy 398 lb-ft. Backed by a six-speed manual gearbox, the combo will swing the speedometer through 100 miles per hour in 7.5 seconds. The upper and lower A-arm suspension is a bit firmer than what you'd expect from an equivalent Ferrari, but it will give you a secure high-speed ride regardless of road surface. —JL

Lamborghini

Jalpa · 1981–1988

Being a Taurus by birthsign, Ferrucio Lamborghini named the vast majority of his beloved supercars after his second greatest passion in life, bullfighting. And the Jalpa is no exception (even if the Silhouette that preceded it is). Designed by Bertone to be the affordable Lamborghini, the Jalpa was powered by a transversely mounted 3.5-liter V-8 that produced a relatively meager (for Lamborghini) 255 horsepower. Even so, it was mid-engined and reasonably lightweight in construction and was far less intimidating to drive than the heavier, altogether hairier Countach of the same era. And it could still top 140 mph and break the seven-second barrier from 0 to 60 mph. When Chrysler bought Lamborghini in 1988 the Jalpa was one of the first casualties, despite paving the way for what would eventually, under Audi, become the idea for the Gallardo. —SS

- The Jalpa was a development of the Silhouette, Lamborghini's answer to the small V-8 Ferrari.

- Official top speed was 145 mph, although numerous magazines recorded more than that in testing.

- Jackie Stewart once owned a Lamborghini Jalpa.

- Frank Sinatra once said, "You buy a Lamborghini when you are somebody."

Engine: 3.5-liter V-10	Top speed: 145 mph
Horsepower: 255	Price when new: $11,000
0–60 mph: 6.8 seconds	Value now: $45,000

- Miura engineer Gian Paolo Dallara produces today's Indycars.

- Another of the Miura's creators was American Bob Wallace.

- And the third father of the Miura, Paolo Stanzani, engineered the Bugatti EB110.

- A total of 764 Miuras were built, 150 of them SVs.

Engine: 3.9-liter dohc V-12	Top speed: 171 mph
Horsepower: 370	Price when new: $19,500
0–60 mph: 6.7 seconds	Value now: $150,000+

Although his mid-engine race cars were quite successful, Enzo Ferrari was reluctant to engineer a mid-engine production car. Not so for his Modenese rival, Ferruccio Lamborghini. For the 1966 Geneva auto show, the upstart exotic car company produced the sleek Miura, which was a landmark car both for its engineering and its luscious bodywork, which is credited to Marcello Gandini. Not only was the V-12 behind the cockpit, it was set in laterally . . . a sidewinder done as one unit with the transmission. Both ends of the monocoque car have race car–like upper and lower A-arm suspensions. Miuras were produced in three forms, the 350-horsepower P400 (1966–1969, the 350-horsepower P400S (1968–1971), and the most prized, the 385-horsepwer P400SV (1971–1972). —JL

Lamborghini

Murcielago   2002–2010

If there's a scarier or more magnificent supercar on the planet than the Lamborghini Murcielago, then best of luck in trying to find it. Then again, as a direct replacement for the legendary Diablo, Lamborghini needed to come up with something special, and how they did that with this car. To begin with the Murcielago seems comically vast when you first approach it, and should you then summon the courage to climb inside it the scare factor is approximately quadrupled. But it's not until you fire up the massive V-12 engine and start driving a Murcielago that the real magic arrives, at which point you'll either have a heart attack or experience pure nirvana behind the wheel. In more ways than one this was, and still is, Lamborghini's finest hour. —SS

- The chief designer of the Murcielago was a Belgian gentleman named Luc Donckerwolke.

- The final and fastest version was called the LP670-4 SV (670 horsepower).

- In the end, Lamborghini produced 4,099 Murcielagos.

- The car was replaced in 2011 by an all-new V-12 machine called the Aventador, also named after a Spanish fighting bull.

(LP670):	
Engine: 6.2-liter V-12	Top speed: 213 mph
Horsepower: 661	Price when new: $455,400
0–60 mph: 3.4 seconds	Value now: Same

- Beneath its demonic-looking skin the Reventon is, in fact, a standard Murcielago LP 670-4 SV.

- Lamborghini claims the styling is influenced by "the fastest airplanes on the planet."

- A Reventon almost beat a Tornado fighter in a standing start race along a 3 km runway.

- The name comes from a bull that killed famous Mexican bullfighter, Felix Guzman, in 1943. It means "explosion" in Spanish.

Engine: 6.5-liter V-12	Top speed: 213 mph
Horsepower: 661	Price when new: $1,300,000
0–60 mph: 3.4 seconds	Value now: $1,500,000+

As if the plain old Murcielago wasn't wild enough, Lamborghini produced a 20-run superspecial version of the car in 2007 and called it the Reventon—and at the same time provided Batman with an entirely appropriate set of wheels with which to clean up Gotham City in the 2008 film *The Dark Knight*. The list price ($1.31 million) was enough all on its own to guarantee that the Reventon hit the headlines, but the car's futuristic (some say slightly vulgar) styling codes also ensured instant fame, as did the fact that its top speed was officially verified at 211.3 mph. Apart from being utterly outrageous, the Reventon's more serious claim to fame is that it paved the way for the styling of future Lamborghinis. Whether you regard that as good or not-so-good news is, in the end, up to the individual. —*SS*

The extraordinary-looking *Sesto Elemento* is named after the sixth element in the periodic table (which just so happens to be carbon), chiefly because it's made out of a material that Lamborghini itself invented, and which is referred to by the company as forged carbon—a new ultralight, ultrastrong, far-cheaper alternative to carbon fiber that may, in time, revolutionize the sports car business. The result is effectively a re-engineered version of the regular Gallardo that weighs (whisper this) just 2,202 pounds. Given that it has 564 horsepower from a mildly tweaked Gallardo V-10 engine, this means the *Sesto Elemento* is mind-bogglingly rapid—far quicker than any other Lamborghini to date. The only downside is that it is a concept car, pure and simple, so no one will ever get to drive it. —SS

- Styling is said to provide a clear indication of what the next Gallardo might look like.

- But even clearer still is the engineering message it carries; this is the future of Lamborghini, plain and simple.

- The V-10 engine's cooling is aided by 10 hexagonal holes in the engine cover.

- Running gear is standard Gallardo LP560-4 and is none the worse for that.

Engine: 5.2-liter V-12	Top speed: 196 mph
Horsepower: 564	Price when new: N/A
0–60 mph: 2.9 seconds	Value now: Priceless

- The pretty Lancia B24 spyders and convertibles used the B20 chassis and driveline.

- B20s finished 1–2–3 in the 1952 Targa Florio.

- The front suspension was an unusual sliding pillar design.

- A total of 3,871 B20s were built.

Engine: 2.5-liter ohv V-6 (4th series)
Horsepower: 118
0–60 mph: 8.5 seconds

Top speed: 115 mph
Price when new: $5,800
Value now: $150,000

These cars are legendary, but little-known in the United States. Italian machines, famed for their road holding, B20s are best remembered for finishing 2nd, 5th, and 7th overall in the rainy 1951 Mille Miglia against much more powerful Ferraris. Italian legend Vittorio Jano designed the B20, which was assembled by Pininfarina. The first two series had 2.0-liter V-6 engines with 75–80 horsepower, while the third series went to 2.5 liters. All these cars had right-hand drive, but with the fourth series B20s, Lancia added left-hand drive, changed to a DeDion rear suspension, and made the cars available in the States. With the fifth and sixth series, the cars became more luxurious but retained the B20's famed ability to maintain high speeds on narrow, windy European highways. —JL

Lancia

Beta Zagato and HPE   1975–1984

- The transmission was a five-speed manual.

- Fun to drive, but not the most reliable of automobiles.

- Though built by Zagato, the Spider was designed by Pininfarina.

- The Spider had a wide B-pillar and short roof section.

Engine: 2.0-liter dohc inline four
Horsepower: 122
0–60 mph: 10.0

Top speed: 108 mph
Price when new: $4,500
Value now: $3,000

During an interlude when Fiat attempted to sell cars in the United States, it also imported several Lancias. By then it owned the once-proud automaker and Lancias had become Fiat clones. The line was called Beta, and two of the best were the front-drive Zagato Coupe and the HPE. The Coupe (*pictured*) had a folding rear window and removable top, while the HPE was a neat junior station wagon in the manner of the Volvo P1800. —*JL*

Lancia

Delta S4   1985–1986

- Group B cars were banned for being too dangerous.

- A Delta S4 won its first event, the 1985 RAC Rally.

- Lancia built 200 road-going S4 Stradales to meet homologation rules.

- S4s featured a midmounted engine and all-wheel drive.

Engine: 1.8-liter supercharged, turbocharged dohc inline four
Horsepower: 480 (rally version)
0–60 mph: 2.3 seconds

Top speed: N/A
Price when new: N/A
Value now: $200,000 (rally version)

This was during the era of the Group B rally cars, some of the most potent race machines ever created. Called the Delta, the S4 had nothing to do with that street machine, but was based on a space frame with long-travel independent suspension and carbon fiber bodywork. However, the amazing element was the engine, a 1.8-liter with both supercharging *and* turbocharging to take it to 480 horsepower. —*JL*

- *Road & Track* called it "a Scorpion without a stinger."

- Torque was a puny 89 lb-ft.

- A quarter-mile required 19.1 seconds.

- Both ends had strut suspensions.

Engine: 1.8-liter dohc inline four	**Top speed:** 104 mph
Horsepower: 81	**Price when new:** $9,943
0–60 mph: 13.4 seconds	**Value now:** $4,950

Here's another sports car best filed under, "It probably seemed like a good idea at the time." Remember the Fiat X1/9? (If you don't, flip back a few pages to refresh your memory.) Nice little car, and Fiat felt it needed a big brother. . . and provided one to corporate stepchild, Lancia. Not a bad idea—a mid-engine sports car with a 2.0-liter four slung sideways. Except it didn't quite work out that way. In Europe, the car was called the Montecarlo, but Chevy had that name in the United States (as two words), so here it was called Scorpion. Another problem: The 2.0 couldn't pass emissions, so U.S. versions got a strangled 1.8 at just 81 horsepower. Other problems: The cars were noisy, the brakes were not all that wonderful, and rust was the Lancia's best friend. What a shame, as it did seem like a good idea. . . . —JL

Lancia

Stratos 1973–1975

The Stratos, with its supershort wheelbase and wraparound windshield, was surely one of the most beguiling cars of all time. Not only did it redefine the world of rallying in the mid-1970s, obliterating all before it in the World Rally Championship from 1974 through 1976, it also provided the basis for one of the most extraordinary road cars the world has ever seen. For starters, the Stratos was tiny relative to just about every other car on the road, and the fact that it was powered by a midmounted Ferrari V-6 engine meant it was as quick in a straight line as it was agile through a series of corners. It may have been tricky to drive near the limit, but, visually, the Stratos was one of Marcello Gandini's finest achievements, and there have been quite a few of those over the years. —SS

- The Stratos made its debut at the Turin Auto show in 1971.
- It was preceded by a concept car called the Lancia Stratos Zero, shown in 1970.
- The first prototype Stratos was painted fluorescent red.
- It was the brainchild of Lancia team manager, Cesare Fiorio, Brit engineer Mike Parkes, and rally driver Sandro Munari.

Engine: 2.4-liter V-6
Horsepower: 190
0–60 mph: 4.9 seconds
Top speed: 144 mph
Price when new: $10,000
Value now: $100,000+

- The LFA has an even 50/50 front-rear weight distribution.

- Toyota will build only 500 LF-As for the world.

- Much of the LFA's handling development was done on Germany's Nürburgring.

- Toyota's LFA was 10 years in the making.

Engine: 4.8-liter dohc V-10	**Top speed:** 202 mph
Horsepower: 552	**Price when new:** $375,000
0–60 mph: 3.8 seconds	**Value now:** Same

Toyota wanted a "halo" supercar to display its technical abilities, and the result, after years of development, is the Lexus LFA. Its soul is a throaty all-aluminum V-10 with 552 horsepower and 354 lb-ft of torque that is matched to a six-speed automated sequential gearbox with paddle shifters. Much of the chassis and bodywork is made of strong, lightweight carbon fiber–reinforced plastic. Suspension designs have upper and lower A-arms at the front, a multi-link design at the back, much of it done in lightweight aluminum. You wouldn't call the LFA's exterior beautiful in the Ferrari/Pininfarina sense, but it is exciting and tuned for max aerodynamic efficiency. Inside is an interior that mixes tech and glamour, driver oriented with a 10,000-rpm tachometer, but finished off in leather. —JL

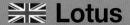

Lotus

Elan   1989–1995

The return of the Elan in the late 1980s/early 1990s was notable for various reasons. A historic name had been revived, and a very fast, capable sports car had been created. But what stopped the purists dead in their tracks was the fact that, shock-horror, the new Elan was front-wheel drive and was powered by, of all things, a turbocharged engine from Isuzu. It didn't matter in the end, though, because what Lotus had created may have been wrong-wheel drive, but it was also one of the quickest cars of its era from point to point—a true homage to the orignal Elan, in other words. Its grip levels were truly incredible, to the point where the car felt much faster than its raw data suggested—even if it was the first and only front-wheel-drive Lotus. —SS

- The front-wheel-drive Elan was codenamed the M100 and was launched in the UK in 1989, in the same week as the Mazda MX-5.

- Its bodyshell was made from glass-reinforced plastic and weighed just 2,400 pounds.

- The shape was designed by Peter Steves, who also did the McLaren F1.

- A spin-off from the car, called the Kia Elan, was created in 1995 for the Korean market.

Engine: 1.6-liter Lotus/Isuzu turbocharged inline four
Horsepower: 162
0–60 mph: 6.5 seconds

Top speed: 137 mph
Price when new: $31,000
Value now: $10,000–$15,000

Lotus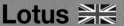

- Since joining Lotus as CEO, ex–Ferrari boss Bahar has pinched several other key staff from his former employer.

- The KERS system on the new Elan will be optional; that's some option.

- Production is currently set to begin in 2013. . .

- . . .although showroom cars aren't likely to be seen in the United States until 2014—at the earliest.

Engine: 4.0-liter V-6	Price when new: $90,000 (approximately)
Horsepower: 350	Value now: N/A
0–60 mph: 4.5 seconds	
Top speed: 165 mph	

Lotus unveiled its new era at the Paris Motor Show in 2010. The all-new management, headed by ex–Ferrari employee Danny Bahar, took the wraps off an entire new range of cars, including an all-new 4.0-liter V-6, mid-engined version of the Elan. And for a minute the car world just stood there in silence, stunned but impressed at the pure ambition behind Lotus' new plans. The Elan itself fits into the range above the next Elise but beneath the new Esprit and is aimed squarely at the Porsche 911. Not only will it weigh as little as 2,800 pounds and be powered by a 350–400-horsepower V-6, it'll also feature a "push-to-pass" kinetic energy recovery system (KERS) that'll give bursts of extra power generated via braking. Definitely a car to drive before you die—so long as you can hold on until 2013. . . . —SS

 # Lotus

Elise 1996–

Lotus is one of those venerable automakers that has had several swings of success over the decades, and seems well on the upswing now. Its several models—the Elise, its fastback cousin the Exige, and the Evora—are highly regarded by enthusiasts. There's an Indy car race program, Formula 1 ties, and a batch of new models under development. The Elise is a modern example of what makes Lotus cars so fun. The engines are small—the standard 1.8 and the 218-horsepower supercharged version—but the Elise weighs just 1,984 pounds. That puts the 0–60 time for the blown version at just 4.3 seconds. Or 4.0 in the Exige, with its 257 horsepower. Mind you, Lotuses are also small, so they can be a bit tight inside, but it sure is a fun ride. —JL

- Torque for the nonsupercharged four is 133 lb-ft.
- This Elise is the basis for the Tesla sports car.
- The transmission has six speeds.
- EPA mileage: 21 mpg city/27 mpg highway.

Engine: 1.8-liter dohc inline four	Top speed: 148 mph
Horsepower: 190	Price when new: $52,970
0–60 mph: 4.7 seconds	Value now: Same

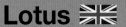
- Lotus produced 998 first-generation Elites.

- Due to its expensive build costs, Lotus lost money on every Elite it made.

- Lotus debuted the Elite at the 1957 Earls Court show in London.

- Both ZF and MG gearboxes were used.

Engine: 1.2-liter Coventry-Climax inline four
Horsepower: 95
0–60 mph: 11.4 seconds

Top speed: 120 mph
Price when new: $4,780
Value now: $60,000

Colin Chapman was famed for his innovative, lightweight race cars, and that philosophy carried over to his production machines. The Elite proved this with a monocoque body made of fiberglass, so the 'glass wasn't just added-on body panels a la the Corvette, but actually the core of the car's structure. The front suspension and engine were supported on a separate steel subframe. This construction provided the hoped-for light weight, though Lotus owners were quite familiar with regularly reattaching some of the metal bits to the body, as some tended to pull loose. Regardless, many owners would argue it was a small price to pay for the joy of driving the pretty little coupe. The engine was the famous aluminum inline four from Coventry Climax, which also produced several series of winning race car engines. —SL

Elite S1   1974–1980

Although you'd be hard-pressed to call the second-generation Elite a full-blown sedan, it was, however, Lotus's first-ever four-seat car. And there were two distinctly different versions, the first known as the Type 75 (because it was launched in 1975, no less), the second the Type 83 (no prize for guessing what the 83 stood for). Both were front-engined, rear-drive machines that looked ever so slightly odd in their proportioning but drove beautifully in their day. Initially, the T75 used the 2.0-liter 150-horsepower version of the infamous Lotus twin cam engine, which later grew to 2.2 liters. Performance wasn't quite breathtaking, despite the Elite's light overall weight, but the steering and road holding were near flawless. Four people and their luggage had never experienced handling like this before. —SS

- Power steering and air conditioning were both optional on the Elite from 1974.
- The Elite was the first Lotus to use the company's own 907 twin cam engine, first used in the Jensen-Healey.
- Quoted curb weight of the Elite was just 2,000 pounds.
- The Elite's steel backbone chassis was an evolution of the original Elan platform.

(2.0-liter):
Engine: 2.0-liter twin cam inline four
Horsepower: 160
0–60 mph: 7.4 seconds
Top speed: 135 mph
Price when new: $8,900
Value now: $5,000–$9,000

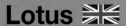
2014–
Elite
(third generation)

- Again there will be an optional KERS system available as an extra on the Elite.

- Top speed will be "in excess of 195 mph."

- With its front mid-engined layout, the Elite has the potential to be the best-balanced handler of all the new-era cars from Lotus.

- The new Elite was unveiled alongside the new Elan and Esprit at the Paris auto show in 2010.

Engine: 5.0-liter Lexus V-8	Top speed: 195 mph
Horsepower: 600	Price when new: $150,000
0–60 mph: 3.5 seconds	Value now: N/A

You're going to have to wait until at least 2014 to drive the new Lotus Elite, so make sure you eat up all your vegetables and take those multi-vitamins each and every morning. However, when it does finally arrive, the new Elite sounds like it will be one heck of a car. Unlike the other new-era machines from Lotus, the Elite will be in keeping with its forebears and will be front-engined (i.e., not mid-engined) and powered by the same 5.0-liter Lexus-sourced V-8 as the new Esprit. If it handles and rides anything like as crispy as the Evora, it'll be a joy to drive, of course, and very quick indeed. Lotus claims 600 horsepower and a 0–60 mph time of 3.5 seconds for this 2+2 machine. Price? Around $150,000, ker-ching. . . . —SS

Lotus

Evora   2009–

For a while, the rest of the world believed that the Evora was, in fact, the new Esprit. But it wasn't. It was a stand-alone model, designed by Lotus and codenamed Project Eagle, to fit between the forthcoming new Esprit and the Elise. And a heck of a fine mid-engined sports car it proved, too, even if its Toyota V-6 engine and cable-operated gear shift did attract one or two sniffs of disapproval from the more cynical types. Truth is, the Evora has one of the very best chassis you'll ever come across, with quite extraordinarily telepathic steering to go with it. It's even built to a reasonably high standard—for a Lotus—and with the supercharged engine option it has the performance to match its looks to boot. —SS

- Yes, there's a pair of rear seats in the back. . .
- . . .but no one over the age of 10 can realistically use them.
- The trunk can fit a set of golf clubs (though not a PGA Tour bag, it must be said).
- Evora is the name of a city in Portugal.
- Other names considered were: Eagle, Exira, and, believe it or not, Ethos.

Engine: 3.5-liter Toyota V-6
Horsepower: 276
0–60 mph: 4.9 seconds

Top speed: 162 mph
Price when new: $59,950
Value now: Same

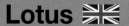
1987–1992 — Esprit Turbo (Third Generation)

- Giugiaro is said to have approved of the redesign. A lot.

- When he finished this car Peter Stevens went on to design the McLaren F1.

- The best and fastest version of this Esprit was the four-cylinder Sport 300, not the V-8.

- Lotus introduced a new patent to produce the car's plastic body, called Vacuum Assisted Resin Injection—or VARI as it became known.

(SE model):
Engine: 2.2-liter turbocharged inline four
Horsepower: 264

0–60 mph: 4.7 seconds
Top speed: 160 mph
Price when new: $42,000
Value now: $25,000–45,000

When Peter Stevens was asked to restyle the Lotus Esprit in 1987—the original having been designed by none other than Giugiaro himself—he was more than a little excited about the task. The resulting car he came up with may have been a more or less angular-looking Esprit, but it also contained all the right design cues—and a fair bit more practicality than Giugiaro's original. It was also faster and better than ever to drive, thanks to a new charge-cooled version of the 2.2-liter turbo engine that in SE trim produced 264 horsepower and could fire the Esprit to 60 miles per hour in 4.7 seconds. They say the steering on this car is among the best there ever was, and the road-holding is pretty mesmerizing too. —SS

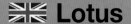

Lotus

Esprit (new generation)

2013–

The first of the new-era Lotus cars, all of which were unveiled at the 2010 Paris motorshow, will be the Esprit. It won't hit the streets until 2013, but when it does, expect the fireworks to really fly. Power will come from a turbocharged version of the 5.0-liter Lexus V-8—with outputs stretching toward 600 horsepower and beyond—allied to a curb weight of little more than 3,000 pounds. The styling, as you can see, is edgy, futuristic, and exciting, featuring LED lights at the front and a very obviously mid-engined feel to the overall proportions. And in price terms the Esprit will make a big leap up the aspirational ladder, costing around $200,000–$250,000, and, in the process, providing some serious competition to the Ferrari 458s and Lamborghini Gallardos of this world. Good luck to them, we say. —SS

- The Esprit's V-8 engine is a development of the Lexus ISF engine.
- KERS will be optional.
- Lotus already claims a 0–60 mph time of 3.4 seconds.
- Power will be fed to the rear wheels (and only the rear wheels) by a seven-speed dual clutch gearbox.

Engine: 5.0-liter Lexus V-8	Top speed: 195 mph
Horsepower: 600	Price when new: $150,000+
0–60 mph: 3.5 seconds	Value now: N/A

Lotus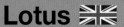

- Lotus Engineering was first based in Hornsey, north London, only later moving to Hethel in Norwich.

- Chapman's first car was based on a lowly Austin Seven platform.

- It used a three-speed transmission lifted straight out of a Ford 8.

- The success of the Mk IV led to Chapman receiving hordes of requests from other private racers to build more cars.

Engine: 71.5-cubic-inch Ford	Top speed: 105 mph
Horsepower: 75	Price when new: $1,500 (approx)
0–60mph: 10 seconds	Value now: N/A

It started life as a humble trials car, built by Lotus founder Colin Chapman on an Austin Seven chassis in the early 1950s, and, somewhat typically for Chapman, it won on its very first outing. And so the foundations for Lotus Engineering had been laid. The Mk IV was actually preceded by the less successful Mk II, but it wasn't until Chapman realized that by using a superlightweight aluminium body with a rounded nose cone that he could get more than enough performance out of Ford's diminutive 71.5-cubic-inch side valve engine. Thus equipped the Mk IV was almost unbeatable by its competition at the time, and the design went on to form the basis of the Lotus Seven, which, of course, still exists today in the form of the (still near unbeatable) Caterham Seven. —SS

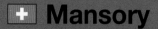

Mansory

Cormeum — 2011

Mansory is a Swiss tuner well known for taking perfectly nice exotic cars and somehow making them, well, different. We offer as evidence the company's Cormeum, which is basically a Mercedes-Benz SLS AMG with reworked body panels done in carbon fiber. No mistaking that the effect of the carbon fiber is visually dramatic and presumably the material is also how they shaved 198 pounds from the car. While the bodywork is none-too-subtle—the mouth is gaping—it is said to increase downforce front and rear. Horsepower is increased from the stock AMG 563 to a claimed 660. Mansory will build only 15 Cormeums. —JL

- An opera aria was the basis for the name Cormeum.
- An 800-horsepower option is planned.
- The center of gravity has been lowered by almost an inch.
- In case this car is too slow for you, Mansory said it is working on an 800-horsepower version. . . .

Engine: 6.2-liter dohc V-8
Horsepower: 668
0–60 mph: Est. 3.2 seconds
Top speed: Est. 203 mph
Price when new: Est. $300,000
Value now: Same

1963–1972   GT

- Marcos showed the GT at the 1963 Earls Court Motor Show.

- The rear axle was from a Ford Capri, the front suspension from Triumph.

- Selling kit cars avoided taxes in England.

- Marcos struggled along in business until 2007.

Engine: 3.5-liter ohv V-8
Horsepower: 114
0–60 mph: N/A
Top speed: N/A

Price when new: $17,000 for the kit minus drivetrain
Value now: $25,000

Another history lesson. Jem Marsh and Frank Costin started Marcos in 1959 to build sports cars. Costin was gone a year later, but Marsh had Dennis Adams design a GT car. It was an interesting car assembled from three large fiberglass pieces on—for the first six years—a wooden chassis. Marsh was a racer, so that purpose and thinking was part of Marcos. Come 1971, Marcos went belly-up, but Marsh wouldn't let go, bought the production equipment back, and a decade later was selling GTs again, now in kit form. The engine? Your choice of Rover V-8 or Ford four or six. You could buy the almost finished car or as a truckload of pieces. Roll up your sleeves and get to work. —JL

Marcos

XP-1   1968

A bit far-fetched for this book? Well, I've driven this car, which belongs to old friends, on public roads. Marcos built this race car in 1968, powered by a Repco Brabham Formula 1 engine. The car has the odd structural feature of a stressed plywood monocoque. The suspensions came from Cooper. And the body, with its huge see-through plastic cockpit cover, is dramatic. The XP raced once at the 1,000 Kms of Spa, but then the project had to be abandoned. The Brabham engine was replaced by a practical Buick V-8. Tom Morris bought the car for $7,100 from an ad in the *Wall Street Journal* 40 years ago. His son Ned restored the Marcos and has driven it in the Goodwood Festival of Speed. —*JL*

- Marcos also built a Mantis road car.

- The radiators are at each side of the cockpit.

- To meet racing regulations, there is room in the nose for a suitcase.

- This famous British car has lived in California for 40 years.

Engine: 215-cubic-inch V-8
Horsepower: Est. 200
0–60 mph: Est. 5.0 seconds
Top speed: Est. 120 mph

Price when new: Last sold for $7,100
Value now: Can't imagine what they'd want for it

Maserati 🇮🇹

- The coupe shown here was done by Zagato.
- Weight was about 1,870 pounds.
- These cars are also known as A6G54.
- Some A6G2000 roadsters were built.

Engine: 2.0-liter dohc inline six	Top speed: 130 mph
Horsepower: 160	Price when new: $6,500
0–60 mph: 10.0 seconds	Value now: $1,100,000

With the end of World War II, sports car racing resumed, and Maserati was back in the thick of it. Competing first in the 2.0-liter class, the Italian automaker created the A6GCS (*below*). . .and a legendary sports racing car. There were customers who wanted closed cars, and the A6GCS Berlinetta was the result. Next step was a car meant to be usable as a race car by privateers, but also driven on the street. This was the A6G2000 (*inset*), and roughly 60 were built. Three of the well-known design houses were given chassis—Frua, Allemano, and Zagato—and those from the latter tend to the prettiest. The cars had a good race history, but have since become known as some of the most desirable of the small-displacement Italian cars from the 1950s. . .hence the hefty prices. —*JL*

Bora   1971–1980

Probably the most famous Maserati road car of all time, and certainly one of the best-looking, the Bora was no less than a revolution in its era, and remains ultra-desirable today. It was powered by a mid-mounted V-8 of either 4.7 or 4.9 liters, both with over 300 horsepower, and it was designed—as so many of the most beautiful cars of that era were—by Giorgetto Giugiaro, who was working for Ital Design at the time. What made the Bora different from its competitors was the fact that it used hydraulics for its brakes, clutch, throttle, and headlights; Maserati's association with Citroën provided the basis for its radical engineering. On the road that meant the Bora was as refined as it was fast, unlike other, more brutish mid-engine sports cars at the time. —SS

- The first test mules of the Bora hit the roads of Modena in 1969.

- The wheels were 15-inch Campagnolo alloys that featured removable polished steel hubcaps.

- The Bora's twin was the Merak, which had a V-6 engine but was otherwise all but identical.

- Just 524 Boras were made in the end: 289 with the 4.7-liter V-8 engine and 235 with the 4.9 V-8.

Tech specs (4.7-liter):	
Engine: 4.7 liter V-8	Top speed: 165 mph
Horsepower: 310	Price when new: $12,000
0–60 mph: 6.5 seconds	Value now: $70,000–120,000

- The Coupé and Spyder were both designed by Giugiaro of Ital Design.

- They are built at the Viale Ciro Menotti plant in Modena, Italy.

- The Spyder's wheelbase is 8.6 inches shorter than the Coupé's.

- Both models use a 4.2-liter V-8 that is similar in design to the engine from the Ferrari California.

Engine: 4.2-liter V-8
Horsepower: 385
0–60 mph: 4.8 seconds

Top speed: 177 mph
Price when new: $100,000
Value now: $25,000–$70,000

Maserati had been absent from the United States for 11 long years when it returned with the Spyder version of its good-looking, great-driving Coupé in 2002. A few months later the Coupé itself went on sale; since then the relationship has blossomed. The Coupé's roots are based firmly on those of the turbocharged 3200 GT, which was only ever available in Europe but was superceded by the nonturbo 4200 GT, effectively the Coupé as we know it today. Perhaps not the most beautiful of Maseratis, the Coupé is nevertheless a great thing to drive, with Porsche 911–rivaling performance and a V-8 engine note to die for. It also has a cabin that is rich in quality, is high on luxury, and makes the car feel like a junior Ferrari inside. Same as it ever was from Maserati, in other words. —SS

■ Maserati

Ghibli 1966–1973

You might not think so, but the Ghibli actually outsold both the Ferrari Daytona and the Lamborghini Miura when it was unleashed upon the world in 1966; since then it has become one of the most highly regarded Maseratis of all time. So much so that it was voted the ninth best sports car of the 1960s by *Sports Car International*. Powered by the same 4.7- or 4.9-liter V-8 used in the Bora, the Ghibli was, just like the Daytona, a front-engined GT car with transcontinental touring aspirations and a level of effortless performance that could sweep it to 60 miles per hour in 6.8 seconds and well past 150 miles per hour on the right road. And as ever it was designed by Giugiaro. It was eventually superceded by the Khasmin. —SS

- The spyder version went into production in 1969, but the coupe outsold it by 10/1.
- The car had two 13.2-gallon fuel tanks, with a filler on each side of the roof pillars.
- A second-generation Ghibli was sold in Europe between 1992 and 1997.
- Giugiaro designed the car for Ghia, but its successor, the less highly regarded Khasmin, was designed by Bertone.

Tech specs (4.9-liter):	
Engine: 4.9-liter V-8	Top speed: 154 mph
Horsepower: 335	Price when new: $12,500
0–60 mph: 6.8 seconds	Value now: $70,000–$90,000

2008–   Gran Turismo and Gran Turismo MC Stradale

- The MC Stradale was unveiled at the Paris motorshow in 2010, and boasts a nice round 444 horsepower.

- Ferrari and Maserati insist that their engines are entirely different—and we'd insist they might be fibbing.

- MC stands for "Maserati coupe," and all MC versions come with a faster (than normal) paddle shift gearbox.

- The regular GT has a drag factor of just 0.33, unusually good for such a big machine.

Tech specs (MC Stradale):	
Engine: 4.3-liter V-8	Top speed: 187 mph
Horsepower: 444	Price when new: $204,000
0–60 mph: 4.6 seconds	Value now: Same

The big Maserati Gran Turismo is surely one of the most elegant sports cars of the modern era, and the best thing about it is that it's not just a pretty face. Essentially a two-door coupe version of the acclaimed Quattroporte V, the GT was unveiled at the 2007 Geneva motor show to a deafening round of applause, its curvaceous and deeply seductive-looking bodyshell clothing a potent V-8 engine that bears more than a little similarity to the one you'll find in a Ferrari California. Which means it's quick, even if it does weigh some 4,100 pounds. No matter, because if less weight, more power, and even greater performance is what you require, the MC Stradale version has the lot—and it's more aerodynamic as well. We like this car, we like it a lot. —SS

Maserati

MC12   2004–2005

At the time—2004—Ferrari owned Maserati, so it was no surprise when Maser created a mid-engine supercar based on the Ferrari Enzo chassis and drivetrain. Called the MC12, it looks quite different that the Enzo, being larger and with a signature Maserati nose. Credit for that exciting design goes to Frank Stephenson. The standard paint scheme—white with a blue stripe—features the U.S. racing colors as used on the very successful Camoradi racing Maseratis in the early 1960s. The MC12 is a bit more civilized than the Enzo, with a carbon fiber and blue leather-finished interior. The racing version, the MC12 Corsa, has proved to be a solid winner in European GT racing for a half decade, taking several FIA GT1 championship titles. —JL

- Torque is listed as 481 lb-ft.
- Maserati built 25 MC12s in 2004 and again in 2005.
- Paddle shifters are used with the six-speed transmission.
- MC12s have a removable Targa top.

Engine: 6.0-liter dohc V-12	Top speed: 205 mph
Horsepower: 623	Price when new: $700,000
0–60 mph: 3.7 seconds	Value now: $1,000,000

1989–1995   **Shamal**

- The Shamal is named after a hot summer wind that blows through Mesopotamia each year.

- Check out the Gandini trademark rear wheel arch design, also seen on the Lamborghini Countach.

- Quoted output for the twin turbo V-8 was 325 horsepower; rumor has it the motor produced rather more than that.

- The gear lever of the Shamal is finished in polished elm.

Engine: 3.2-liter twin turbo V-8	**Top speed:** 168 mph
Horsepower: 325	**Price when new:** $50,000
0–60 mph: 5.3 seconds	**Value now:** $50,000–$65,000

Designed for Maserati by Marcello Gandini at a time when Maserati had faded almost into total obscurity, the Shamal was truly one of the wildest cars of its era (it was built in miniscule numbers during its six-year run). With a short wheelbase and similarly puglike proportions from one side of its muscular body to the other, the rear-drive Shamal looked a recipe for snap-oversteer before you even fired it up. And when you did, the driving experience became so intense (courtesy of a peaky but deliciously potent 3.2-liter twin turbo V-8 motor) that quite a few examples ended up either scaring their owners into submission or gracing the scenery in and around its Modenese homeland or, occasionally, both. Mad name, even madder car. —SS

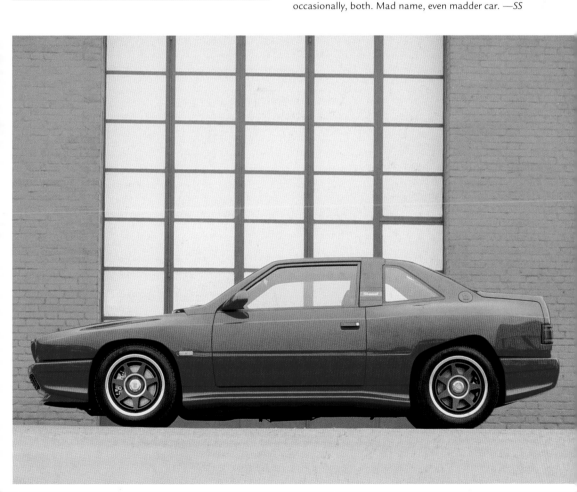

Cosmo   1967–1972

This is such a cool machine, and for several reasons. To start, it was the world's first twin rotor Wankel engine car. This was very important at the time, as automakers were looking at alternatives to the classic piston engine, and Felix Wankel's idea of a mill that spins in the same manner as the rest of the drivetrain seemed to make sense. And the engine was tiny, with just 982ccs of displacement (that's two 491cc rotary chambers) creating 110 horsepower. But also the look of the Cosmo was so period, like it had been shaped for a Godzilla movie. Mazda hand-built these sports cars at a rate of about one per day and used it as a showcase for their rotary engine. —JL

- If you don't recall ever seeing this car before, it's because only about a half dozen were known to have been exported to the United States. . .

- . . .and one of the two of those believed to be still running belongs to entertainer Jay Leno.

- Several other Mazdas have borne the name Cosmo over the years, including coupes and touring cars.

- The Cosmo was also known as the 110S.

Engine: 982cc twin rotor Wankel	**Top speed:** 115 mph
Horsepower: 110 (later 128)	**Price when new:** $4,100
0–60 mph: 9.0 seconds	**Value now:** $80,000

1989–ㅤㅤㅤMiata (NA, NB, NC)

- The word *Miata* is Old High German for "reward."

- In Japan, the Miata is called the Eunos Roadster; Eunos is Mazda's luxury nameplate.

- Guinness World Records declared the Miata the world's best-selling two-seater sports car in 2000, when production reached 531,890 units.

- The first-generation Miata is known as the NA. The second generation, NB. And so on. . . .

(NA):
Engine: 1.6-liter dohc inline four
Horsepower: 115
0–60 mph: 8.6 seconds

Top speed: 115 mph
Price when new: $13,800
Value now: $7,000

(NB):
Engine: 1.8-liter dohc inline four
Horsepower: 140
0–60 mph: 7.3 seconds

Top speed: 130 mph
Price when new: $22,098
Value now: $10,000

(NC):
Engine: 2.0-liter 16-valve dohc inline four
Horsepower: 170

0–60 mph: 6.5 seconds
Top speed: 130 mph
Price when new: $23,110
Value now: Same

Bob Hall grew up riding in his father's British sports cars. He was fascinated with all things Japanese and learned to write and speak the language as an exchange student. Hall was convinced that if anyone was going to build an affordable, modern roadster, it would be a Japanese car company.

Mazda took Hall up on his idea, turning him from automotive writer to product planner and putting him on a small team in California that included engineer Norman Garrett III and designers Tsutomu "Tom" Matano, Masao "Mark" Yagi, Koichi Hayashi, Taiwan-native Wu-Huant Chin, and Mark Jordan to work on project P729, which late in 1989 was launched into production as the Mazda MX-5 Miata.

Since then, Mazda has produced three generations of Miatas—a world-record for sports cars at 900,000 and counting—that are still fun to see and even more fun to drive, and these cars, unlike their British inspiration, don't leak fluids or suffer electrical failures in the middle of the night.

An important element of the Miata's success is that Mazda has remained faithful to the original theme of the car and not given in to calls for a little more room, a coupe version, etc. Unlike the Pontiac Solstice or Saturn Sky, the Miata has been kept simple, though constantly refined.

(continued on next page)

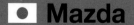

There have been changes from one generation to another, like forsaking the pop-up headlights for fixed lamps. One of the very nice additions came with the introduction of the optional folding steel hardtop on the third generation that is power operated and needs just 12 seconds to go up or down...perfect for use at stoplights.

Mark Jordan's first sketch of the car had it outfitted for racing, and the Miata has become the most popular race car in history, competing in various classes, including Miata-only series that sees starting fields of up to 85 cars. —JL

- Mazda introduced the RX-7 in Japan as the Savanna in 1978.

- In 1979, Mazda RX-7s finished first and second in the GTU category—and fifth and sixth overall—in the 24 Hours of Daytona race. A Ferrari 365 was second overall, and all of the other top 17 finishers were Porsches.

- RX-7s won the IMSA (International Motor Sports Association) GTU class season championship seven years in a row.

- Optional on first-generation RX-7s were a pair of dealer-installed second-row seats.

Engine: 1.1-liter rotary	Top speed: 120 mph
Horsepower: 100	Price when new: $7,200
0–60 mph: 9 seconds	Value now: $5,700

Mazda had produced more than 930,000 rotary-powered cars by the time it rolled out, including what may be the most sensational of them, the RX-7. Here was a genuine sports car, both in its design and in its dynamic capabilities. Those dynamic capabilities were enhanced by the fact that the car's little 70-cubic-inch twin rotor engine was mounted behind the front axle. The RX-7 was also affordable, starting at less than $7,200, or some $2,600 less than a Datsun 280ZX and some $3,000 less than a Chevrolet Corvette. Though the rotary powerplant spun out only 100 horsepower, the car was fast and nimble—and could achieve 30 miles per gallon while cruising on the highway. And it looked good while doing so. The RX-7's design featured a long, low hood and short, fastback roofline. The sleek styling was enhanced by hidden headlamps that popped up when needed. This was the beginning of something special. —*LE*

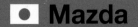
RX-7
(second generation)

1986–1991

Mazda made the second generation RX-7 more civilized than the first. You could see this in the exterior design, which looked more sophisticated and refined and, some still argue, a bit more Porsche-like. Ditto the interior, which had a more finished feeling to it. The live rear axle was swapped out for a proper independent rear suspension, the steering was now rack and pinion, and the brakes were upgraded. The rotary engine came in two flavors, normal and turbocharged, the latter bumping up on 200 horsepower. There was both a coupe and a somewhat complex convertible, the roadster sported the first-ever windblocker to minimize turbulence in the cockpit. Where the first RX-7 was a somewhat raucous little hot rod, the second gen was very much the touring car. So what did Mazda do with the next generation? Revert to the racer in its corporate heart. . .read on. —JL

- The second-gen RX-7 was named *Motor Trend*'s Import Car of the Year for 1986.
- In the second-gen RX-7's first model year, Mazda sold more than 56,000 units in the United States alone.
- Second-gen RX-7s were some 80 pounds heavier than the originals.
- There was an optional (but rare) rear seat.

(Series 4 turbo):	0–60 mph: 6.7
Engine: 1.3-liter turbocharged rotary	Top speed: 142 mph
	Price when new: $20,000
Horsepower: 182	Value now: $4,000

1992–2002

RX-7
(third generation)

- In 1991 Mazda became the first Japanese automaker to win the 24 Hours of Le Mans race.

- The third-generation RX-7 was built only as a coupe.

- The third-generation RX-7 is a popular car for drifting competition. Youichi Imamura won the 2003 D1 Grand Prix Championship driving an RX-7.

- Mazda replaced the RX-7 with the four-seat, four-door RX-8 "coupe."

Engine: 1.3-liter twin-turbocharged rotary
Horsepower: 255
0–60 mph: 4.9 seconds

Top speed: 156 mph
Price when new: $32,500
Value now: $17,000

With a pair of sequentially operating turbochargers on its rotary engine, and with a smooth new design and a more compact chassis, the third-generation Mazda RX-7 transformed from sporty coupe to true sports car. In a way, Mazda reached back to the RX-7's original version for inspiration and added elements of its Le Mans–winning sports prototype to produce a contemporary and truly world-class sports car. With its little rotary engine turbocharged to spin out 255 horsepower, the third-generation RX-7 was as fast as the big V-8–powered Chevrolet Corvette—at least from a standing start and through a quarter-mile sprint. The new RX-7 was both smaller—an inch and a half shorter—and lighter—a significant 200 pounds lighter—than its predecessor and had a wider stance. It rode on racing-style double-wishbone suspension and Z-rated tires. Some called it a street-legal race car. —LE

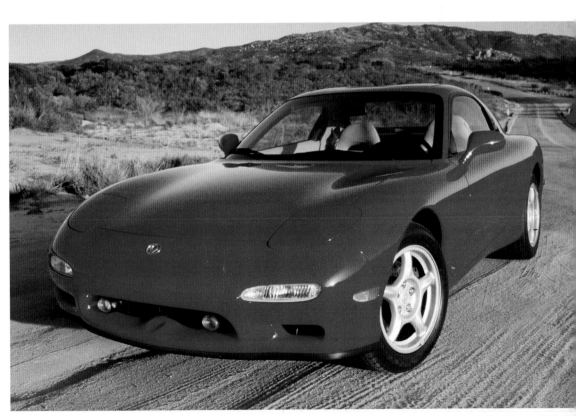

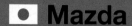
RX-8 — 2003–

A four-door sports car? When Mazda claimed to have one in the works, the critics were skeptical. And yet the RX-8 is a fine machine, a sports car that is quick and handles so nicely the driver could be unaware he has passengers tucked (if somewhat tightly) in the back seats. Access to those seats is aided by a pair of rear-hinged half doors. This is the only Wankel rotary engine car sold in the United States. Horsepower depends on the transmission, as those with the six-speed manual have 232 horsepower, while the automatic transmission cars have 212. This also explains the pair of 0–60 times. There are three versions of the RX-8: Sport is the basic, the Grand Touring adds luxury extras, and the R3 is the boy racer. —JL

- RX-8s have been raced very successfully in the Grand-Am series in the United States.
- The best-known RX-8 racer is actor Patrick Dempsey.
- The small rotary engine allows for a front mid-engine layout.
- Torque is 159 lb-ft with the manual or automatic gearbox.

Engine: 1.3-liter rotary
Horsepower: 212 or 232
0–60 mph: 6.5 or 6.0 seconds
Top speed: 148 mph
Price when new: $26,795
Value now: $8,600

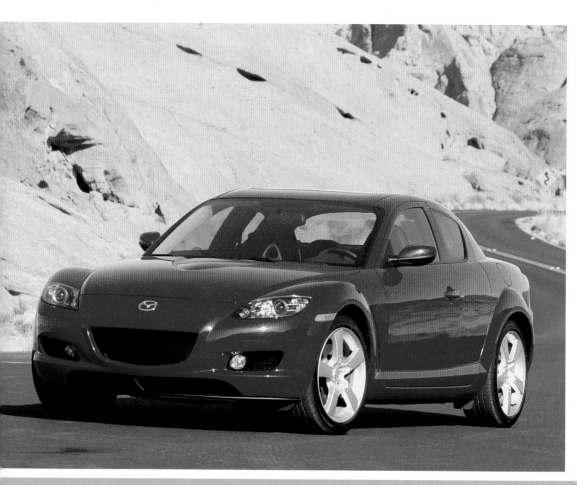

McLaren 🇬🇧

- McLaren built 64 "standard" street F1s, the total with other versions added up to 106.

- The V-12's torque is 480 lb-ft.

- One F1 has sold for $4,100,000.

- Time to 200 mph: 28 seconds.

Engine: 6.1-liter dohc V-12	**Top speed:** 231 mph
Horsepower: 627	**Price when new:** $810,000
0–60 mph: 3.2 seconds	**Value now:** $2,500,000

Gordon Murray is one of history's most creative automotive engineers, and his dream was to build the ultimate sports car. Many experts will tell you he did just that, in the form of the mid-engine McLaren F1. Peter Stevens did the exterior shape, carefully aero tuned to avoid exterior downforce devices. The chassis monocoque was formed in carbon fiber, and the finished F1 is dramatic, with its swing-forward doors. Inside is an unusual layout with a central driving position and places for passengers to the sides and slightly rearward. BMW supplied the 627-horsepower V-12 for McLaren, while the six-speed transmission was designed in California by Weismann. —JL

F1 LM | 1996

Although McLaren had not built the McLaren F1 with racing in mind, several owners pressed the company to create a competition version. Called the F1 GTR, the cars finished 1st, 3rd, 4th, 5th, and 13th at Le Mans in 1995. To celebrate this finish, McLaren built five special LM versions incorporating elements of the race cars. Most obvious is the added rear wing, and they are fitted with the GTR BMW V-12 minus the air intake restrictors required at Le Mans. This bumped horsepower from the standard F1's 627 to 680. Inside, the F1 LM is stripped of many of the amenities, like the audio system, sound deadening, and comfy seat coverings. Those of us who have ridden in LMs recommend noise-canceling headphones. Also gone are the suspension's rubber bushings, so the handling and ride are firmer. —JL

- Curb weight of the F1 LM is just 2,341 pounds.
- The transmission is a transversely mounted six-speed.
- F1 LMs are painted papaya orange to honor founder Bruce McLaren.
- An F1 LM will get you to 100 mph in a mere 6.7 seconds.

Engine: 6.l-liter dohc V-12
Horsepower: 680
0–60 mph: 3.9 seconds
Top speed: 225 mph
Price when new: $1.25 million
Value now: $2.5 million

- The race car–based M6GT weighed 1,765 pounds.

- A ZF five-speed gearbox was used.

- The monocoque was in aluminum, the body in fiberglass.

- It's said one owner drove his kids to school in his M6GT.

Engine: 5.7-liter ohv V-8	Top speed: 180 mph
Horsepower: 370	Price when new: N/A
0–60 mph: 4.2 seconds	Value now: N/A

By 1969, New Zealander Bruce McLaren had already established himself as a winning F1 driver and constructor, not to mention the builder and driver of fearsome Cam-Am machines. Seeking new worlds to conquer, he decided to build a machine to compete in the FIA's Group 4 series. Basis for the coupe would be the successful Can-Am M6 mid-engine chassis, with the power coming from a small-block Chevrolet V-8. The FIA's rules initially called for 50 examples to qualify for the series. This was later dropped to 25, which brought Porsche in with the 917 and Ferrari with the 512. This essentially ended McLaren's project, but a total of three M6GTs were built, including one for McLaren to drive. The New Zealander's untimely death during a testing crash in 1970 brought an end to the project, although his team still lives on today. —JL

McLaren

MP4-12C   2011–

The MP4-12C might not be McLaren's first-ever foray into the world of road cars, but it is certainly its most committed attempt so far, as well as its best. The twin-turbo, mid-engined car is so thoroughly engineered, so powerful (592 horses), and its seven-speed dual clutch gearbox so fast in its operation that it's actually quicker where it counts than the legendary F1. Yet at the same time it has a multi-adjustable chassis and suspension that can transform it from boulevard cruiser one minute to incisively honed track monster the next—and pretty much anything you'd like it to be in between. Bottom line, McLaren is hoping to out-Ferrari Ferrari with the 12C, and from the way it drives they should have no trouble at all. —SS

- The 12C's 0–100-mph time is 0.2 seconds faster than Autocar magazine recorded for the F1.
- The car has no anti-roll bars, its roll being controlled by hydraulics and active dampers instead.
- It has been unofficially timed at four seconds faster than a Ferrari 458 around *Top Gear*'s test track.
- It will be joined by an even-faster GTR version and an open-top model in the fullness of time.

Engine: 3.8-liter twin-turbocharged V-8
Horsepower: 592
0–60 mph: 3.1 seconds
Top speed: 206 mph
Price when new: $229,000
Value now: Same

- *SL* stands for "Sport Leicht," German for "Sport Light."
- 300 represents the 3.0-liter engine.
- Mercedes built 1,400 300SL coupes.
- Mercedes built roadster versions of this 300SL.

Engine: 3.0-liter sohc inline six	Top speed: 149 mph
Horsepower: 175	Price when new: N/A
0–60 mph: N/A	Value now: N/A

When Mercedes-Benz returned to racing after World War II, it was not to the Grand Prix circuits, but to sports cars. Basis for the cars was a somewhat complex but light and stiff tubular space frame. When Mercedes decided for aerodynamic reasons to race a coupe instead of a roadster, it was the high sides of this frame that inspired the use of gullwing doors. At the front of the chassis were double A-arm suspensions, while at the back was a swing axle design. Watching their Deutsche Marks, Mercedes went to its new production inline six to develop the engine for the 300SL. On the track, the coupes were quick and reliable, the best proof coming with a 1–2 win in the 1952 24 Hours of Le Mans and again in Mexico's rugged Carrera Panamericana. Those early 1950s cars were built solely for racing, but their success inspired Mercedes to build production versions. —JL

═ Mercedes-Benz

300SLR coupe   1954–1955

Ah, another dream car. After Mercedes-Benz reentered racing, one of its most important machines was the 300SLR. This open sports car was in many ways a two-seat version of the company's famed W196 Grand Prix car with the unique desmodromic-valve straight eight opened to 3 liters. Sadly, a 300SLR was involved in the tragic 1955 Le Mans disaster and Mercedes pulled out of competition for decades. But the company had already begun development of a coupe version of the 300SLR for use on events like Mexico's Carrera Panamericana road race. Only two were built before Le Mans, which ended their development. Legendary Mercedes race engineer Rudolf Uhlenhaut used one of the coupes as a road car. What a drive that must have been. . . . —JL

- 300SLRs had a rear-mounted five-speed transaxle.
- Desmodromic valves use the camshaft to open and close the valves.
- You can see a 300SLR Coupe in Mercedes' museum in Stuttgart.
- 300SLR bodies were formed in a magnesium alloy called elektron.

Engine: 3.0-liter dohc inline eight	**Top speed:** Est. 175 mph
Horsepower: 310	**Price when new:** N/A
0–60 mph: N/A	**Value now:** Truly invaluable

- Sophia Loren drove a 560SL. Perfect.

- Between 1986 and 1989 the list price rose by an incredible $16,030.

- The 5.6-liter V-8 was detuned by Mercedes to be as economical as possible!

- Internally, Mercedes-Benz referred to the 560SL as chassis R107.

Engine: 5.6-liter V-8	Top speed: 134 mph
Horsepower: 227	Price when new: $61,130
0–60 mph: 8.5 seconds	Value now: $45,000

The 560SL was a U.S. market–only car as far as Mercedes-Benz was concerned, and a deeply, lovely, eminently seductive piece of Teutonic automotive engineering it was, too. Standard equipment included everything you could ever want, and then just a little bit more on top, with gorgeous leather seats playing the starring role in a cabin that was rich with class and atmosphere. But the business end of the car was up front, where the 5.6-liter V-8 sat, mated to one of the smoothest, most robust automatic gearboxes ever produced. Despite its big capacity motor, the 560SL was more about wafting than it was drag racing. You reached your destination graciously in a 560, rather than in a cloud of smoke. And when got there you had most definitely arrived. —SS

Mercedes-Benz

C111 | 1969–1970

Automakers, independent design studios, and coachbuilders were experimenting with all sorts of exotic, wedge-shaped vehicles in the late 1960s. Among them was Mercedes-Benz, which devised an engineering research vehicle known by its internal codename, C111. The car was built around a racing-style, midmounted engine architecture with gullwing doors, and, as a test bed, at various times and in various versions—there were at least six C111 prototypes and, a year later, an updated C111-II and then a C111-III. At various stages, they carried Wankel (rotary), diesel, or turbocharged powerplants.

The C111 had a fiberglass body. Initially equipped with a three-rotor Wankel engine, the car could accelerate from 0 to 60 mph in less than five seconds on its way to a speed of 170 miles per hour. Later, the C111-II, with a four-rotor engine, approached 190 mph. With a coefficient of drag of a mere 0.191 and a turbocharged diesel, the car exceeded 200 miles per hour. —LE

- Mercedes called the C111's bright orange color "weissherbst."
- The C111 was designed by Bruno Sacco, who would go on to design many of the company's most iconic models into the 21st century.
- One benefit of the C111 program was the creation of a new front suspension system that did go into production on Mercedes' S-class sedans.
- The C111 pictured here is the original Wankel-powered machine.

Engine: Wankel rotary and turbocharged diesel
Horsepower: Up to 500
0–60 mph: Less than 5 seconds
Top speed: 250 mph

Price when new: Factory experimental vehicle not for sale
Value now: Factory experimental vehicle not for sale

2005   **CLK-DTM AMG**

- *DTM* stands for "Deutsche Tourenwagen Masters" (German Touring Car Masters), a European-based racing series that currently features hopped-up Audis and Mercedes.

- Mercedes built just 100 fixed head and 80 convertible CLK DTMs.

- In Germany, the car cost €236,000, including taxes.

- Actual DTM cars of the same era used a highly tuned 4.0-liter V-8 and had less than 500 horsepower.

Engine: 5.4-liter V-8	Top speed: 200 mph
Horsepower: 582	Price when new: $450,000
0–60 mph: 3.8 seconds	Value now: $500,000+

Apart from the ultrarare, ultraexpensive CLK GTR, the DTM is probably Mercedes most-extreme-ever road car, hence the reason why ex–F1 world champion Jenson Button used to own one and why they remain so very desirable, despite being produced in extremely limited numbers (fewer than 200 were made) and only in 2005. The engine is a 582-horsepower supercharged 5.4-liter V-8 that also develops 800 lb-ft of torque. It sends power to the rear tires via a paddle shift–controlled gearbox and a limited slip diff that provides the perfect platform for delivering 200-yard power slides. And the styling is almost comical in its aggression, with vast wheelarch extensions only just managing to contain tires wide enough to help the DTM develop 1.35g of lateral grip. Only the brave and/or exceedingly wealthy need apply. —SS

Mercedes-Benz

FAB Design SLS AMG   2011

There are any number of European tuning firms that bring in Mercedes-Benz, Porsche, and BMW models and then take them another step. One is the Swiss company FAB, and what you see here is their take on Mercedes' gullwing SLS AMG. Not surprisingly, the engine has been heavily breathed upon, upping horsepower from the SLS's 563 to 615. Torque climbs from 480 lb-ft to 509. Suspension changes firm things up to go with the added power. FAB also goes about changing the exterior, adding what it calls its "widebody" look. This means redone fenders, quarter panels, and sills to make the SLS look even more aggressive. —SS

- 0–125 mph takes just 11 seconds.
- Among the engine modifications is a low-pressure exhaust.
- Three-piece 20-inch Evoline wheels are fitted.
- Carbon fiber is used for the new side sills.

Engine: 6.2-liter dohc V-8
Horsepower: 611
0–60 mph: 3.5 seconds
Top speed: 202 mph

Price when new: As customized as the car, but a lot
Value now: Same

- The SL65 develops so much torque it has to make do with Mercedes' older five-speed gearbox because the new seven-speeder can't cope.

- *Car and Driver* recorded a 0–60 mph time of 3.6 seconds for the SL65, despite the official quote of 4.2 seconds.

- Just 350 Black series cars were made, each one costing 250,000 euros plus local taxes.

- The Black series version weighs 550 pounds less than the regular SL65, thanks to its carbon fiber body panels.

Tech specs (SL 65 Black Series):	
Engine: 6.0-liter twin turbo V-12	Top speed: 206 mph
Horsepower: 661	Price when new: $500,000
0–60 mph: 3.6 seconds	Value now: $550,000

The SL65, particularly the "is it a car, is it a cartoon" Black Series edition, is one of those experiences in life that you really should try to sample before shuffling off your mortal coil. Both are powered by the same 6.0-liter twin turbo V-12 engine, the only difference being that in the regular 65 (*left*) you get a mere 604 horsepower, whereas in the more highly tuned Black (*below*) you have 661 horsepower beneath your right foot. Yet in reality it's the torque, not the power, of this engine that leaves its mark—and in both cars there is a quite astonishing 1,000nm of the stuff available—from little more than 2,000 rpm onward. That's enough to bend an entire forest should you feel the need, and in the Black model, with its track-focused chassis and monster tires, you might well need an entire forest in which to slow down should you get it wrong. —SS

SLK   1996–

The Mazda Miata renewed interest in small, two-seat sports cars. Ford (Australian-built Mercury Capri), General Motors (Japanese-built Geo Metro), Honda (Civic del Sol), and Toyota (MR2) were quick to follow. So were the European luxury carmakers. BMW rolled out its Z3 for 1996, while Porsche and Mercedes-Benz followed with the Boxster and SLK, respectively, for 1997. At Mercedes, the S stood for "sports," the L for "lightweight," and the K for both "short" (in length) and "supercharged" (Kompressor)—the car's 2.3-liter four-cylinder engine boosted to 185 horsepower. The SLK was also distinctive because it was both a solid-topped coupe and an open-air roadster, thanks to a retractable hardtop system that, at the push of a button, folded the hardtop and stowed it beneath the rear deck lid. With a base price of less than $40,000, the SLK was Mercedes' first "affordable" two-seater since the 190SL of the 1960s. —LE

- The SLK was previewed by concept cars in 1994.
- For 2004, AMG created an SLK 32 AMG model powered by a hand-built, 3.2-liter V-6 that provided 354 horsepower.
- The second-generation SLK came equipped with a seven-speed automatic transmission or a six-speed manual.
- For the second-generation SLK, AMG upped the ante with a 5.4-liter V-8 engine.

Engine: 2.3-liter supercharged inline four
Horsepower: 185
0–60 mph: Less than 7 seconds
Top speed: 138 mph
Price when new: $39,700
Value now: $7,000

- The SLR's aerodynamics are enhanced by side exhaust outlets in the rocker panels that allow for a flatter undercarriage.

- The SLR was previewed at the 1999 Detroit auto show by the Vision SLR concept car.

- SLR engines were hand-built by AMG.

- Despite all of its performance potential, the SLR sips only about 15 miles per gallon while puttering around town.

Engine: 5.4-liter supercharged V-8	**Top speed:** 207.5 mph
Horsepower: 617	**Price when new:** $450,000
0–60 mph: 3.6 seconds	**Value now:** $300,000

Mercedes-Benz and its partner in Formula One racing, McLaren, designed the SLR as a supercar you could drive on a daily basis—though you have to wonder how many people had a daily commute that called for a car capable of speeds of more than 207 miles per hour, not to mention one that was equipped with a rear airfoil braking system. The SLR McLaren was a throwback to the gullwinged 300SL coupes of the 1950s, right down to the straked and checkerboard-design air vents built into the bodywork behind the front wheels. However, the new SLR doesn't have gullwing doors, but rather "swing-wing" doors hinged into the car's A-pillars. The front-engine layout makes the SLR more of a true Grand Touring car and allowed for nearly 10 cubic feet of luggage space. —LE

SLS AMG   2010–

The SLS, Mercedes' successor to the SLR McLaren, is the first supercar Mercedes-Benz has produced following the (amicable) dissolution of its partnership with McLaren. The SLS was designed in Germany by AMG. The SLR aside, Mercedes likes to think of the SLS as the true grandson of its famous 300SL gullwing sports car, hence the flip-up doors, although what's under the hood would amaze original SL owners. How about an AMG dry-sump V-8 with 563 horsepower and 480 lb-ft of torque? The transmission is a seven-speed dual-clutch paddle shifter "automatic." If that's not enough, hang in there for the SLS AMG E-Cell. This will put an electric motor at each wheel for a combined 525 horsepower and 650 lb-ft of torque. —JL

- Carbon-ceramic brakes are an option.
- A rear wing rises to add downforce at high speed.
- There is a GT3 race version of the SLS.
- The SLS E-Cell is fitted with a 400V lithium-ion battery.

Engine: 6.2-liter dohc V-8	Top speed: 197 mph
Horsepower: 563	Price when new: $183,000
0–60 mph: 3.7 seconds	Value now: Same

- Trossi's Mercedes is now owned by Ralph Lauren.

- This car has won Best of Show at Pebble Beach.

- Max torque is said to be more than 500 lb-ft.

- Quick as it is, the SSK weighs two tons.

Engine: 7.1-liter supercharged sohc inline six	**Top speed:** 145 mph
Horsepower: 300	**Price when new:** N/A
0–60 mph: N/A	**Value now:** $10,000,000?

Arguably the most famous pre–World War II supercars were Mercedes' SSKs. Designed by Ferdinand Porsche before he went off and started his own company, the big cars were actually shortened versions of the Model S. The acronym name stands for "Super Sport Kurz," the last word meaning "short." Under that long hood is a supercharged 7,069cc straight six that produces up to 300 horsepower. We can attest that when the accelerator is floored and the blower kicks in it creates a howl that will make you jump. Successful race cars, several SSKs were converted to street use after their competition years. This is not one of those, but rather an unsold chassis that was eventually purchased by Count Carlo Trossi of Italy, who had that exciting body built by Willie White. —JL

Mercer

Type 35 Raceabout   1911–1914

So you think the sports car is a modern invention? Wrong, and many experts have dubbed Mercer's Type 35 Raceabout the first American sports car. Considering that one of the founding families of Mercer, the Roeblings, was also famous for the Brooklyn Bridge, you might not think their goal would be a low, fast automobile, but that was the brief given to engineer Finley Robertson Porter. This did not lead to a particularly civilized machine, but it was a quick one, a favorite of rich young men around the country. And of race drivers, who won scores of contests in Mercers. The Raceabout's big rival was another great classic, the Stutz Bearcat. —*JL*

- Mercer was named for Mercer County, New Jersey, where the cars were made.
- That 58 horsepower peaked at 1,900 rpm.
- A scion of the Roebling family, Washington Augustus Roebling II, died on the Titanic.
- Of the 1,000 or so Raceabouts built, fewer than 20 are believed to still exist.

Engine: 4.9-liter side-valve inline four
Horsepower: 58
0–60 mph: N/A

Top speed: 100 mph
Price when new: $2,250
Value now: $2,000,000

Mercury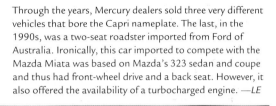

- The first (1970s) Mercury Capri was a svelte and sporty coupe imported from Ford of Germany.

- Later in the 1970s, the Capri nameplate went on Mercury's version of the Ford Mustang.

- The 1990's Capri featured a back seat with a seat back that could be folded down to increase the cargo capacity of the trunk.

- The Mercury Capri XR2 came with a turbocharged engine with 132 horsepower.

Engine: 1.6-liter inline four	Top speed: N/A
Horsepower: 100	Price when new: N/A
0–60 mph: N/A	Value now: $1,000

Through the years, Mercury dealers sold three very different vehicles that bore the Capri nameplate. The last, in the 1990s, was a two-seat roadster imported from Ford of Australia. Ironically, this car imported to compete with the Mazda Miata was based on Mazda's 323 sedan and coupe and thus had front-wheel drive and a back seat. However, it also offered the availability of a turbocharged engine. —LE

Messerschmitt

Okay, this one is an oddball, but can't we have a little fun here? After World War II, warplane-builder Willy Messerschmitt wasn't allowed to produce aircraft, so when Fritz Fend showed him plans for a small car, Messerschmitt bought into the project. The unique car was not just economical, but provided a car for injured veterans to drive. The Fichtel & Sachs two-stroke engine is mounted in back. Reverse "gear" means starting the engine "backward," so there were four gears forward and four in reverse. —JL

- Curb weight of the KR200 is a mere 506 pounds.

- The KR201 is a roadster version.

- Just over 41,000 KR200s were built between 1955 and 1964.

- The canopy roof offered great visibility, but heated up the interior on sunny days.

Engine: 191cc single-cylinder two-stroke	Top speed: 56 mph
Horsepower: 10.2	Price when new: $600
0–60 mph: 7.5 seconds	Value now: $25,000

MG

MGA 1955–1962

Come the mid-1950s, the traditional (some might say pre-war) look of the MGTF was costing MG. But it turns out they already had an answer. For the 1951 Le Mans race, the company had built a special-bodied car, more streamlined than the current models. Called EX 172, it was a design theme used for 1955 when the company shook off its old clothes. MG would go on to build more than 100,000 MGAs, many of which were exported stateside. Most were convertibles, but there were also coupes, and in time the engine was increased from 1,489cc to 1,588cc, and, finally 1,622cc. There was also a twin cam version of the engine, though it had a reputation for being unreliable. These much-loved MGs were a backbone of the U.S. sports car movement. —JL

- MG first showed the production MGA at the 1955 Frankfurt Motor Show.
- Elvis drove an MGA in the 1961 film *Blue Hawaii*.
- The 1500 roadster pictured is painted Orient Red.
- MG built 52,478 1500 roadsters from 1955 to 1959.

Engine: 1.5-liter ohv inline four
Horsepower: 72
0–60 mph: 15 seconds
Top speed: 90 mph
Price when new: $2,550
Value now: $16,000

- It is believed that 51 Airline Coupés were built.

- The car pictured here is 1 of 14 built on a PB Midget chassis.

- The transmission was a four-speed.

- A rare six-cylinder MB chassis Airline could fetch $450,000 today.

Engine: 938cc ohv inline four	**Top speed:** 75 mph
Horsepower: 43	**Price when new:** $37,000
0–60 mph: 23 seconds	**Value now:** N/A

There is something particularly sweet and graceful about the MG Airline Coupés. The shape was an attempt to be somewhat aerodynamic, though one suspects the barn door nature of the stand-up MG grille thwarted that a bit. Still, these stand out as exquisite examples of MG in the 1930s. Built in a variety of MG chassis, the cars feature steel bodies formed around ash frames. They had sliding roofs, and one can only imagine the joy of rushing along English hedge-lined lanes on a spring day in an Airline Coupé. Mind you, it wouldn't be a major rush, as most Airlines were built on four-cylinder chassis with sub-1-liter engines. A few were done on six-cylinder chassis, and these are quite valuable today. —JL

MGB

1962–1980

If you're looking for a classic British sports car for a reasonable price, check eBay for an MGB. Around a half million "Bs" were assembled during its long production run, so there are still plenty of them around. They come in two forms, the roadster and MGB GT coupe (pictured). There are also early chrome bumper cars and those with the U.S. "rubber" safety bumpers. The late-1960s MGC, which looked like the MGB with a bulging hood, was powered by a 3.0-liter, 145-horepower inline six. Still another form was the MGB GT V-8, which used a former aluminum GM engine built by Rover. The V-8 cars were never sold in the United States. MGs suffered from British Leyland's inability to meet the U.S. safety and emissions standards of the early 1970s. —JL

- One option was an electronically actuated overdrive.
- Some U.S. MGs have three windshield wipers.
- The MGB GT's upper body was designed by Pininfarina.
- A restyled non-U.S. version called the MG RV-8 was built from 1993 to 1995.

Engine: 1.8-liter ohv inline four	**Top speed:** 99 mph
Horsepower: 95	**Price when new:** $3,400
0–60 mph: 12 seconds	**Value now:** $5,000

- Just 33 K3 Magnettes were produced in 1933–1934.

- Many K3s were rebodied as single seaters for racing.

- The transmission was a four-speed Wilson preselector.

- K3s weighed around 2,000 pounds.

Engine: 1.1-liter supercharged sohc inline six	**Top speed:** 110 mph
Horsepower: 118	**Price when new:** $3,975
0–60 mph: Est. 12 seconds	**Value now:** $250,000

Many MG experts will tell you the K3 Magnette was the greatest of all MGs. It certainly did much to establish the company's racing reputation. The K3's supercharged six was bolted to a chassis that featured a beam front axle and live rear axle. All this in a body that epitomizes MG and the era. The K3's potential was proved in the rugged Mille Miglia in 1933, where MG won the team prize. This impressed Tazio Nuvolari, one of the greatest race drivers of all time, and he used a K3 to win its class in the Tourist Trophy. While Americans have always had the luxury of big-displacement cars, Europeans put great value on the small racing classes, so a win in a sub-1100cc class was honored. And that's where the K3 was so successful. —JL

MG

TC 1945–1949

Young sports car fans have trouble believing it, but this is the car that started the post–World War II sports car movement in the United States. Granted, these little machines were antiquated; they were based heavily on the pre-war MG TB, though with a 4-inch-wider body. The TC certainly didn't offer much in terms of creature comfort—rain leaked through the doors and roof—and the horsepower was puny compared to American cars. The front suspension had a beam axle, the rear a live axle; both sat on semi-elliptic springs. Still, the MG TC was light, handled nicely, and was great automotive fun at a time when returning servicemen deserved to have some fun, which is how some 2,000 were sold in the United States, even though they were all right-hand drive. And it whetted American's appetite for the TC's successor, the TD. —JL

- Ten thousand MG TCs were built from 1945 to 1949.
- The MG TC put out just 64 lb-ft of torque.
- Only the top three speeds in the four-speed gearbox had synchromesh.
- TCs had a steel body over a wood frame.

Engine: 1.25-liter ohv inline four
Horsepower: 55
0–60 mph: 22 seconds
Top speed: 80 mph
Price when new: $2,395
Value now: $30,000

- The car pictured here is an early TD.

- The T Series MGs were also known as Midgets.

- Just 1,656 of the 29,664 MC TDs made were sold in the U.K.

- The TD was followed by the far less successful TF.

Engine: 1.25-liter ohv inline four	**Top speed:** 77 mph
Horsepower: 57	**Price when new:** $1,855
0–60 mph: 18.2 seconds	**Value now:** $30,000

If the MG TC whetted Americans' appetite for sports cars, its successor, the TD, allowed them to indulge. MG records state that, of the 29,664 TDs built, almost 23,500 were exported to the United States. MG had learned its lesson from the TC, and the TD offered left-hand drive, better weather protection, proper bumpers, a more substantial frame, and independent double wishbone/coil spring front suspension. The new model still used the TC engine, though it was soon upgraded to 57 horsepower. At the same time, bucket seats had replaced the one-piece seat back/individual seat cushions. If there was one complaint from the traditionalists, it was the substitution of steel wheels for wire wheels, though wire was still offered as an option. No doubt the TD was much more civilized than the TC. —JL

Cooper S   2001–

When BMW reinvented the MINI at the beginning of this century, it could have had no idea how popular the car would turn out to be. Or how many versions it would be possible to create out of one single—albeit rather smart— re-branding idea. And the best of the lot, arguably, is the Cooper S, a turbocharged version with a six-speed manual geabox that has the performance to match the car's name and its cheeky good looks. Designed by Frank Stephenson, who went on to work for Ferrari and later McLaren, the "new" MINI was always crying out for the power to unlock its hilarious front-wheel-drive chassis, and the supercharged 1.6-liter Cooper S provided it—even more so when they turbocharged it and released yet more power (175 horsepower) for the 2007 model year. —SS

- Designer Frank Stephenson genuinely had doubts whether the new MINI would work in the beginning.

- An even-hotter, 200-plus horsepower version called the John Cooper S Works was launched alongside the S.

- The S can be distinguished by twin exhausts that exit under the rear valance.

- The United States and Australia were never offered the basic MINI version, only the Cooper and Cooper S models.

Engine: 1.6-liter turbocharged inline four
Horsepower: 181
0–60 mph: 6.7 seconds

Top speed: 140 mph
Price when new: $23,000
Value now: same

1953–1961   **750 Gran Sport**

- The transmission is Moretti's own four-speed unit.

- These cars weighed less than 1,100 pounds.

- Morettis had aluminum bodies over tube frames.

- Redline for the little engine was 7,000 rpm.

Engine: 750cc dohc inline seven	**Top speed:** 100 mph
Horsepower: 80	**Price when new:** N/A
0–60 mph: 15.5 seconds	**Value now:** $220,000

Here's another tip of the hat to the little guys. Could there be a more Italian name than Giovanni Moretti? Founder of a company in Turin, Italy, that made all sorts of small-displacement vehicles, plus motorcycles, Moretti created a dual overhead cam engine with 750cc. Sounds perfect for racing, which he did with a series of lightweight Gran Sport automobiles. Where other makers of small Italian cars were well known for using Fiat parts, during the time of the Gran Sport, Moretti took great pride in creating his own parts. And those parts were highly regarded for excellent workmanship. Michelotti designed the pretty little body, and those of us who have driven a Gran Sports can attest to the remarkable amount of interior room despite the small exterior size. —JL

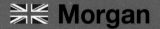
Aero Supersports 2011–

Updating tradition ain't easy, and there's no more traditional car company in England than Morgan. Still, the company needed to step into the 21st century. Hence the Aero Supersports. You can see the basics of the Morgan shape, now hunkered down on 19-inch wheels and tires, the headlamps blended into the fender forms, and the car's overall form looking, as its name implies, rather aero. There are removable roof panels so the car can be a coupe or open Targa-style machine. Those body panels are superformed in aluminum and, in company tradition, laid over ash wood on a bonded aluminum chassis. Morgan went to BMW for the V-8 and matches it to a six-speed manual or automatic transmission. Interior appointments include leather upholstery and polished wood trim; there's even an optional navigational system. —JL

- Torque from the BMW V-8 is 370 lb-ft.
- Only 200 Aero Supersports will be made.
- On a scale the Morgan hits just 2,600 pounds.
- You can buy a track-ready Morgan SuperSport GT3.

Engine: 4.8-liter dohc V-8	Top speed: 170 mph
Horsepower: 367	Price when new: $185,000
0–60 mph: 4.2 seconds	Value now: Same

1968–2004   **Plus 8**

- All Morgans are hand-built in the company's factory in Malvern Link, Worcestershire, England.

- That's Peter Morgan pictured, the son of company founder H. F. S Morgan.

- Peter's son Charles is the company's third-generation owner.

- Oh, and you can choose from 40,000 different colors.

Engine: 3.0-liter dohc V-8
Horsepower: 228
0–60 mph: 4.9 seconds
Top speed: 140 mph

Price when new: $80,000
Value now: Many years from which to choose. . .

This isn't so much an automobile as a history lesson. It began in 1911 when H. F. S. Morgan built a three-wheeled vehicle for himself. The car caught the public's imagination and production began. In 1936, Morgan began to build four-wheel sports cars in a style that has not changed a great deal since then. Today's Morgans are modern enough, meeting all current safety and emissions rules, but all five of the "traditional" models retain the look of their predecessors. And that's how we can show a photo of a 1988 model and still be (pretty much) up-to-date in 2011. Today's versions come as two- or four-seat models with engines from 1.6 to 3.0 liters. And you can choose from a list of options ranging from leather upholstery to a carbon fiber hardtop. —JL

Metropolitan 1953–1961

Okay, not strictly a sports car to some, but so lovable. This two-seater—okay, maybe a three-seater—was the brainchild of Nash Motors and built on a wheelbase that was shorter than a VW Beetle's. Nash was trying to meet what it thought would be a postwar need for small cars. It made little financial sense to build the Metropolitan in the United States, so production was done in England by Austin Motor Company, using that firm's A40 engine. Both coupes and convertibles were built in four series between 1953 and 1961. And, yes, some might call the Metropolitan homely, but it was fun to drive in its era, and while that 0-60 time looks slow, it was faster than the Beetle. —JL

- In 1956, the engine size was increased to 1.5 liters.
- Metropolitans were sold under both the Nash and Hudson nameplates.
- Styling of the Metropolitan was based on William Flajole's NXI concept car.
- A total of 83,442 Metropolitans were sold in the United States.

Engine: 1.2-liter ohv inline four
Horsepower: 42
0–60 mph: 19.3 seconds

Top speed: 75 mph
Price when new: $1,445
Value now: $10,000

1951–1954   **Nash-Healey**

- The Pinin Farina Nash-Healey debuted at the 1952 Chicago auto show.

- In 1952, horsepower went to 140.

- A total of 506 Nash-Healeys were built, and Nash lost money on every one.

- Donald Healey created competition Nash-Healeys for Le Mans.

Engine: 4.1-liter ohv inline six	**Top speed:** 104 mph
Horsepower: 140	**Price when new:** $5,908
0–60 mph: 9.8 seconds	**Value now:** $175,000

You never know what might come from a great dinner. Like the one on the ocean liner the *Queen Elizabeth*, when Donald Healey met George Mason, CEO of Nash-Kelvinator. Healey was looking to expand production; Mason wanted a "halo" car to promote Nash automobiles. The result was the Nash-Healey. Nash provided the drivetrain from its Ambassador model, and Healey upgraded it from 112 to 125 horsepower. The first model (1951) was a bit homely, so for 1952 they went to Pinin Farina (spelled as two words back then), which reshaped the body in both roadster and coupe form. The cars were pricey; the Nash drivelines were shipped to England to be installed in the chassis, which then went to Italy to be bodied, then sent to the United States. —*JL*

 # Nissan

300ZX (Z31)   1983–1989

It was still called a Datsun in the United States (it became a Nissan in 1985), but 1983 brought the third generation of the now legendary Z sports cars. Code-named Z31, the all-new 300ZX was powered by an all-new 3.0-liter V-6 engine, and marked the series' first major exterior styling change, forsaking the Z's roundness for a more wedgelike look. Some complained that the somewhat ungainly 300ZX took the Z series too far from its basic sports car roots, but sales were as strong as ever. . . ! —JL

- Paul Newman won the 1985 SCCA GT1 title driving a 300ZX.
- Curb weight was 3,080 pounds.
- That weight was distributed 51/49 front to rear.
- Wheelbase was 81.3 inches.

Engine: 3.0-liter turbocharged dohc V-6
Horsepower: 200
0–60 mph: 6.9 seconds

Top speed: 135 mph
Price when new: $18,199 (base)
Value now: $8,000

1989–2000   **300ZX (Z32)**

- Curb weight was 3,435 pounds.

- Four-wheel steering was an option with the Z32 turbo package.

- The turbo Z32 ran a quarter-mile in 15.0 seconds at 96.0 mph.

- Electocmotive based their winning race cars on the 300ZX.

Engine: 3.0-liter turbocharged dohc V-6	**Top speed:** 155 mph
Horsepower: 300	**Price when new:** $33,000
0–60 mph: 5.5 seconds	**Value now:** $6,000

Come the end of the decade, those complaints about the Z31 were still being heard. But Nissan was listening, and when they launched the new fourth-generation car in 1989, those whiners were too busy drooling to say anything. The new (Z32) body shape was rounded, smooth, and sexy. Ditto inside, like the model of a modern sports car interior. Best yet, the V-6 now had twin cams, 222 horsepower in base form, and a solid 300 when turbocharged. —JL

350Z and 370Z
2002–2009 and 2008–

At the Detroit auto show in 1999, Nissan unveiled the *Z Concept*, an evolutionary interpretation of the original 240Z. Its creation had been a clandestine operation within Nissan's North American headquarters in southern California. The Japanese automaker was struggling financially and had just entered a partnership with Renault of France, which brought in Brazilian-born Carlos Ghosn to lead a Nissan revitalization. In a wonderful twist of fate, it turned out that Ghosn himself had once owned a 240Z. Add in the overwhelming acclaim enjoyed by the *Z Concept* and the car was approved in the form of the stunning 350Z production car and its successor, the 370Z. —LE

- The internal code for the 350Z was Z33; for the 370Z it was Z34.
- The original *Z Concept* was designed by Ajay Panchal.
- A roadster version of the 350Z was unveiled for the 2004 model year.
- The 370Z was equipped with a—you guessed it—3.7-liter V-6.

(350Z):
Engine: 3.5-liter V-6
Horsepower: 287
0–60 mph: 5.5 seconds

Top speed: Est. 155 mph
Price when new: $35,000
Value now: $10,000

Nissan

GT-R

- The GT-R's nickname is Godzilla, and with good reason.

- Nissan's internal chassis code for the car is R35.

- The GT-R set lap records during testing at Germany's famed Nürburgring circuit.

- Nissan invited Polyphony Digital, the producers of the *Grand Turismo* video game series, to participate in the GT-R's development.

Engine: 232 cubic-inch V6	Top speed: Est. 190 mph
Horsepower: 480	Price when new: $81,000
0–60 mph: Est. 3.5 seconds	Value now: Same

The Skyline GT-R is a legend among American automotive enthusiasts. Or maybe *mythical* is a better word—the car was never officially exported to the American market. For the most part, Americans only could dream of driving what was generally regarded as the world's best all-around, all-wheel-drive, all-wheel-steering, twin turbocharged inline six-cylinder sports car. But then, in 2001, at the Tokyo auto show, Nissan showed a concept for a new Skyline GT-R, and four years later it updated the concept and dropped strong hints that not only would the concept go into production, but it would be sold in the United States. In 2007, Nissan showed the production version of the car—the GT-R (no longer Skyline), which in 2008 finally made its way to American shores, ready to tear up the pavement with its twin turbocharged V-6 rated at 480 horsepower—but without all-wheel steering. —*LE*

Nissan

R390 GT1   1997–1998

- Torque came in at 470 lb-ft.

- R390 GT1s featured launch control. . .thank goodness.

- Included is a six-speed sequential transmission.

- It'll cover the quarter-mile in just 11.9 seconds.

Engine: 3.5-liter twin-turbo V-6	**Price when new:** $1,000,000. . .
Horsepower: 550	but good luck buying it
0–60 mph: 3.9 seconds	**Value now:** N/A
Top speed: N/A	

Regulations at the time required an automaker to build at least one street example for its GT1 race cars to qualify for 24 Hours of Le Mans. Nissan went to Tom Walkinshaw Racing in England, where Ian Callum, later Jaguar's design director, shaped the R390 GT1. Callum actually managed to include a sense of Nissan's road cars of the time in the supercar. . .but underneath, it was a mid-engine race car. Nissan didn't win in 1998, but nailed down four of the top ten finishing spots. —JL

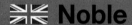
Noble

M600   2010–

- The Volvo/Yamaha V-8 creates 604 lb-ft of torque.

- Noble expects to build 50 M600s each year.

- The gearbox is a six-speed manual.

- The M600 can generate more than 1g on the skid pad.

Engine: 4.4-liter twin-turbo dohc V-8	**Top speed:** 225 mph
Horsepower: 650	**Price when new:** $325,000
0–60 mph: 3.0 seconds	**Value now:** Same

The British firm Noble has been building mid-engine supercars for more than a decade. Their newest is the M600, which wraps a pretty carbon fiber body around a steel space frame. Noble keeps their cars simple; they even make ABS and traction control optional. The result is a lightweight car—2,800 pounds—that is very quick, if not as civilized as, say, a Ferrari or Lamborghini. —JL

General Motors' European arm, Opel, said it had no intention of actually building the sporty little Opel GT concept car it put on display in 1965 at the Paris and Frankfurt auto shows, but three years later the car that looked like a mini-Corvette went into production. The Opel GT, which was sold through Buick dealerships, had a surprisingly roomy interior that included a lever used to manually rotate the hidden headlights into their "on" position. —*LE*

- Opel built 103,373 GTs in the car's relatively brief production run.

- Production of the Opel GT ended when the Opel Kadett on which it was based was redesigned on a new chassis for 1972.

- The GT had no external trunk lid; luggage had to be loaded and unloaded through the driver or passenger doors.

- Bodies for the Opel GT were manufactured by French coachbuilder Brissoneau & Lotz.

Engine: 1.9-liter inline four	**Top speed:** 115 mph
Horsepower: 67	**Price when new:** $3,395
0–60 mph: 12 seconds	**Value now:** $9,300

Yes, a bit obscure, but there has to be an OSCA in this book. The letters stand for Officine Specializzate Construzione Automobili, a company founded by three of the Maserati brothers. They built small-displacement sports cars—from 750 to 1,500cc—but the cars were light and quick. Stirling Moss and Bill Lloyd drove this OSCA MT4 to win the 1954 12 Hours of Sebring overall. Let's hear it for the little guy. —*JL*

- Weight came in at around 1,300 pounds.

- OSCA was eventually sold to the MV Agusta motorcycle company.

- The transmission was a four-speed manual.

- OSCAs were known for the high quality of their construction.

Engine: 1.5-liter ohv inline four	**Top speed:** 116 mph
Horsepower: 130 horsepower	**Price when new:** N/A
0–60 mph: N/A	**Value now:** N/A

Pagani

Zonda F and S   1999–

Horacio Pagani traveled from his native Argentina to work in the exotic car business near Modena, Italy. He went to work for Lamborghini, eventually heading the composite materials department before striking off on his own in 1988. A decade later, Pagani launched the Zonda, a mid-engine supercar of his own design. The shape—made as a coupe or spyder—is meant to suggest the feeling of a jet fighter and is built with a combination of carbon fiber, aluminum, and other lightweight materials. When Pagani went looking for an engine, his countryman (and hero) Juan Manual Fangio suggested he contact Mercedes-Benz. Which is why Zondas are powered by variations of the V-12 from AMG. Both the exterior and interior are noted for their excellent detailing, such as its distinctive four-pipe exhaust. —JL

- *El Zonda* is the name of a seasonal wind that blows down through the Andes Mountains in Argentina.

- Pagani has used Mercedes-AMG V-12s that have ranged from 6.0 to 7.3 liters.

- The body shape is designed to add high-speed downforce.

- The newest Pagani is the $1.4 million Huayra.

Engine: 7.3-liter dohc V-12	**Top speed:** 214 mph
Horsepower: 602	**Price when new:** $1.2 million
0–60 mph: 3.6 seconds	**Value now:** Same

Panoz 🇺🇸

2005   **Esperante GT**

Don Panoz made his fortune in pharmaceuticals, but racing became his passion. He founded the American Le Mans Series, bought the Sebring, Mosport, and Road Atlanta racetracks, and began building cars. One aim was to win races, but his Esperante is also a credible street machine. Powered by Ford-supplied V-8 engines, the Esperante has a front mid-engine layout for optimal weight distribution. —*JL*

- GTLM Esperantes have a 420-horspower supercharged V-8.
- GTS Esperantes are built to SCCA race specs.
- Panoz Esperante race cars have proven themselves at Sebring and Le Mans.
- The torque of the GT's V-8 is 320 lb-ft.

Engine: 4.6-liter dohc V-8	**Top speed:** 150 mph
Horsepower: 305	**Price when new:** $92,256
0–60 mph: 5.1 seconds	**Value now:** $50,000

Parradine 🇬🇧

1990   **Pegasus V-12**

John Parradine was an English millionaire who wanted to build his own automobiles. Designed by Richard Oakes, it had a Kevlar/carbon fiber bodyshell sitting on a tube space frame. Nicely finished outside, the interior was done in fine leathers. . .quite luxurious. Parradine caused a stir with the car, leading to an offer for a factory in France. Sadly, the project died in 1991. —*JL*

- Jaguar was supporting the project.
- Parradine presented the car at the 1990 Geneva show.
- Parradine's original plan called for 50 cars per year.
- It's estimated that 19 cars were built; only two still on the road.

Engine: 5.3-liter dohc V-12	**Top speed:** 173 mph
Horsepower: Est. 330	**Price when new:** N/A
0–60 mph: N/A	**Value now:** $35,000

Z-102   1951–1958

Best known for its trucks and buses, the Spanish firm Pegaso also built sports cars. The Z-102 was designed by Wilfredo Ricart of Alfa Romeo fame, who also did the 1940 mid-engine Alfa 512 Grand Prix car. His engine for the sports car was an all-aluminum V-8 with dual overhead cams. This was done as 2.5, 2.8, or 3.2 liters, some with a supercharger, horsepower ranging from 165 to 360. The five-speed gearbox was mounted in back as a transaxle. To keep weight down the bodies were done in aluminum; the best-looking were designed by Touring in Italy. For all their potential, Pegasos set some speed records, but didn't have a great competition history. However, some of the more flamboyant bodies are well-known on the concours circuit. —JL

- Only 86 Pegaso Z-102s are believed to have been built.
- The rear suspension is a de Dion design.
- Pegaso debuted the Z-102 at the 1951 Paris auto show.
- Z-102s weighed around 2,200 pounds.

Engine: 3.2-liter dohc supercharged V-8	Top speed: 140 mph
	Price when new: N/A
Horsepower: 360	Value now: N/A
0–60 mph: 8.3 seconds	

1967   Ferrari *Dino 206 Competizione*

- Paolo Martin was 23 when he designed the Dino.

- The structure is an aluminum body over a steel space frame.

- This is one of the rare Pininfarina cars to be sold to a private owner.

- The name *Dino* refers to Enzo Ferrari's son.

Engine: 2.0-liter dohc V-6	**Top speed:** N/A
Horsepower: 175	**Price when new:** N/A
0–60 mph: N/A	**Value now:** A great amount

Ever dream of driving a show car on the street? It would be unusual, as few are ever sold, but Pininfarina sold its famous *Dino 206 Competizione* to American James Glickenhaus. Lucky guy. The basis for the 1967 concept car was Dino 206 chassis #10523, a sister to competition 206s that raced throughout Europe. Paolo Martin penned the gullwing body shape that nicely mixes the excitement of the Dino race cars with the 206 production Dino of that time. Unveiled at the 1967 Frankfurt auto show, the aluminum-bodied Competizione was an immediate success. Under that yellow skin is the racing 206 chassis that wasn't well known stateside, but was famous in Europe for often outrunning much larger-engined race cars on tracks like the twisty Nürburgring. —JL

■ Pininfarina

Modulo 1970

Pininfarina's *Modulo* concept car was designed as what Pininfarina called an expression of culture, culture in a world if not changed then certainly affected by the 1969 Academy Award–winning movie *2001: A Space Odyssey*. Designed by Paolo Martin over mechanical components from the Ferrari 512S, *Modulo* stood only three feet tall. It comprised a shell-like body with upper and lower sections and a sliding canopy. The upper and lower sections of the body were joined at a seam that ran around the circumference of the car. To access the cockpit, the front section of the canopy—including the windshield, roof, and side glass—slid forward, and the driver and passenger stepped over the foot-high sills. *Modulo* explored the relationship between full and empty volumes and also modular construction, with the potential for interchangeable body panels to turn the coupe into a convertible or sedan. —LE

- Pininfarina said the *Modulo* featured "intentional geometricity."

- *Modulo* won nearly two dozen design awards and is still considered among the most significant concept cars of its era.

- Technically, the car is considered a Ferrari, but we filed it under Pininfarina for obvious reasons.

- *Modulo* currently resides at the Pininfarina Museum near Turin, Italy.

Engine: 5.0-liter V-12
Horsepower: 550
0–60 mph: N/A
Top speed: N/A

Price when new: Impossible to guess
Value now: Priceless

Pininfarina

Ferrari *Mythos*

Pininfarina's Ferrari concept cars hold a special place on the list of show cars. The Ferrari *Mythos* from 1989 was a jaw-dropper. Based on the production Testarossa, the *Mythos* is such a sublime design, so simple and yet so beautiful. Those side vents feed air to the rear-mounted flat-12 engine. At speed, the rear wing rises, and a front lip spoiler moves out to increase downforce. —JL

- The *Mythos* was debuted at the 1989 Tokyo Motor Show.
- One *Mythos* resides in the Abarth Gallery in Japan.
- It's said the Sultan of Brunei owns two *Mythos*.
- The *Mythos* body and doors are made of carbon fiber.

Engine: 4.9-liter dohc flat 12
Horsepower: 390
0–60 mph: 4.9 seconds
Top speed: 180 mph

Price when new: Impossible to guess
Value now: Priceless

Plymouth/Chrysler

Prowler

Yes, this isn't strictly a sports car, but it's an open two-seater with a lot of flair and fun. Besides, it isn't like its intended audience wrapped their arms around this retro hot rod. They objected to the fact it didn't have a V-8, but no one could deny it is a dramatic design with the front cycle fenders. And it does have an interesting layout, the V-6 power running through a crankshaft-speed driveline to the rear-mounted transmission. —JL

- Much of the chassis is aluminum.
- Early Prowlers are Plymouths, but after that brand was discontinued in 2001 they were sold as Chryslers.
- You could buy a lookalike Prowler trailer to supplement the limited trunk space.
- Chrysler's design chief at the time, Tom Gale, is a well-known hot rodder.

Engine: 3.5-liter sohc V-6
Horsepower: 253
0–60 mph: 5.9 seconds

Top speed: 118 mph
Price when new: $38,300
Value now: $30,000

Pontiac

Fiero   1984–1988

- In Italian, *fiero* is Italian for "proud" or "valiant."

- In Spanish *fiero* means "fierce" or "ferocious."

- The Fiero served as pace car for the 1984 Indianapolis 500-mile race.

- A more powerful V-6–powered GT version was introduced for 1985, and a new Ferrari-style fastback roofline followed in 1986.

Tech specs (base 1984 model):
Engine: 2.5-liter inline four
Horsepower: 92
0–60 mph: 8.5 seconds

Top speed: 105 mph
Price when new: $7,999
Value now: $14,000

Conceived during the gasoline crisis of the late 1970s, the Pontiac Fiero was designed as a fuel-efficient but fun-to-drive car for commuters, one Pontiac hoped would appeal to driving enthusiasts who dreamed of driving a Chevrolet Corvette. To reduce drag and enhance dynamics, the engine—GM's four-cylinder "Iron Duke"—was mounted behind the two seats. Plastic body panels reduced weight. Initially, supply couldn't keep up with demand, but the car had issues (including fires in the engine compartment), and production ended after five model years. —LE

Pontiac

Solstice   2005–2009

- Saturn dealers got their own version of the car, the Sky, for the 2007 model year.

- GM divisions Opel and Daewoo also produced their own versions.

- A high-performance, turbocharged version of the Solstice—the GXP—was introduced as a 2007 model.

- Solstices (or were they Solsti?) won SCCA national sports car racing class championships in Showroom Stock and Touring classes.

Engine: 2.4-liter inline four
Horsepower: 177
0–60 mph: 7.5 seconds

Top speed: 120 mph
Price when new: $20,000
Value now: Est. $16,000

When Bob Lutz became gasoline guru at General Motors, he realized the company needed to be shaken awake; within just a few weeks of taking over, he pushed through the creation of a stunning sports car concept that was unveiled at the Detroit auto show in 2004. Solstice went from concept into production for the 2006 model year and eclipsed the Mazda Miata in styling. GM saw it as a reasonably priced junior Corvette for budding driving enthusiasts, but the car's run ended with Pontiac's dissolution. —LE

Porsche

1949–1965

356 and 356 Continental

- The silver car pictured is the very first 356 built. The white coupe is a Continental.

- Porsche produced 7,627 copies of the original version of the 356.

- The 356A (1955–1959) featured upgraded suspension, steering, and smaller wheels.

- The 356B (1959–1963) and 356C (1963–1965) benefited from revised styling and numerous upgrades to the chassis, engine, and suspension.

Tech specs (original version):	0–60 mph: Est. 14 seconds
Engine: 1.1-liter air-cooled flat four	Top speed: 84 mph
	Price when new: $3,000
Horsepower: 40	Value now: $160,000

Ferdinand Porsche was not only the father of many cars—among them the Volkswagen "Beetle"—he was also the father of Ferdinand "Ferry" Porsche, who after World War II finally put the family name on an automobile. And not just any automobile, but the first in a succession of sports cars that continues to this day. The first Porsche was the 356, so named because it was the 356th design project for the Porsche engineering company. Engineer Karl Rabe and body designer Erwin Komenda worked with "Ferry" Porsche to build a truly sporty car around VW components. They modified the rear-mounted, four-cylinder, air-cooled engine. They enhanced the car's suspension and other components. And they wrapped it all up in stunning coupe, cabriolet, and "speedster" bodywork. In 1955, Porsche produced the 356 Continental, a special version for the car for the American market. However, a lawsuit from Ford, which owned the (Lincoln) Continental name, quickly halted the application of Continental badges to the front fenders of the 356. —LE

Porsche

356 Speedster   1954–1957

In 1952, Porsche produced an upgraded 356 S (Super) called the America. The car was a roadster with a lightweight aluminum body and basically was designed for sports car racing in the United States. Though spartan, the car cost some $4,600. Reportedly, only four were sold to Americans in 1952, and total two-year production was perhaps as few as two dozen. But that didn't deter American importer Max Hoffman, who convinced Porsche to produce yet another racy lightweight, the 356 Speedster. Based on the 356 roadster, the Speedster had a canvas top and side curtains in place of the regular padded convertible top and roll-up windows, and its windshield height was reduced by 3 1/2 inches—and the windshield could be removed for racing. Again, the interior was spartan, but the price was only $3,000. The Speedsters handled well, were relatively quick up to 80 miles per hour, and did very well in amateur sports car racing. —LE

- Bengt Sonderstrom drove a Porsche Speedster to the SCCA F-Production national championship in 1955.

- While the 356 Americas had aluminum bodies, the 356 Speedsters had steel shells.

- A speedometer and temperature gauge were the only standard gauges in the 356 Speedster, though seemingly every one of them was equipped with an optional tach.

- Porsche built more than 4,000 356 Speedsters.

Tech specs (1500 Super):
Engine: 1.5-liter air-cooled flat four
Horsepower: 70

0–60 mph: Est. 10 seconds
Top speed: 106 mph
Price when new: $3,000
Value now: $210,000

1953–1955   **550 Spyder**

- The 550 Spyder was so low-slung that Hans Herrmann reportedly drove it beneath a railroad crossing gate during the 1954 Mille Miglia.

- Zora Arkus-Duntov was one of the drivers of the Le Mans class–winning Porsche 550 Spyder of 1954.

- Legendary actor James Dean was driving a 550 Spyder when he died in a crash on a California highway.

- Porsche reportedly built some 70 examples of the 550 Spyder.

Tech specs (1.5-liter):	0–60 mph: N/A
Engine: 1.5-liter air-cooled flat four	Top speed: 135 mph
	Price when new: N/A
Horsepower: 135	Value now: $1 million+

Spurred on by the 356's success in racing, Porsche created a special version of the car, called the 550 Spyder, in 1953. With a lighter but stronger space-frame chassis and a 130-horsepower engine, the 550 Spyder (actually, the lighter but stronger 1956 550A version) secured Porsche's first major racing victory when Umberto Maglioli beat a Maserati by some 15 minutes to win the 1956 Targa Florio. But the Spyder had made a big impression even before that victory. A 550 coupe won the 1,101–1,500cc class in the 24 Hours of Le Mans in 1953, and a Spyder repeated that feat in 1954. Then, in 1955, 550 Spyders won not only their class but two other categories as well by finishing third, fourth, and fifth overall at Le Mans behind a pair of Jaguars and an Aston Martin. —*LE*

Porsche

911 Carrera (Type 997) 2005–

For the 2005 model year, Porsche introduced its next-generation 911 (code 997), and for the first time since 1977, the car was available with the buyer's choice of two engines. The 911 Carrera came with a 325-horsepower 3.6-liter six-cylinder engine, while the 911 Carrera S carried a 3.8-liter flat six with 355 horsepower. The cars were available as coupes or convertibles. Like its predecessor, the 996, this 911 had a liquid rather than air-cooled powertrain. Compared to the 996, the 997 had a wider stance, variable-ratio steering, a new six-speed manual transmission and new computerized suspension controls, and an onboard lap-timer. Standard equipment on the 2005 911s included the new Porsche Active Suspension Management technology with normal and sport modes. In testing on Germany's Nürburgring, the sport setting reduced lap times by five seconds. —LE

- To make the 911 lighter and even more nimble, it came without a spare tire.

- Jeremy Clarkson wrote that driving the 997 "is like making love to someone you care for in the bridal suite of the George V hotel in Paris."

- For the first time, Porsche developed the 997 coupe and convertible simultaneously, instead of starting with the coupe.

- The 2005 911 Carrera and Carrera S convertibles introduced side airbags that emerged from the window sills in case of an impact.

Engine: 3.6-liter boxer six-cylinder
Horsepower: 325
0–60 mph: Est. 4.9 seconds
Top speed: Est. 177 mph
Price when new: $69,300
Value now: $35,000

2010 — 911 GT3 R Hybrid

- The GT3 is the high-performance racing version of the Porsche 911, dating to the 1971 911 RS model.

- The GT3 name comes from a racing class for normally aspirated cars.

- The car also raced in a 24-hour event at the Nürburgring, leading the field for more than 8 hours and completing 22 hours, 15 minutes of the overall event.

- Porsche reportedly worked with the Williams F1 team in developing the flywheel energy system.

Engine: 4.0-liter flat six, plus two 60 kW electric motors
Horsepower: 480 (engine)
0–60 mph: Est. 3.5 seconds
Top speed: Est. 193 mph
Price when new: N/A
Value now: N/A

Early in 2010, and 110 years after Ferdinand Porsche engineered what is considered the original hybrid vehicle—the Lohner Porsche—the company that bears the Porsche family name rolled out the newest version of its 911-based GT3 racers, a GT3 R with a hybrid drivetrain. While a 480-horsepower flat six-cylinder engine powers the rear wheels of the GT3 R, a pair of 60-kilowatt electric motors turns the front axle. By the way, those motors aren't turned by traditional batteries but by an electrical flywheel power generator that resides inside the car next to the driver's seat. Porsche said the flywheel generator is basically an electric motor with a rotor capable of spinning at speeds of 40,000 rpm. The rotor stores energy mechanically and is charged whenever the brakes are applied. The power stored in the flywheel system can be used to boost the car's horsepower for a 6–8-second burst. The system also reduces fuel consumption, even in racing conditions. —LE

911 Speedster (Type 997)   2011

At the Paris auto show in 2010, Porsche unveiled the 911 Speedster, an homage to the original 356 Speedster. The homage included the fact that only 356 such cars would be built. The 911 Speedster is energized by a 408-horsepower version of the 3.8-liter flat six-cylinder engine. The two-seat car features a shortened and more dynamically raked windshield, double-hump tonneau cover, wider rear bodywork, and special front spoiler and rocker sills. The new Speedster is the fourth version of Porsche Speedsters. The first was the 356 Speedster in 1953. Next came the 911 Carrera-based Speedster of 1988. The third Speedster was produced in 1993–1994. The fourth Speedster was designed to coincide with the 25th anniversary of the Porsche Exclusive department that specializes in the individualization of all Porsche models and in the creation of limited-edition series. A special "Pure Blue" exterior paint color was created for the latest version of the Porsche Speedster, though the car also will be available in Carrera White. —LE

- The top of the windshield in the 911 Speedster is 1.73 inches lower than in the standard 911.

- Among special options available on the new Porsche Speedster are hand-finished, smooth-finish leather seats with checkerboard-pattern seating area and side bolsters in the car's exterior color.

- The new Porsche Speedsters are equipped only with Porsche's double-clutch PDK transmission.

- Standard equipment for the new Porsche Speedster includes Porsche Active Suspension Management and Porsche Ceramic brakes.

Engine: 3.8-liter flat six	**Top speed:** Est. 190 mph
Horsepower: 408	**Price when new:** $204,000
0–60 mph: Est. 4.2 seconds	**Value now:** Same

- The 911 pictured is a 1988 3.3-liter model.

- In addition to the characteristic whale tail, some turbocharged 911s featured aerodynamically enhanced "slant nose" front ends.

- A turbocharged 911, the Carrera RSR, finished second overall at Le Mans in 1974, and by 1977 Porsche was producing turbocharged, 911-based 935 race cars to teams competing in various sports car series.

- The 2011 Porsche 911 Turbo provides drivers with 500 horsepower, sprints to 60 mph in 3.2 seconds, and can reach a top speed of 194 mph.

Tech specs (1988 3.3-liter U.S.):	0–60 mph: Est. 5.5 seconds
Engine: 3.3-liter turbocharged flat six	Top speed: Est. 157 mph
	Price when new: $69,300
Horsepower: 282	Value now: $39,000

In 1975 in Europe and the following year in the United States, Porsche offered a turbocharged version of its 911 sports car. Sold as the Turbo Carrera, the car was known within Porsche as the 930, and was known on the streets as the "whale tail" because of its enlarged rear spoiler. While the normally aspirated 911 provided 157 horsepower, the turbocharged version boasted 234. By 1978, the engine had been enlarged and power boosted to 253. But the fun was short-lived. Because of U.S. emission regulations, Porsche withdrew the 930 from the American auto market after the 1979 model year. But for 1988 the Porsche 911 Turbo was back, and now with 282 emission-legal horsepower. Again, however, the car's availability was brief, offered only in 1988 and 1989. —LE

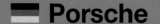

Porsche

911 Turbo S (Type 997) 2011–

At Geneva in 2010, and after a five-year absence from the lineup, Porsche brought back a 911 Turbo S model, in both coupe and cabriolet body styles. The Turbo S gets boosts of 30 horsepower and 37 lb-ft of torque over the non-S Turbos, yet the car is rated at 25 miles per gallon when cruising at highway speeds. Also standard on the Turbo S are all-wheel drive, Porsche's seven-speed, twin-clutch PDK gearbox, ceramic brakes, dynamic engine mounts, torque vectoring with a standing mechanical differential lock on the rear axle, launch control, dynamic cornering lights, center-lock RS Spyder wheels, and adaptive sports seats. The interior features two-tone leather in black and cream or black and titanium blue. —LE

- Porsche has said that about 30 to 40 percent of its Turbo customers upgrade their cars with optional carbon-ceramic brakes.

- The Turbo S was created to compete against the Ferrari 458 Italia, Audi R8 V-10, Lamborghini Gallardo LP560-4, and the Mercedes-Benz SLS AMG.

- Torque is 516 lb-ft.

- In 2011, Porsche offered 19 different 911 variants, from the "base" 911 Carrera to the 911 GT3 RS racer.

Engine: 3.8-liter turbocharged flat six-cylinder
Horsepower: 530
0–60 mph: Est. 3.1 seconds
Top speed: Est. 195 mph
Price when new: $160,000
Value now: Same

- The 914 was available with a four-cylinder engine or as the 914/6 with a boxer six.

- In Europe, the 914 was considered not only a replacement for the Porsche 912 but for the VW Karmann Ghia. In the U.S., it was badged only as a Porsche.

- Karmann built the bodies for both the VW and Porsche versions.

- Two eight-cylinder 914/8s were built in 1969. One was tested as a possible racer; the other was presented to Ferry Porsche for his 60th birthday.

Engine: 1.7-liter flat four	Top speed: Est. 110 mph
Horsepower: 80	Price when new: $3,600
0–60 mph: Est. 12 seconds	Value now: $15,000

In the mid-1960s, Porsche introduced an entry-level version of its 911. Called the 912, the car looked like a regular 911, but had a four-cylinder rather than six-cylinder engine. The car didn't really thrill anyone. So, at the Frankfurt auto show in 1969, Porsche showed a new entry-level car, the 914. This car was no faux 911. In fact, it was a collaboration between Porsche and Volkswagen, although it didn't look like either parent. The mid-engine 914 had its own unique, extremely low-slung design, dominated by seemingly board-flat surfaces instead of graceful curves. The roof was a removable Targa top, allowing the car to be driven open or closed. —LE

918 Spyder   2013–

At the Geneva auto show in 2010, Porsche unveiled the 918 Spyder, its concept for a plug-in hybrid supercar. A year later, it began accepting orders (cost: $845,000) with production, limited to 918 cars, scheduled to begin in September 2013. Exact specifications are still to be determined, but propulsion will come via a V-8 engine of at least 4.0 liters with 500-plus horsepower; this will be assisted by a pair of electric motors that will together add another 218 horsepower to the equation. Porsche says the car will be able to sprint to 60 miles per hour in 3.1 seconds yet will also be capable of traveling up to 16 miles on battery power alone; in routine road driving, the 918 may get something in the range of 80 miles per gallon. —*LE*

- In the ultimate package deal, buyers who pay $1 million will receive both a Spyder and a special edition 911 Turbo with the same production number.

- The V-8 engine will be based on the Porsche RS Spyder mill that has raced at the 24 Hours of Le Mans.

- Porsche says it expects the 918 Spyder to lap the Nürburgring two seconds faster than Porsche's previous supercar, the Carrera GT.

- With an electric motor for each axle—front and rear—the 918 Spyder will feature all-wheel drive.

(estimated):
Engine: 4.0-liter V-8 with two electric motors
Horsepower: 718

0–60 mph: 3.1 seconds
Top speed: Est. 199 mph
Price when new: $845,000
Value now: Same

- The 928 was designed by Tony Lapine, a Russian native and head of Porsche's automotive design studio.

- The 928 featured Porsche's most luxurious interior with a glove box cooled by the car's air-conditioning system.

- In the early 1980s, Porsche introduced a 928 S version with a larger and more powerful V-8 engine.

- The car pictured is a 1987 S4.

(1987 S4):	
Engine: 5.0-liter V-8	**Top speed:** Est. 168 mph
Horsepower: 320	**Price when new:** $28,500
0–60 mph: 6.4 seconds	**Value now:** $15,000

In the early 1970s, the Porsche 911 was approaching its second decade, and Ralph Nader had Americans worried about rear-engined cars. Looking to try something new and different, the company developed a front-engined car, one with—oh, by the way—American-style V-8. Porsche unveiled the 928 at the Geneva auto show in 1977, not as replacement for the 911, but to be sold alongside it. Although the styling was not to everyone's taste, the 928 was an excellent performer. It was fast—at one point it was the fastest car sold in the United States—but it also was expensive. When it was introduced it cost as much as a Ferrari 308 GTB and more than twice as much as a Chevrolet Corvette. —*LE*

Porsche

944   1982–1991

In 1977, Porsche replaced its entry-level 914 with the 924, which featured a Volkswagen/Audi four-cylinder engine mounted in front of the passenger compartment. By the early 1980s, Porsche had developed its own liquid-cooled four-cylinder engine—basically one half of the block from the 928's V-8—and bolted this to a reworked and restyled 924 platform to create the 944. The new car was not only faster than the 924, it was faster to 60 miles per hour than the turbocharged 924. In 1986, Porsche offered a turbocharged version, which boosted horsepower from 188 to 217. Soon after, a 944 S was inserted between the normally spirated and turbocharged versions; it got the unblown engine—though with twin cam, 16-valve heads and several turbo styling features. Next to join the lineup were a 944 Turbo S with more than 240 horsepower and, finally, a 944 convertible. —LE

- The 944 pictured is a 1989 Turbo.

- The 924 had originally been designed by Porsche to be a Volkswagen model.

- The 944 was never a rocket, but the automotive press praised its balanced handling.

- Porsche was working on a third-generation, 944 S3 version of the car but halted development to work on the 944's replacement, the 968.

Tech specs (1989 Turbo):
Engine: 2.5-liter inline four
Horsepower: 220
0–60 mph: 6.5 seconds
Top speed: 162 mph
Price when new: $19,000
Value now: $6,000

- Porsche built more than 300 examples—prototypes and production units—of the 959.

- Porsche showed a concept for the 959 at the Frankfurt show in 1983 and the production version two years later.

- The 959 was not certified for use on American streets until 2003, when Bruce Canepa tweaked the powertrain for U.S. emission regulations.

- Microsoft's Bill Gates and Paul Allen were early 959 owners, as was comedian Jerry Seinfeld, even though they couldn't legally drive their cars.

Engine: 2.9-liter twin turbocharged flat six	**Top speed:** Nearly 200 mph
Horsepower: 444	**Price when new:** $225,000
0–60 mph: 4 seconds	**Value now:** $350,000

Today, a car with a sequential twin turbocharged engine, six-speed transmission, four-wheel drive, tire-pressure monitors, and computer-controlled suspension that adjusts for various road and weather conditions might seem ordinary, but in 1989 the Porsche 959 was revolutionary. Here was a supercar that could approach speeds of 200 miles per hour on pavement—the road-racing 961 version was seventh overall and first in the GTX class in the 24 Hours of Le Mans—yet it also won the grueling Paris-Dakar off-road rally race. In fact, 959s were 1–2 at the finish in the race across the desert dunes of northwest Africa. The 959 was built around a six-cylinder "boxer" engine that combined an air-cooled block with liquid-cooled heads and turbochargers. The engine was developed for the "whale-tailed" 930 race car and was modified for Porsche's Indy car racing effort. —LE

Boxster Spyder — 2010–

There have been minimalist Porsches before—the original Speedster, for example—so when Porsche stripped the Boxster down by 176 pounds it was no surprise. They started with the top, replaced by a two-piece fabric affair that weighs a mere 13 pounds and takes a bit of work to erect, but holds out the water. When it's down—as it should be whenever possible—you get a pair of slick headrests for driver and passenger. Thanks to such items as aluminum doors and a smaller fuel tank, still more weight is shed. To trim still more, choose the carbon fiber seats and ask Porsche to forsake the radio and air conditioning system...all part (or, rather, not part) of the Spyder package. That's the sort of thinking that makes this the lightest Porsche in their fleet and helps explain the 0–60 mph time of 4.1 seconds. —LE

- The Boxster Spyder's curb weight is less than 3,000 pounds.
- Using a canvas top allowed designers to save an estimated 33 pounds compared to a typical convertible roof.
- Door handles, cup holders, and storage containers are all absent in an effort to keep weight down.
- The car's standard exterior paint options—Carrara White, Guards Red, and Black—all harken back to Porsches of the 1960s.

Engine: 3.4-liter 24-valve dohc flat six
Horsepower: 320
0–60 mph: 4.1 seconds
Top speed: 160 mph
Price when new: $62,150
Value now: Same

- The Carrera GT's fiber-reinforced plastic monocoque "tub" chassis weighs a mere 220 pounds.

- The car's internal code was 980.

- The Carrera GT can sprint from 0 to 100 and then stop within 882 feet.

- The cars were built entirely by hand at Porsche's Leipzig factory.

Engine: 5.7-liter V-10	**Top speed:** 205 mph
Horsepower: 605	**Price when new:** $440,000
0–60 mph: Est. 3.9 seconds	**Value now:** $350,000

In the late 1990s, Porsche's racing department had a new 10-cylinder, 5.5-liter engine in development in anticipation of a return to Le Mans. But Porsche had more pressing matters with which to contend—namely, the company's financial and corporate independence—so instead of racing at Le Mans, Porsche raced to produce the Cayenne sport utility vehicle, which may not have looked like a Porsche but kept the company in business and independent. But the work done on that new engine didn't really go to waste. It simply went into an all-new Porsche supercar, the Carrera GT, which was presented as a concept on the eve of the 2000 Paris auto show and then went into production for the 2003 model year. In production, the engine was enlarged to 5.7 liters and boosted to more than 600 horsepower, enough to propel the car to 205 miles per hour. —LE

Cayman R   2010–

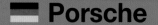

For the 2006 model year, Porsche added a new sports car to its model line. Based on the mid-engine Boxster roadster, the Cayman S was a coupe so aerodynamically slick that it had some people wondering if the 911's days were numbered. They weren't. The 911 was still king of the garage at Porsche. Nonetheless, the Cayman was more than just some new kid on the block. In 2010, Porsche launched an even-higher-performance version called the Cayman R. While the R shares its 3.4-liter boxer six-cylinder engine with the Cayman S, the R lump is tuned to provide 10 more horsepower. Combined with a lower suspension to reduce the drag and increase downforce, along with some weight trimming and—*voila!*—performance is enhanced. Porsche says the Cayman R sprints to 60 miles per hour a full two-tenths of a second faster than the Cayman S. —*LE*

- The lighter Cayman R has a 14.3-gallon rather than the standard 17.1-gallon fuel tank.

- Aluminum doors and lightweight wheels also made the car lighter.

- Weight is also reduced inside the Cayman R with a basic dashboard, pull-strap door handles, and lighter seats.

- Air conditioning and a radio are not standard equipment on the Cayman R.

Engine: 3.4-liter flat six	Top speed: 175 mph
Horsepower: 330	Price when new: $66,300
0–60 mph: 4.6 seconds	Value now: Same

- The Panamera's powertrains are so efficient that no version carries a gas-guzzler tax.

- For minimal consumption, the car's start/stop technology allows the engine to shut down when the car is stopped.

- The Panamera was designed to include back seats that could handle someone as tall as 6 feet 6 inches.

- The Panamera launched with normally aspirated and turbocharged V-8s.

(Turbo):
Engine: 4.8-liter twin-turbocharged V-8
Horsepower: 500

0–60 mph: Est. 4.0 seconds
Top speed: 188 mph
Price when new: $132,600
Value now: Same

Even with the financial success of its Cayenne, the vehicle that finally put the sport into sport utility, people were skeptical when Porsche announced plans to build its first four-door sports car, the Panamera. Skeptical, that is, until they actually drove one and discovered that this luxurious four-door sedan was, indeed, not only sporty enough to be considered a sports car, but was *indeed* a Porsche in both its design and its dynamics. And while those back seats were roomy and luxurious, the car's dynamics ensured that driving enthusiasts wanted to sit only where they could have the steering wheel in their hands. The Panamera launched with engines ranging up to a twin-turbocharged, 500-horsepower V-8 with a Formula One–style launch system that provides absolute acceleration that has rarely, if ever, been enjoyed by as many as four people and their luggage. —LE

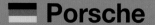

Type 64   1938

Alphabetical order requires us to run the very first Porsche last. Before World War II, a number of city-to-city races were held in Europe, and for the 1939 Berlin-to-Rome event, Ferdinand Porsche designed the Type 64. The thinking was that, as many of the miles were on Germany's new Autobahn system, smooth aerodynamics would be an advantage. And so Porsche shaped the rear-engined racing coupe to slip through the air with a shape resembling the Volkswagen but also presaging the form of the 356 that would come along after the war. Sadly, the car never had a chance to compete, as the outbreak of war canceled the event. —*JL*

- Only three Porsche 64s were built.
- Weight? A mere 1,100 pounds.
- The surviving Type 64 is in Porsche's museum in Germany.
- A four-gear nonsynchro gearbox was used.

Engine: 1.1-liter flat four	**Top speed:** 81 mph
Horsepower: 32	**Price when new:** N/A
0–60 mph: N/A	**Value now:** N/A

1965 — R380

Before the Prince automobile company was combined with Nissan, it created the first of the Skyline series. When a Skyline was defeated by a Porsche 904 in the second Japanese Grand Prix, Prince purpose-built the mid-engine R380, using a 200-horsepower version of the Skyline engine. In the 1966 GP, the R380s defeated the Porsche 906s. When Nissan merged Prince in 1966, Nissan continued to develop the car as the R380-II with a new exterior design. —JL

- R380s were used to set land speed records.
- A five-speed Hewland gearbox was behind the inline six.
- This is the first of the modern Japanese pure race cars.
- The R380 weighed 1,452 pounds.

Engine: 2.0-liter dohc inline six	Top speed: N/A
Horsepower: 200	Price when new: N/A
0–60 mph: N/A	Value now: N/A

Qvale ▮

2000–2002 — Mangusta

- The Mangusta had front-engine rear-wheel-drive layout.
- Marcello Gandini did the exterior design.
- The chassis was designed by ex–F1 designer Enrique Scalabroni.
- A-arm suspensions were used front and rear.

Engine: 4.6-liter dohc V-8	Top speed: 158 mph
Horsepower: 320	Price when new: $78,900
0–60 mph: 5.3 seconds	Value now: $36,500

Originally meant to be a De Tomaso created in the spirit of the TVR Griffith, funding problems put the car in the hands of the Qvale family. The well-known San Francisco-based Qvales proceeded with the production of the car in Modena, Italy. Powered by a Ford V-8, the car had a unique top with a removable center section and a rear glass area that would rotate behind the seats. —JL

 **Ruf**

CTR 3   2007–

- Torque is an impressive 657 lb-ft.

- There's a sequential-shift six-speed transmission.

- Each turbo has its own intercooler.

- The interior is finished in leather and Alcantara.

Engine: 3.8-liter twin-turbo flat six
Horsepower: 700
0–60 mph: 3.1 seconds

Top speed: 234 mph
Price when new: $525,000
Value now: Same

Although Germany's Ruf Automobile is famous for its rear-engine models based on Porsche's 911, it also has a "homebuilt" mid-engine machine, the CTR 3. Basis for the supercar is a steel structure with a built-in rollcage. Most of the bodywork is of Kevlar–carbon fiber. The suspension is a MacPherson strut–type up front, the rear a race-type with pushrod-actuated shocks. The whole package weighs 3,086 pounds. —JL

 Ruf

CTR "Yellowbird"   1987–1996

Easily the most famous of Ruf's various tuned Porsches, the Yellowbird—as it's affectionately known—set the tone for an entire career in making fast cars go faster still. It was and remains one of the craziest road cars you could ever wish to drive, its twin turbo 3.4-liter flat six producing 469 horsepower in an era when 350 horsepower seemed like 50 too much in a car as small and light as a 2,579-pound Porsche 911. —SS

- The name "Yellowbird" was coined by *Road & Track* magazine testers.

- Ruf filmed a famous video of the Yellowbird being driven around the Nürburgring by a gentleman known as Dr. Drift.

- The car was based on a 1987 model year Porsche 911, not a 930 as has occasionally been reported.

- The car recorded a 0–100 mph time of 7.8 seconds and 0–125 mph in 11.4 seconds, and once held the road car lap record at the Nürburgring.

Engine: 3.4-liter twin turbocharged flat six
Horsepower: 469
0–60 mph: 3.7 seconds

Top speed: 211 mph
Price when new: $223,000
Value now: $300,000

- The V-8 has a 180-degree "flatcrank" crankshaft.

- The RGT-8's torque is 369 lb-ft.

- Ruf adds a six-speed manual gearbox.

- The brakes are carbon ceramic.

Engine: 4.5-liter dohc V-8
Horsepower: 550
0–60 mph: N/A

Top speed: N/A
Price when new: In production soon
Value now: N/A

Alois Ruf is legendary for the manner in which he has been modifying Porsches for decades. After years of upping the horsepower of the famous flat sixes from Zuffenhausen, Ruf created his own engine. It fits in the back of the 911-based machine, a lightweight and compact V-8 packing 4.5 liters and 550 horsepower and looking quite natural under the 911's rear deck lid. —JL

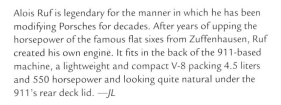

Ruf

Rt12 — 2004–

Alois Ruf is not a man who does things by halves, although lately his wild interpretations of production-ready Porches have, it must be said, begun to show a sign of greater maturity. And the Rt12 is perhaps the very best of them so far, partly because it represents an entire model range of upgrades available on the 997 version of the 911. The most potent of these is the infamous (and utterly insane) 685-horsepower version of the 997 GT2, a car so fast in a straight line that it'll easily take care of any road car made by Ferrari in 2011. Top speed is said to be 220 miles per hour with a 0–60 time of 3.2 seconds. Ask Herr Ruf to fit taller gearing and the car is then good for 227 miles per hour—and all at a snip of the price of an Enzo Ferrari at "just" $400,000. —SS

- You can have a 530-, 560-, or 685-horsepower version of the Ruf Rt12.
- The model was introduced at the Essen motorshow in 2004, just after the 997 911 had gone on sale.
- The 3.6 engine is bored out to 3.8 liters.
- Ruf offers an upgrade on the factory carbon-ceramic brakes, just as well with a 227 mph top speed.

Engine: 3.8-liter twin-turbocharged flat six
Horsepower: 685
0–60 mph: 3.2 seconds
Top speed: 219 mph
Price when new: $400,000
Value now: Same

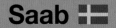
1966–1974   **Sonnet**

- The cars pictured here are Sonnet IIs.

- *Saab* is short for "Svenska Aeroplan AB" and was created in 1937 to build aircraft for the Swedish air force.

- Saab's first attempt at a sports car was the Sonett I, a fiberglass-bodied roadster produced in 1956–1957.

- Sonnet sales may have been hurt by an American advertising campaign that noted that *Sonett* was Swedish for "expensive toy."

(Sonnet II):	
Engine: 1.5-liter Ford V-4	**Top speed:** 90 mph
Horsepower: 65	**Price when new:** $3,500
0–60 mph: Est. 15 seconds	**Value now:** $20,000

Saab launched its idea of a sports car late in 1966, when it also introduced four-stroke engines to its powertrain lineup. The front-wheel drive Sonnet shared many mechanical components with the new Monte Carlo 850 sports coupe, including a 60-horsepower, three-cylinder engine, and in 1968 a 73-horsepower V-4 from Ford of Germany. Technically, this was the Sonnet II. In 1970, Saab introduced the redesigned, smoother, and longer Sonnet III with hidden (pop-up) headlights and a larger V-4. —*LE*

Saleen

S7   2000–2004

Steve Saleen was already famous for his modified Mustangs when he decided to build a mid-engine exotic car. Phil Frank penned the dramatic exterior—which is formed in carbon fiber—with its swing-up doors. Ray Mallock in England developed the mid-engine chassis. Though it looks like a race car, the S7 has a leather-upholstered—if tight—interior. Needless to say, the S7 is a hoot to drive, but Saleen went one step further with a twin turbo version that had 750 horsepower and 700 lb-ft of torque. Now 60 miles per hour comes up in 2.8 seconds on to a top speed of 248. Next came a racing version of the Twin Turbo with some 1,000 horsepower. Pure racing editions are called S7-Rs and accumulated an impressive list of wins, mostly in Europe. —JL

- Torque of the nonturbo engine was 525 lb-ft.
- Price of the S7 included first-class airfare to the factory to be fitted to the car.
- Curb weight: 2,870 pounds.
- The quarter-mile goes by in 11.8 seconds at 120 mph.

Engine: 7.0-liter ohv V-8
Horsepower: 550
0–60 mph: 3.3 seconds

Top speed: 220 mph
Price when new: $395,000
   (original nonturbo)
Value now: $550,000

Saleen 🇺🇸

2010   SMS 570 Challenger

Steve Saleen's newest company, SMS, will add horsepower to your Mustang, Camaro, or, here, Dodge Challenger. The "basic" car, the 570, has a 500-horsepower supercharged 5.7-liter V-8, while a step up is the 700-horsepower blown 6.4-liter Hemi in the 570X. Best gearbox choice for either engine is the six-speed Tremec manual. To go with the added power, SMS adds its own specific shocks, springs, and anti-roll bars. —JL

- Torque? 570: 520 lb-ft; 570X: 650 lb-ft.
- Good idea: Order the optional $2,000 integrated radar detector.
- SMS will custom-paint your SMS Challenger for $18,000.
- The Mustang and Camaro models are the SMS 302 and SMS 620, respectively.

Engine: 5.7-liter supercharged ohv V-8	Top speed: N/A
Horsepower: 500	Price when new: $67,581
0–60 mph: 4.5 seconds	Value now: Same

Sbarro ➕

2010   Autobau

Franco Sbarro is a Swiss designer whose display vehicles and technical ideas at each year's Geneva auto show range from the sublime to the strange. The latter would include the Autobau from 2010. How do you get into this odd machine? The center section of the car tilts forward and you settle into semi-reclining seats. Mounted behind the cockpit is a Ferrari V-12. Very strange. —JL

- Sbarro built the Autobau to honor Swiss race driver Fredy Lienhard.
- Franco Sbarro founded his company in 1971.
- The car was designed by Sbarro but built by students.
- Weight of the Autobau is around 3,200 pounds.

Engine: Ferrari V-12	Price when new: What would you pay for this?
Horsepower: 550	
0–60 mph: Est. 4.5 seconds	Value now: Same
Top speed: Est. 120 mph	

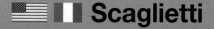

Scaglietti

Three well-known American racers, Carroll Shelby, Jim Hall, and Gary Laughlin, figured it was possible to compete against Enzo Ferrari with an American-based car. So they shipped three 1959 Corvette chassis to Modena, Italy, and convinced longtime Ferrari bodymaker Sergio Scaglietti to build bodies for the chassis. As always, Scaglietti's work was magic, and the result looked rather like a Ferrari 250 Tour de France. Problem was that General Motors refused to get behind the project. Shelby went off and worked with Ford, eventually creating the Cobra. Hall put his efforts behind his highly successful Chaparral project. And Gary Laughlin tells us the quality of the finished machine was not up to his expectations. Still, the car is beautiful, and being some 400 pounds lighter than a stock Corvette, it is quick. —*JL*

- Sergio Scaglietti had to work to keep the Corvette project a secret from Enzo Ferrari.
- Car number one was finished in Italy, while the others were completed in the United States.
- The interior is classic Italian for the era, with gauges stretching across the dashboard.
- The project took three years, and the first car didn't arrive in the United States until 1961.

Engine: 283-cubic-inch Chevrolet V-8
Horsepower: 315
0–60 mph: N/A

Top speed: N/A
Price when new: $9,200
Value now: $750,000

- The 4.3-liter (260-cubic-inch) Cobra V-8 has 269 lb-ft of torque.

- The 4.7-liter (289-cubic-inch) Cobra V-8 has 314 lb-ft of torque.

- Shelby introduced the first Cobra at the 1962 New York auto show.

- The first of the many Cobra race wins came in January 1963.

Engine: 260-cubic-inch ohv V-8	Top speed: 145 mph
Horsepower: 260	Price when new: $5,995
0–60 mph: 5.5 seconds	Value now: $500,000

After General Motors turned him down, retired race driver Carroll Shelby went to Ford looking for a small V-8 that he could install in the AC Ace to create a new sports car. Ford saw a chance to trump the Corvette and agreed to supply its new thin-wall, 260-horsepower V-8. This became the first series Cobra, which weighed in just over 2,000 pounds and had (for then) fierce acceleration. Thus began the Shelby Cobra legend, on both roads and tracks throughout the world. The second series Cobras used a 289-cubic-inch, 271-horsepower V-8. Both ends of the car have an independent suspension with a transverse leaf spring. Cobras are quick, of course, but also look the part and have very faithful owners clubs. —JL

When the small-block Cobra wasn't quick enough, Carroll Shelby and Ford developed the next series, the famous Cobra 427 with a 7.0-liter V-8. The car looks faster with its widened body and fat tires filling the wheelwells. The changes added only a few hundred pounds, and the big engine knocks more than a second off the 289's 0–60 time. To go with the added power, the 427 has a stiffer frame and coil spring suspension all around. Like the 289, the 427 Cobra was as famous on the track as on the road, and the sight of a well-driven 427 drifting around a quick corner is a sight to be relished. For all its excitement, the 427 was not a financial success, but it has been a historical success and remains the most treasured of the street Cobras. —JL

- The 427 Cobras have 480 lb-ft of torque.

- Shelby's personal supercharged 800-horsepower Super Snake Cobra sold at auction for $5.5 million.

- Some "427" Cobras have tamer 428-cubic-inch V-8s.

- Production of the Cobra 427s began on January 1, 1965.

Engine: 7.0-liter ohv V-8	Top speed: 165 mph
Horsepower: 425	Price when new: $7,495
0–60 mph: 4.2 seconds	Value now: $1 million

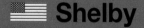

Shelby

Cobra Daytona coupe   1964–1965

Carroll Shelby wanted to beat Enzo Ferrari on his home turf, Europe, but the standard Cobra body was too aerodynamically inefficient. To go against the likes of the Ferrari 250GTO, Shelby had Peter Brock design an aero body that is smooth and rounded with a flat Kamm rear end. Powered by the 4.7-liter Ford V-8 the Cobra coupes went on to win their class in, among other events, the 24 Hours of Le Mans, 12 Hours of Sebring, and the 24 Hours of Daytona. Better yet, the coupe allowed Shelby to beat Ferrari in the 1965 World Manufacturers Championship. Six Daytona Coupes were built, and several are used regularly in vintage races such as the Rolex Monterey Motorsports Reunion at Mazda Raceway Laguna Seca. —JL

- The Daytona Coupes have the transverse-leaf suspension of the 289 Cobras.
- Designer Peter Brock penned the Daytona Coupe and the original Corvette Stingray race car.
- One Daytona Super Coupe with a 427 was started, the project was abandoned, and was then completed in 1981.
- Carroll Shelby is one of the world's oldest and longest-living heart transplant recipients.

Engine: 4.7-liter ohv V-8	Top speed: 191 mph
Horsepower: 385	Price when new: N/A
0–60 mph: 4.4 seconds	Value now: $8 million

- The six-speed transmission was rear-mounted in the transaxle.
- The minimal interior had no radio or air conditioning.
- How about 501 lb-ft of torque?
- Curb weight was 3,075 pounds.

Engine: 6.4-liter dohc V-10	Top speed: 260 mph (theoretical)
Horsepower: 605	Price when new: N/A
0–60 mph: 3.9 seconds	Value now: N/A

Hey, if wishes were fishes, eh? At the 2004 Detroit auto show, Ford presented its interpretation of a modern Shelby Cobra. It all seems like a pipe dream now, but at the time it seemed so real. This was because Ford dipped into the Ford GT program to commonize as much as possible. . .which had us hoping for Cobra production. Even though the GT had a midmounted engine, Ford was able to adapt much of its structure to the front-engine Cobra. Also adapted was the independent suspension, the Brembo brakes, and the steering rack. With crosstown rival Chrysler using a V-10 in its Viper, Ford did the same for the Cobra, creating a V-10 from its family of modular engines. Best of all, arguably, was the exterior, which looked like the Cobra updated. . .but alas. —*JL*

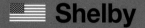
Ford Mustang GT500   2010–

Yes, it is a Mustang, but it will run rings around many two-seater sports cars. Here's why: Begin with the all-aluminum supercharged V-8 and its 550 horsepower and 510 lb-ft of torque. . .and a nice growl from its low-pressure exhaust system. Matched to a six-speed gearbox that gets that quick 0–60 time, the quarter-mile is gone in just 12.6 seconds. But this isn't just a straight-line machine. Thanks to fat Goodyear Eagle F1 Supercar G:2 tires (19s up front, 20s in back), the GT500 will circle a skid pad in a remarkable 1.0g. When *Road & Track* tested the 2011 GT500, they found it came away with better test results than the Ford GT. Just a Mustang indeed. If you see one of these snarly grilles with the Shelby snake in your rearview mirror, move over. —*JL*

- Weight? 3,820 pounds.
- The GT500 goes from 0 to 100 in 9.2 seconds.
- The 155 mph top speed is electronically limited.
- EPA mileage for the GT500 is 15 mpg city/23 mpg highway.

Engine: 5.4-liter supercharged dohc V-8
Horsepower: 550
0–60 mph: 4.4 seconds

Top speed: 155 mph
Price when new: $48,645
Value now: Same

- Some 28 percent of GT350s are said to have been painted in white with blue stripes.

- The Paxton supercharger option cost $670.

- GT350s could be specified with optional valve covers with the word Cobra embossed on them.

- The GT350 was the famous Hertz car, which some racers rented for a weekend of unusually affordable motorsport.

Engine: 289-cubic-inch Ford V-8	**Top speed:** 135 mph
Horsepower: 306	**Price when new:** $3,500
0–60 mph: 6.4 seconds	**Value now:** $60,000–$200,000

It wasn't until 1966 that this most iconic of American muscle cars car dropped the Mustang from its title and became known simply as the Shelby 350 GT. At the same time you could finally purchase your GT in a different color other than white, and other options became available such as—shock, horror!—an automatic gearbox and, much more appropriately, a Paxton supercharger to boost the 289-cubic-inch Ford V-8's output from 306 to 440 horsepower. Shortly before the bigger GT500 was introduced in 1967, the 350 got the high-performance 289 motor, which was nice, but by then the legend had already been set in stone. Carrollc Shelby's sports coupe become a bona fide homegrown hero of downtown USA, and rightly so if you ask us. —*SS*

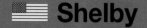

Shelby

Series 1 — 1999–2003

Carroll Shelby has been involved in many very cool, successful projects. This isn't one of them. The body of his Series I is interesting but a bit ungainly, done in a combination of carbon fiber and fiberglass. Under that is an aluminum frame that is reinforced by aluminum honeycomb panels. The convertible top stows behind the passenger compartment. This was a well-featured car with power windows, air conditioning, and a good sound system. Shelby offered two versions of the very nice Oldsmobile Aurora V-8: normally aspirated at 320 horsepower or supercharged up to a reported 600 horsepower. After failing to meet the changing government rules—plus some financial troubles—not all the Series I cars were completed, but they could be bought as Series II "kit cars" minus the driveline. —JL

- Shelby Series I production: 249.
- The gearbox is a six-speed ZF.
- Supercharged versions are said to get to 60 mph in 3.2 seconds.
- The first plan was to use the Oldsmobile engine developed for the Indy Racing League.

Engine: 4.0-liter V-8
Horsepower: 320
0–60 mph: 4.3 seconds
Top speed: 170 mph
Price when new: $200,000
Value now: $125,000

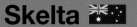

2010   G-Force

- Skelta was founded by an Australian rally driver.

- The name Skelta comes from the Beatles' "Helter Skelter."

- Two body styles: open two-seat Spyder or gullwing Targa-top G-Force.

- The supercharger is a Rotex.

Engine: 2.0-liter supercharged dohc inline four
Horsepower: 230
0–60 mph: N/A

Top speed: N/A
Price when new: $131,000
Value now: Same

Bet you've never heard of this one. Made in Australia with an aim toward winning rallies comes the superquick Skelta. Designed to be as light as possible, the G-Force is built on a chrome-moly steel tube space frame with added stiffening from a carbon fiber–aluminum sandwich used for the central tunnel and sidepods. This is then wrapped in a carbon fiber body best described as functional. Suspension is upper and lower A-arms—a traditional race car design— and the brakes are ventilated discs. So now you have a car that weighs in at around 1,600 pounds complete with drivetrain. Two choices are offered for that drivetrain: a 2.0-liter Honda four with a mere 340 horsepower or a Hartley V-8 with a torrid 460 horsepower. In either case, power is routed through a six-speed Honda gearbox. —JL

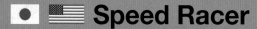

Speed Racer

Mach 5 — 2008

So how many of you have sat through the *Speed Racer* cartoons (oops, anime) and wondered at that pointy-nosed and, for that matter, pointy-tailed, Mach 5? The true *Speed Racer* fans can tick off all the car's many features, several operated through seven buttons (A to G) in the middle of the steering wheel, just like the automatic transmission buttons in an Edsel. When *Speed Racer* was turned into a movie in 2008, the Mach 5 was created and tested for *Road & Track* magazine by *Speed Racer* aficionado Sam Mitani. We're rather certain the story is made up (it's in the April issue), but we would love to know if Yokohama made "tire crampons" for the ultimate in tire traction. —JL

- Jacks under the car allowed it to leap over obstacles.
- There were also saw blades for cutting trees.
- Claimed torque was 1,400 lb-ft.
- The suspension A-arms were in carbon fiber.

Engine: 8.0-liter quad-turbo dohc V-12
Horsepower: 1700
0–60 mph: 0.6 seconds

Top speed: 305 mph
Price when new: $5,000,000
Value now: Sorry—it isn't for sale

2009– **C8 Aileron**

- The C8's engine is a tuned version of the Audi S4's 4.2-liter V-8.

- This is the only car that comes with bespoke Luis Vuitton luggage (at a cost of $20,000).

- Styling of the C8 is said to be influenced by the engines on a jet aircraft.

- Spyker briefly did Formula One before giving that up to buy Saab!

Engine: 4.2-liter V-8	Price when new: $350,000
Horsepower: 395	Value now: Same
0–60 mph: 4.5 seconds	
Top speed: 187 mph	

The C8 Aileron is Dutch company Spyker's latest and, undoubtedly, greatest road car creation. It emanates from the same fearless men of orange who have also done Formula One, bought Saab, and produced some of the world's weirdest supercars. Spyker is not, it is fair to surmise, your typical sports car company. And their motto is: *Nulla Tenaci Invia Est Via*, which means "for the tenacious, no road is impassable." As in, anything in life is possible—so long as you've got the balls for it. And the 395-horsepower V-8 Aileron certainly has plenty of cojones. Capable of 187 miles per hour and 0–60 mph in 4.5 seconds, the C8 has a longer wheelbase and is much sweeter to drive than Spyker's other cars, plus it has an interior to die for. Oh yes, and JLo drives one, too. —SS

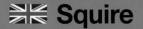

Squire

Vanden Plas Sports Tourer
1935–1937

You may have never heard of the Squire, but among those who treasure pre–World War II British sports cars it's a star. Adrian Squire was just 21 when he decided to build his dream car. He sourced the engine from the British-Italian company Anzani, which added a supercharger. Vanden Plas was commissioned to create bodies for the proposed two- and four-seat cars. Under that body was a conventional but quite strong chassis that made the Squires known for their excellent handling. I recall helping road test a Squire, and the young tester just couldn't believe that the machine, which has quite large magnesium brake drums, could stop as quickly as a modern Corvette. Sadly, the company went under in the mid-1930s, and Adrian Squire, 30, was killed during a bomb attack in 1940. —JL

- The transmission is a preselector.
- Seven Squires were competed.
- The Anzani engine has a cast-iron block and head.
- One of the Squires was missing for 25 years.

Engine: 1.5-liter supercharged dohc inline four
Horsepower: 110
0–60 mph: 12.0 seconds

Top speed: 100 mph
Price when new: $5,978
Value now: N/A

- Only 14,257 SVXs were sold in the United States.
- It's estimated Subaru lost $3,000 on every SVX it built.
- To lower the SVX's price, Subaru developed a front-drive version.
- In Japan, the SVX was known as the Alcyone.

Engine: 3.3-liter dohc flat six	**Top speed:** 154 mph
Horsepower: 230	**Price when new:** $24,445
0–60 mph: 7.3 seconds	**Value now:** $5,600

Having lunch with the editor of Japan's famous *Car Graphic* magazine in 1993, I asked what he thought of Subaru's SVX. He replied, "Ah, our hidden treasure." After failing with its awkward-looking XT coupe, Subaru went to famous Italian designer Giorgetto Giugiaro to draw its successor, the SVX. It is a rather dramatic shape, with side windows-in-windows, à la the DeLorean. Up front was a strong twin cam flat-six going through all-wheel drive. The SVX was, in its day, an excellent performer, but no one seemed to notice. Subaru was famous for smaller, rock-rugged machines, not luxury/performance cars, and the SVX never caught on. Soft economic times and the fact that the car's price rose to over $36,000 by the time it was discontinued in 1997 didn't help. The SVX will always be a hidden treasure. —JL

GT Street Turbo R
2010

For those who find the regular 911 Turbo a little too predictable, allow us to introduce the Techart GT Street Turbo R. It may sound like a renegade from one of the *Fast and Furious* movies, but it's a highly credible machine, engineered to deliver that little bit more in every way—visually, on the road, in mind, and at the track. It has 660 horsepower and a top speed way north of 200 miles per hour, but its true backyard is at the Nürburgring, near the company's headquarters in Germany, around which the Street GT R is all but unbeatable by any other car with number plates, a roof, and more than one seat. It's not for the fainthearted, but for the truly committed there's little that comes close. —SS

- The car is based on the second-generation 997 series 911, not the first.
- Torque is an incredible 860nm, even though the internals of the engine are untouched.
- Techart was founded in 1987 by Thomas Behringer.
- The company is based in the small hamlet of Leonberg in the middle of the Adenau forest.

Engine: 3.6-liter turbocharged flat six
Horsepower: 660
0–60 mph: 3.5 seconds

Top speed: 210 mph
Price when new: $400,000
Value now: $400,000

Tesla 🇺🇸

Roadster

- The warranty of the electric roadster is three years/36,000 miles.
- Rev limit of the motor is 13,000/14,000 rpm.
- Recharge time on 220 volts is three to four hours.
- EPA mileage: 231 mpg city/224 mpg highway.

Engine: Single three-phase, four-pole AC induction electric motor
Horsepower: 248
0–60 mph: 4.0 seconds
Top speed: 121 mph
Price when new: $109,000
Value now: Same

If electric cars are the future, Tesla's Roadster is the pioneer. Well before Nissan unveiled its Leaf electric sedan, Tesla was assembling its electric car in California. What you see is actually a Lotus that is assembled in England, minus the drivetrain. When it arrives in Palo Alto, California, the lithium-ion battery pack and the 248-horsepower motor are installed and the car is finished off. Being a Lotus, the Roadster is small but comfortable once you're in. What matters is not that horsepower number but the 276 lb-ft of torque, which is available from zero rpm, this being an electric car. So you whisper off from a dead stop, but you're at 60 miles per hour in just four seconds. That's Ferrari-like acceleration, and, being Lotus-based, the Tesla handles like, well, a Lotus. —JL

Tojeiro-Jaguar   1956

John Tojeiro's most noted contribution to the sports car world was arguably a design he sold to AC Cars, which became the AC Ace, which evolved into the Shelby Cobra. After founding Tojeiro Automotive Developments, he was approached to create a race car with a Jaguar 3.4-liter engine. He laid out the design of a tubular space frame, adding an upper and lower A-arm front suspension and de Dion rear layout. Around all this was a body that looked a bit like a squished D-type. The Tojeiro-Jags were light, and this made them quick against such opposition as Jaguar-powered Listers and HWMs. Many of the great drivers of the day raced Tojeiro-Jags, among them Formula 1 champions Jim Clark, Graham Hill, and Jack Brabham. —JL

- The drivetrain included a Moss gearbox and Salisbury ZF differential.
- Disc brakes were used, the rears mounted inboard.
- One team using a Tojeiro-Jaguar was the famed Ecurie Ecosse.
- Though quick, these cars had a reputation for being twitchy.

Engine: 3.4-liter dohc inline six	**Top speed:** 153 mph
Horsepower: N/A	**Price when new:** N/A
0–60 mph: 5.4 seconds	**Value now:** $600,000

- Fewer than 65 of the 337 2000GTs came to the United States; no more than 38 remain.

- A 2000GT won the 24-hour race at Mount Fuji Speedway in 1967.

- Carroll Shelby prepped a trio of 2000GTs and boosted their power output to 250 horsepower for the SCCA's C-Production class for the 1968 season.

- Two 2000GT convertibles were crafted for the James Bond movie *You Only Live Twice*, which was filmed in Japan.

Engine: 2.0-liter inline six	Top speed: 135 mph
Horsepower: 150	Price when new: $6,800
0–60 mph: Est. 10 seconds	Value now: $350,000

The 2000GT was the first Japanese supercar, and was designed to wear a Nissan badge. The design was done by Count Albrecht Goertz, a U.S.-based German whose work had included the BMW 507 (see that car's profile). Japanese motorcycle and engine manufacturer Yamaha commissioned Goetz to design a world-class, high-performance sports car that it thought would be built as a Nissan. But Nissan declined the project, so Yamaha went to Toyota, which ended up ordering 337 of the cars. The 2000GT has a long, low, muscularly exotic and aerodynamic aluminum body with pop-up headlamps and a wraparound windshield. It takes its name from its 2.0-liter, inline six-cylinder engine built for Toyota by Yamaha. The engine was tuned to spin to more than 6,000 rpm and propelled the 2000GT to a succession of international speed records, including one 72-hour stint in the mid-1960s during which the Toyota supercar averaged nearly 130 miles per hour. —*LE*

MR2   1984–2007

Toyota was experimenting with vehicle architecture in the 1970s. One experiment involved taking the powertrain from the front-drive Corolla and mounting it just behind a two-person passenger compartment. Suddenly—well, after a lot of engineering and development work—Toyota had an entry-level sports car, the MR2. Production began in 1984 and would continue through various generations until 2007. The first generation was angular in design, powered in Japan by a 112-horsepower engine but in the United States by a twin cam version with 128 horsepower. Soon, a Targa-style roof was available, as was a supercharged engine boosted to 145 horsepower. The MR2 was all-new for 1989, and a 200-horsepower turbocharged engine seemed to befit the car's Ferrari-like redesign. The third generation launched in 1999 with the car now labeled as the MR2 Spyder, a roadster with a normally aspirated engine that provided less than 140 horsepower. —LE

- The MR2 was previewed in the form of the SV-3 concept car at the Tokyo auto show in 1983.

- Former Grand Prix and Indy racer Dan Gurney was involved in the development of the MR2 in its various generations.

- Also involved in development of the original MR2 was Lotus, which at the time was partially owned by Toyota.

- Why *MR2*? It was short for "mid-engine runabout two-seater." Many people simply referred to the car as "Mister Two."

Tech specs (first generation, U.S.):	0–60 mph: Est. 8.7 seconds
	Top speed: N/A
Engine: 1.6-liter inline four	Price when new: $14,000
Horsepower: 128	Value now: $3,000

1965–1969 — **Sports 800**

Toyota launched its first car, the Publica sedan, in 1961 and a year later showed a prototype for a Publica-based sports car with a removable roof. That car didn't advance into production until 1965, but it still beat Porsche as the first with what we now know as a Targa top. The car was the Sports 800, so named because of its sporty design and its 799cc two-cylinder, horizontally opposed and air-cooled engine. —LE

- In addition to a top speed of 90 mph, the S800 could get 50 miles on a gallon of gasoline.

- In Japan, the S800 was called the *Yota-Hachi*, a combination of the last letters of Toyota and the Japanese word for "800."

- In 1965, a Sports 800 won the All Japan Car Club Championship race.

- Fewer than two dozen Sport 800s were imported to the United States.

Engine: 799cc inline two	Top speed: 90 mph
Horsepower: 45	Price when new: N/A
0–60 mph: N/A	Value now: N/A

Treser

1987 — **T1 Roadster**

Here's a car so rare, one can only ask: ever heard of it? Walter Treser was instrumental in the early successes of Audi's Quattro rally car. He left the company to build his own automobile, the T1. Many of the wedgy car's parts were sourced from Volkswagen and Audi. A Golf GTI 16V was behind the cockpit in the mid-engine coupe/roadster. Sadly, the car drove Treser into bankruptcy. —JL

- The transmission was a five-speed manual.

- Torque measured 127 lb-ft.

- Most guesses put production at five road-going T1s.

- T1s were to be built in Berlin.

Engine: 1.8-liter dohc inline four	Top speed: 140 mph
Horsepower: 170	Price when new: N/A
0–60 mph: 8.6 seconds	Value now: N/A

Triumph

GT6 — 1966–1976

- Its rear suspension was not the original GT6's finest hour, allowing huge oversteer if you backed off at the wrong moment.

- Chief rival to the GT6 was the MGB, but the Triumph was comfortably quicker in its final M3 form.

- To begin with, the GT6 was known as the poor man's E-type.

- The car was based on the Triumph GT4, which was designed by Giovanni Michelotti.

(Mk II):	
Engine: 2.0-liter inline four	Top speed: 104 mph
Horsepower: 104	Price when new: $1000
0–60 mph: 10.6 seconds	Value now: $5,000–$12,000

It may have stretched the Spitfire's chassis to within an inch of its life, but the bigger-engined, straight-six-powered GT6 was, in its day, quite a plausible attempt to produce an English alternative to the Datsun 240Z. It was quick-ish, decent-looking, and affordable; and if its 2.0-liter engine had to be worked hard to produce its 95 horsepower (raised on the Mk II model to a more rousing 104) it didn't really matter in the end. The GT6 was about having fun first, speed second, and it got that balance just right. —SS

Triumph

Spitfire — 1962–1980

- There were five incarnations of the Spitfire, the Mk I, II, III, IV, and 1500.

- The car pictured is a U.S.-spec Mk III.

- The 1500, made between 1974 and 1980, sold almost as many as the other four put together.

- It was based on the Standard Triumph of 1957 and made its debut at the London motor show in 1962.

(1500):	
Engine: 1.5-liter inline four	Top speed: 100 mph
Horsepower: 71	Price when new: $5,995 (1980)
0–60 mph: 13.2 seconds	Value now: $3,000–$10,000

There's something about Giovanni Michelotti's small, simple, but curiously beguiling little Spitfire that Amercia fell in love with in the 1960s. It wasn't especially fast (the biggest engine it ever got was a 1.5-liter four-cylinder), and it didn't go round corners on rails, either, but as an overall experience it just worked, and Triumph ended up selling over 300,000 as a result, the majority of them in the United States. —SS

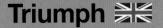

1955–1962   **TR3/3A/3B**

- Accessories included a hardtop and small rear seat.

- There was an optional 2,138cc engine.

- TR3s were very popular with club racers.

- Many of the U.S.-only TR3Bs had the 2.1-liter engine of the upcoming TR4.

Engine: 2.0-liter ohv straight four	**Top speed:** 110 mph
Horsepower: 100	**Price when new:** N/A
0–60 mph: 10.8 seconds	**Value now:** $13,500

This was one of the automobiles that created the sports car movement in the United States in the late 1950s. In fact, of the many TR3s built, the great majority were sold stateside. The successor to the TR2 and a competitor of the MGA, the TR3 was a simple, reliable sports car. There were several types of TR3: The first came in 1955 and separated itself visually from the TR2 by having a near-flush grille. Come 1957, the car got disc brakes, and the next year the wide-grille TR3A was sold, featuring, believe it or not, door handles. These are basic sports cars, not all that weatherproof in the rain and with minimal creature comforts, but a great deal of fun to drive. —JL

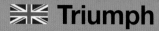

Triumph

TR4/4A 1961–1968

Triumph modernized its sports car with the TR4, adding such niceties as roll-up windows and a much larger trunk than the TR3. This was a good-looking sports car in its age, and the upgrades from the TR3 made it more acceptable in the United States, where most of the TR4s were sold. Like the TR3, the engine was based on a one-time tractor unit, now at 2,138 cc, and those of us who owned TR4s can attest to the drivetrain's ruggedness. One of the cool options was the electrically engaged overdrive with the excellent name Laycock de Normanville. With overdrive in the top three ratios, you effectively had a seven-speed gearbox. In 1965, Triumph replaced the live rear axle with an independent rear suspension to create the TR4A. —JL

- TR4s were quite successful in U.S. racing thanks to Kas Kasner and Bob Tullius.
- Italian coachbuilder Michelotti designed the TR4 exterior.
- A Targa-style hardtop was optional.
- A supercharger was available for the TR4.

Engine: 2.1-liter ohv inline four	Top speed: 120 mph
Horsepower: 105	Price when new: $2,995
0–60 mph: 10.7 seconds	Value now: $22,000

James Mann

Triumph 🇬🇧

- Triumphs were assembled in Coventry, England.
- There was an optional steel hardtop.
- The suspension was independent front and rear, with front disc brakes and rear drum brakes.
- Triumph used the now-dated body-on-frame design for the TR6.

Engine: 2.5-liter ohv inline six
Horsepower: 104
0–60 mph: 8.2 seconds
Top speed: 120 mph
Price when new: $3,400
Value now: $12,000

There was a Triumph TR5 in the rest of the world, but the U.S. got a model called the TR250. Both cars looked like the TR4, but had six-cylinder engines. While the engine was fuel injected in the TR5s, it was carbureted for the emissions-conscious United States. Triumph took that basic package and restyled it for 1969 as the TR6, the main differences being the squared-off front and rear ends of the car. While the UK TR6s continued with fuel injection and got as much as 150 horsepower, U.S. versions carried on with carburetors and just 104 horsepower. The transmission still had four speeds and the option of overdrive. Like previous Triumph sports cars, these were rugged, dependable machines that gave their drivers many enjoyable miles. —JL

Triumph

TR7/8 1975–1981

When Triumph's TR6 had run its course, it was replaced by the TR7 with a wedge-shaped body designed by Harris Mann. . .or apparently doodled and then taken seriously. A few loved it. . .many found it odd-looking. While the TR7 was a bit anemic with its four-cylinder engine, Triumph went to Rover for its 3.5-liter V-8 and stuffed that in the car to create the TR8. There's no denying the car is quick, but the British auto industry was in turmoil at the time, while the likes of Datsun with its Z cars had found their legs in America. There were a few coupe TR8s, but most were convertibles, and the vast majority sold were in the United States. The TR8 was a sad ending to the history of Triumph sports cars. —JL

- The V-8 was originally a General Motors design.
- Some 112,368 TR7s were built.
- About 2,500 TR8s were built.
- TR7s and TR8s were not known for high quality.

Engine: 3.5-liter ohv V-8
Horsepower: 148
0–60 mph: 8.0 seconds

Top speed: 134 mph
Price when new: $11,000
Value now: $15,000

1991–2002 — Griffith

You haven't really lived unless you've wrestled with a TVR Griffith, ideally along a winding country road, lined with trees to bounce the outrageous V-8 exhaust note off. The Griffith may have been a monster capable of over 160 miles per hour, but it was also TVR's finest hour, with elegant good looks to match its superhero powertrain. It also worked because it used the tried and tested Rover (formerly Buick) V-8 engine rather than one of TVR's less reliable homegrown motors. They don't make 'em like this anymore (which may be a good thing for the rest of us. . .) —SS

- It's said that the boss's dog, Ned, was involved with the styling of the car; it took a bite out of the clay model and the designers liked what they saw.
- The Griffith was mechanically similar to the far less attractive Chimaera.
- The Griffith played a starring role in the *Gran Turismo* and *Gran Turismo 2* video games.
- The car was partly designed by a Scottish gent named Ian Robertson, who later worked for *Autocar* as a journalist.

(Griffith 500):
Engine: 5.0-liter Rover V-8
Horsepower: 340
0–60 mph: 4.1 seconds

Top speed: 169 mph
Price when new: $50,000
Value now: $25,000–$35,000

M932 OKO

Motoring Picture Library/Alamy

Vector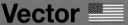

1980 — W2

There's no denying Gerry Wiegert had a terrific idea. He had designed a mid-engine supercar that, in its day, had a shape that blew the competition away. This combination of auto and airplane thinking was a leader, powered by a twin turbo Chevrolet-based V-8. The car offered such promise. Wiegert kept searching for funds, American car fans kept waiting, and Europeans loved the Vector. . .but the project kept misfiring. . . . —JL

- The name? W for "Wiegert," 2 for the number of turbos.
- Vector Motors headquarters is located in Wilmington, California.
- Vector Motors still exists and is trying to build the WX8.
- Gerry Wiegert was involved in the design of the original Jet Ski and the four-wheel ATV.

Engine: 5.7-liter twin-turbo ohv V-8
Horsepower: 600
0–60 mph: N/A

Top speed: 200 (claimed, never proven)
Price when new: N/A
Value now: N/A

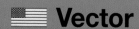

Vector

W-8 — 1989–1993

The Gerry Wiegert saga ground on, and he created the W-8, which was said to contain so much aeronautical technology the company called itself Vector Aeromotive. The styling was dramatic, if over the top, done in carbon fiber over a semi-monocoque of aluminum honeycomb. The interior also echoed an aircraft theme, but for all the promises of speed, Vector never truly delivered the goods. —JL

- Vector built 17 W-8s for the public.
- Production lasted from 1989 to 1993.
- The transmission was a three-speed automatic.
- Torque rating: 630 lb-ft.

Engine: 6.0-liter twin-turbo ohv V-8	**Top speed:** 242 mph
Horsepower: 625	**Price when new:** $455,000
0–60 mph: 4.2 seconds	**Value now:** $250,000

Vector

M12 — 1995–1999

The Vector saga got even stranger when Megatech, the Indonesian company that then owned Lamborghini, bought the company. Vector was moved from California to Florida and developed the M12, which mixed elements of the WX-3 with the Diablo V-12 engine and other components from the Italian company. Lamborghini helped with some of the work, but sales sputtered and the company went through still another disruption. —JL

- Just 14 production M12s were assembled.
- Tommy Suharto, son of Indonesian President Suharto, was a principal in the company.
- The V-12 had 425 lb-ft of torque.
- M12s were built from 1995 to 1999.

Engine: 5.7-liter dohc V-12	**Top speed:** 189 mph
Horsepower: 492	**Price when new:** $184,000
0–60 mph: 4.8 seconds	**Value now:** $115,000

Voisin

- Voisin used a sleeve-valve engine.

- This was among the first monocoque-bodied race cars.

- Four cars were assembled originally, and a replica has since been built.

- A front-mounted propeller spins a water pump.

Engine: 2.0-liter inline six	**Top speed:** 109 mph
Horsepower: 80	**Price when new:** N/A
0–60 mph: N/A	**Value now:** N/A

Frenchman Gabriel Voisin had an aeronautical background, so when he turned to automobiles, it wasn't surprising that he brought that thinking with him. Voisin's entry in the 1923 French Grand Prix was this wonderfully odd machine called the Laboratoire. Its profile is meant to mimic that of an aircraft wing section, and the advanced aerodynamics include a full belly pan. The car is quite light, with an aluminum body over a wood-and-steel chassis. The car's weak point was its engine, which just couldn't hold the pace against the likes of Sunbeam and Bugatti. Of the four cars entered in the GP only one finished, and that was in last place. Still, you have to have a soft spot in your sporting heart for Voisin's "laboratory." —*JL*

Volvo

A sports car from Volvo? At least it's a sporty-looking car. The P1800 was designed by Pietro Frua and Pelle Pettersson, whose father was an engineer who pushed Volvo to do such a car. Originally, the P1800 was built in England by Jensen, but after the first 6,000 were finished, production shifted to Sweden, where the next 41,000 were built. With the move to Sweden, the name changed from P1800 to 1800S, and in 1970 to 1800E when fuel injectors replaced the SU carburetors. In 1972, a wagon-styled 1800ES joined the lineup. —*LE*

- The original plan was for Karmann to build the car in Germany . . .

- . . . but Karmann's biggest customer, Volkswagen, vetoed it.

- The P1800 was featured in the British television series *The Saint*, starring Roger Moore . . .

- . . . but the show's producers had been hoping Jaguar would provide an E-type.

Engine: 1.8-liter inline four	**Top speed:** 105 mph
Horsepower: 100	**Price when new:** $4,000
0–60 mph: Est. 12 seconds	**Value now:** $10,000

Acknowledgments

With a book that covers 365 cars, you'd need about that many acknowledgments just to encompass all of those who provided automobiles to be photographed, so there must be a general thanks to all of them. Jane Barrett at *Road & Track* was as helpful as always as I tried to ferret out the few images that weren't in my collection. The magazine's editor-in-chief—and my old friend—Matt DeLorenzo was kind enough to provide an opening for this book. If you've ever taken on a project as all-inclusive as this alone you know it can turn your brain to oatmeal, and the assistance of Larry Edsall and Steve Sutcliffe in writing their share of the profiles helped me retain my sanity. . .while also adding some welcome balance to the book. And a thousand thanks to my editor, Jeffrey Zuehlke, not just for his editing and perseverance in nailing down those most evasive of facts and photos, but for his patience.

Regards to all,

John Lamm, Summer 2011